Praise for *Pathogenesis*

"[Kennedy] wrangles an astonishing breadth of material into easily accessible, plain prose. . . . Even readers familiar with the material will find *[Pathogenesis]* fascinating. . . . Kennedy will leave readers galvanized by the time they flip to the last page, having assured us that we could win the narrative back from germs—if we're able to muster the political will to do so. *Pathogenesis* puts us in our rightful tiny place in the universe as this great, big—and terrifying, at times—world spins. But, Kennedy reminds us, we are not helpless."

—*The Washington Post*

"Powerfully argued . . . *Pathogenesis* sets out, like Yuval Noah Harari's *Sapiens* or Peter Frankopan's recent *The Earth Transformed*, to reinterpret the entire history of mankind. . . . A fascinating and pacey run through the history of humanity from an unfamiliar perspective."

—*The Times* (U.K.)

"A compelling account of the role of bacteria and viruses in world history. Mr Kennedy marshals a dizzying range of material, from the transition from feudalism to capitalism in Europe to the rise of the slave trade. . . . An entertaining read."

—*The Economist*

"I love this surprising, learned, fascinating book which brings human arrogance into sharp relief, reminding us that the real masters of the universe are microbes. Jonathan Kennedy fast-forwards through history, unpicking everything we thought we knew; we are but the pawns and playthings of viruses and bacteria. . . . Mind-blowing stuff."

—CAL FLYN, author of *Islands of Abandonment*

"Kennedy is right to state that pandemics and plague outbreaks have had a big influence throughout human history. Such dramatic episodes get written up by historians, and Kennedy describes their accounts with verve. . . . Well written."

—*Nature*

"Well-timed . . . [and] compelling . . . Kennedy's book manages to end on a somewhat hopeful note. Yes, our trajectory is defined by microbes. But it's also influenced by our reactions to them—and our acknowledgment of their power."

—*The Atlantic*

"How a virus might have written human history . . . This is a fascinating, readable, and superbly researched account of how infectious diseases have shaped our history, from the Paleolithic Era to Covid."

—DAVID CHRISTIAN, author of *Origin Story*

"Our very existence and success as a species, Kennedy argues in this fascinating book, has been shaped by bacteria and viruses."

—*The Guardian*

"[Kennedy] retells the story of human civilization from its earliest prehistoric roots to the current decade, not from the perspective of its Great Men so much as its Great Diseases—the bacteria and viruses that have dogged us since *Homo sapiens* emerged as a species. . . . What the book

reveals is the plain fact that humans are often not the only actors on the great stage of history that we assume we are, and that we may not even be the most important."

—*The New Republic*

"From the fall of Rome to the Spanish conquest of the Americas to the industrial revolution, germs have played as much a role in history as guns, generals, and 'great men.' In a timely updating of William McNeill's *Plagues and Peoples*, Jonathan Kennedy restores the microbes of infectious disease to their rightful place in the story of human evolution and the rise and fall of civilizations. . . . Bio-history at its best."

—MARK HONIGSBAUM, author of *The Pandemic Century*

"[*Pathogenesis*] shines when it brings cutting-edge science to bear on these questions, something that Kennedy treats with great care."

—*Financial Times*

"Kennedy debuts with a virtuoso analysis of the fallout from encounters between deadly viral and bacterial pathogens and human populations that lacked immunity. . . . He marshals a wealth of surprising scholarship in lucid and succinct prose. The result is a fascinating look at history from the perspective of its tiniest protagonists."

—*Publishers Weekly*, starred review

"After recent years you don't need us to tell you that infectious diseases have the power to change history. . . . A compelling case."

—*GQ*

"Thrilling and eye-opening . . . From neolithic diseases to Covid-19, Jonathan Kennedy explores the enormous role played by some of the tiniest life on Earth: the power of plagues in shaping world history."

—LEWIS DARTNELL, author of *Being Human*

"It's not often you pick up a book that promises to alter your entire understanding of the story of humanity."

—*Lit Hub*

"The fluency of Kennedy's narration is remarkable, weaving Tolkien, *Game of Thrones,* and *Monty Python* into memorable and accessible explanations of genetics, evolutionary biology, and demography. . . . Impressive and enjoyable."

—*The Spectator*

"[*Pathogenesis*] offers a different lens to view many of the big events of the past."

—*Associated Press*

"This book challenges some of the greatest clichés about colonialism and leaves you wondering why you ever gave them the time of day. . . . A revelation."

—Sathnam Sanghera, author of *Empireland*

"[A] wonderfully written survey of eight major outbreaks of infectious disease . . . Sobering."

—*Air Mail*

"*Pathogenesis* makes a convincing case that germs did help mold history—and that history in turn affected how germs evolved and traveled around the globe with ferocious efficacy. Kennedy's final chapters are cautionary but not pessimistic. What has happened in the past can happen again—but not necessarily in the same way. With this knowledge, perhaps we can be better armed when, not if, the next plague emerges."

—*BookPage*

"[Full of] lessons to ponder for our own pandemic-hobbled time."

—*Kirkus Reviews*

"The word 'pathogenesis' means the ways in which a disease develops and progresses, and Jonathan Kennedy's hopefully contagious thesis examines all manner of dreadful illnesses and their gruesome effects; not just on individuals, but on entire societies."

—*Sydney Morning Herald*

"Jonathan Kennedy condenses a huge amount of information into *Pathogenesis* and does so in a very vivid and engaging fashion. . . . [It] is an excellent read, thought provoking and engaging in ways that are both eloquent and insightful. . . . I suspect [this book] will educate, excite and stimulate a deeper appreciation of the role that pathogens have had in human history for at least the next 50 years."

—*Nature*

Pathogenesis

Pathogenesis

A History of

the World in

Eight Plagues

Jonathan Kennedy

Crown
New York

2024 Crown Trade Paperback Edition

Copyright © 2023 by Jonathan Kennedy

Published in the United States by Crown, an imprint of the
Crown Publishing Group, a division of Penguin Random
House LLC, New York.

CROWN and the Crown colophon are registered trademarks of
Penguin Random House LLC.

Originally published in hardcover in the United States by Crown,
an imprint of the Crown Publishing Group, a division of Penguin
Random House LLC, in 2023.

LIBRARY OF CONGRESS CATALOGING-IN-PUBLICATION DATA
Names: Kennedy, Jonathan, author.
Title: Pathogenesis / Jonathan Kennedy.
Description: First edition. | New York: Crown, 2023. | Includes index.
Identifiers: LCCN 2022052387 (print) | LCCN 2022052388 (ebook) |
ISBN 9780593240496 (paperback) | ISBN 9780593240489 (ebook)
Subjects: LCSH: Epidemics—History. Plague—History. | Diseases
and history.
Classification: LCC RA649 .K46 2023 (print) | LCC RA649 (ebook) |
DDC 614.4—dc23/eng/20221114
LC record available at https://lccn.loc.gov/2022052387
LC ebook record available at https://lccn.loc.gov/2022052388

Printed in the United States of America on acid-free paper

crownpublishing.com

9 8 7 6 5 4 3

Book design by Simon M. Sullivan

For Farrah and Zaha

Contents

Pathogenesis

Introduction

Where the telescope ends, the microscope begins.
—Victor Hugo

Through the Looking-glass

According to Sigmund Freud, there have been three great revolutions in Western science and each of these dealt a blow to humans' belief in their special status—or what he referred to as our "naive self-love."[1] The first, which began with Copernicus, was the revelation that the earth is not the center of the universe but just one of several planets revolving around the sun. After this setback, we could still console ourselves with the *Book of Genesis'* claim that God created humans in his own image and gave us dominion over the land, sea and animals— albeit in a location that was astronomically peripheral. Then Charles Darwin came along and pointed out that humans are just another species of animal and that we share a relatively recent common ancestor with apes. The third great scientific revolution, according to Freud, was his own discovery of the unconscious. The realization that we aren't even in control of our thought processes was, he argued, the "most irritating insult" to "the human mania of greatness."

Freud's suggestion that psychoanalysis is more significant than the Copernican or Darwinian revolutions seems a little, well, egotistic.[2] But his general point—that the more humans learn about the world, the more insignificant we realize we are—is insightful. For example, advanced telescopes have revealed that earth is an infinitesimally small rock rotating around an unremarkable star in a galaxy of at least 100 billion stars, which itself is just one of many billions of galaxies in the universe. In addition to this, there have been other scientific revolutions that have further undermined our species' high opinion of itself. To my mind, the most important of these is the discovery of a world as vast as outer space, and yet so tiny that it is invisible to the naked eye: the realm of bacteria, viruses and other microbes.[3]

In the early seventeenth century, Galileo realized that when he reversed the order of the lenses in his telescope, very small things became visible.[4] For the first time in history, humans had the technical capacity to see microbes. But Galileo preferred to focus his efforts on observing the stars and planets in the sky, and it wasn't until fifty years later that a haberdasher from Delft in the Netherlands began to explore the microscopic world. Antonie van Leeuwenhoek initially developed his lenses to inspect the quality of the textiles he bought and sold. But after a while he turned his gaze upon the natural world. His letters to the Royal Society in London describe how everything from a drop of water to the plaque on our teeth is alive with what he called "animalcules." He was enraptured: "No more pleasant sight has ever come before my eyes."[5] In all of history, Leeuwenhoek's discovery of the microscopic realm might well be the closest anyone has come to falling down the rabbit hole, climbing through the looking-glass, or stepping into a wardrobe and finding oneself in a world of fantastical creatures.

It wasn't until the second half of the nineteenth century—a full 200 years later—that scientists finally began to comprehend the significance of the new world that Leeuwenhoek had stumbled into. And it's only quite recently that researchers have begun to appreciate how bacteria and viruses perform a wide range of roles that are vital to the functioning of our planet, bodies and even our minds. Human life—indeed, complex life in any form—is inconceivable without microbes.

The Tree of Life

In the summer of 1837, fresh from a five-year voyage around the world on HMS *Beagle*, Darwin made a sketch in his notebook under the words "I think." The unassuming doodle of what looks like the branch of a tree neatly captures the main features of what would develop into his theory of evolution by natural selection: when populations from a single species find themselves living in different surroundings, random variation—combined with natural selection for traits that provide an advantage in each particular environment—eventually result in them splitting into separate species. This process, repeated again and again over hundreds of millions of years, accounts for the kaleidoscopic variety of life forms on our planet that looks like a vast tree when mapped out on paper.

If we trace the Tree of Life to the base of its trunk, we find the Last Universal Common Ancestor (LUCA): a single-celled, bacterium-like organism that is the distant progenitor of all living things, humans included. This one shared antecedent is the reason why everything from blue whales to giant redwoods to bacteria have inherited common features such as DNA to store genetic information and a molecule called ATP that is the universal source of energy. Moving up the tree, the trunk splits into three boughs that represent the great domains of life. Two of these consist of organisms invisible to the naked eye: bacteria and archaea—single-celled microbes that resemble bacteria.* The third branch depicts eukaryotes, which are distinguished by storing their DNA in a nucleus and using specialized structures called mitochondria to produce energy. This category encompasses all complex life including animals, plants and fungi, but it makes up only a few small twigs in the vast Tree of Life. There are about 8.7 million species of animals, plants and fungi on earth,[6] compared to an estimated 1 trillion—1 million million—types of bacteria and archaea.[7] Less than 0.001 percent of all species on the planet are eukaryotes.

The American paleontologist Stephen Jay Gould argues that "on any possible, reasonable, or fair criterion, bacteria are—and always have been—the dominant forms of life on earth."[8] One reason for this is the sheer length of time they have existed. Our planet was formed around 4.6 billion years ago. About a billion years later, the first evidence of bacterial life appears in fossils. Single-celled eukaryotes emerged some

* Archaea were only identified in 1977. Until then it was believed that the Tree of Life had two main branches: bacteria and eukaryotes.

1.8 billion years ago, but it took more than a billion years for the oldest multicellular animals to evolve and even then they were tiny, worm-like creatures. Humans are relative newcomers: we diverged from chimpanzees between 6 and 8 million years ago,[9] and the earliest evidence of *Homo sapiens* dates back about 300,000 years.[10] Such immense periods of time are hard for the human brain to conceptualize, but if we compressed 4.6 billion years into one calendar year then bacteria evolved in early spring. Humans don't appear until about half an hour before midnight on 31 December.[11]

Bacteria are everywhere. They have been found in Antarctic glaciers and on the ocean floor where boiling hot water surges out of the center of the earth. They live miles below ground and miles above it, where they influence the formation of clouds and possibly even lightning.[12] They are so numerous that, despite their tiny size, the total mass of all bacteria on the planet is thirty-five times that of all the animals and 1,000 times the weight of all humans.[13] But bacteria are not just ubiquitous: they have also had a profound impact on our planet.

About 2.5 billion years ago our world was almost completely submerged in water, with the exception of the odd volcanic peak piercing through the sea.[14] Methane in the atmosphere created a greenhouse effect that kept the planet far hotter than it is today. There was little or no free oxygen in the water or air, as it was all locked up in other molecules. Life on earth consisted of anaerobic bacteria. Then the world began to change with the emergence of cyanobacteria—blue-green algae that use the sun's rays to power photosynthesis. This made cyanobacteria much more effective at generating energy, giving them a huge evolutionary advantage. Their numbers boomed. Over a period of several hundred million years, they pumped vast amounts of oxygen—a by-product of photosynthesis—into the oceans and atmosphere.

This Great Oxygenation Event transformed the planet.[15] Some of the oxygen combined with methane in the air to form carbon dioxide, a much less effective greenhouse gas. As the planet cooled, ice sheets crept as far as the tropics. The sea level fell and land emerged from the water. Eukaryotic organisms appear in the fossil record shortly after oxygen became abundant in the atmosphere. This is not a coincidence. All plants and animals produce energy through aerobic respiration, which is twenty times more efficient than anaerobic respiration—and therefore much better suited to supporting large, multicellular organisms.[16]

Microbes continue to play a crucial role in maintaining an atmosphere that can support complex life. Cyanobacteria in the oceans still contribute to the oxygen in the atmosphere. In total, phytoplankton—photosynthesizing microorganisms in the sea—account for at least half of the oxygen produced by living organisms.[17] And bacteria perform a variety of other vitally important functions. They convert carbon, nitrogen, sulfur and phosphorus into nutrients that can be used by animals, plants and fungi. When these organisms die, they return the compounds to the ecosystem through decomposition. It's no exaggeration to say that bacteria have made the planet habitable for complex life, including humans. It's a bacterial world, and we're just squatting here.

Going Viral

Viruses tend not to be included in the Tree of Life because they occupy an ambivalent state between the worlds of the living and the lifeless. Unlike bacteria, archaea and eukaryotes, they are not made up of cells, the basic building blocks of life that are capable of generating energy and reproducing. Instead, viruses consist of genetic material—in the form of DNA or its sister molecule RNA—coated in protein. On their own they are an inert arrangement of matter. But when they manage to enter—or infect—the cell of a living thing, they take over its machinery to reproduce copies of themselves, bursting into life. This process is often deadly to the host.

Viruses are tiny, even by the standards of microbes. They can be hundreds of times smaller than the average bacterium. Viruses are so minuscule that they haven't left a mark on the fossil record. Their origins remain unclear. They may have emerged prior to, soon after, or even from early single-celled life. In any event, for most if not all of the 3.5 billion years that life has been around, viruses have been capable of infecting it. They are found anywhere that life is present and far outnumber all forms of life on earth—even bacteria. A liter of seawater contains over 100 billion virus particles, and one kilogram of dried soil somewhere in the region of a trillion.[18] The total number on the planet is estimated at about 10^{31}—that is, one followed by thirty-one zeros.[19] But only about 220 types of virus are known to be capable of infecting humans.[20] Most are so-called bacteriophages or phages—from the Greek "to devour." Phages kill between 20 percent and 40 percent of all bacteria every day, which maintains balance in a variety of ecosystems, from the oceans to our own bodies, by ensuring that no one strain of bacteria can become too numerous.[21]

A retrovirus is a specific type of virus that reproduces by inserting a copy of its DNA into the genome of the host cell. But when a retrovirus infects a sperm or egg cell, something remarkable happens: viral DNA is then passed on to every cell in every subsequent generation. An astonishing 8 percent of the human genome is made up of such genes.[22] Many of these DNA sequences don't seem to do anything in the human body, but retrovirus infections allowed our distant ancestors to acquire the capacity to perform functions that are fundamental to human existence. One remarkable example is a gene inherited from a retrovirus infection about 400 million years ago that plays a crucial role in memory formation. The gene does this by coding for tiny protein bubbles that help to move information between neurons, in a manner similar to the way that viruses spread their genetic information from one cell to another.[23] In the laboratory, mice that had this gene removed are unable to form memories.

Another mind-blowing example of a function that human ancestors acquired from retroviruses is the ability to give birth. When animals first evolved, they reproduced by laying eggs, and most creatures in the animal kingdom continue to give birth this way. Then, between 100 million and 200 million years ago, a shrew-like creature developed the capacity to gestate her young inside her own body—an extraordinary evolutionary advance because a fetus is much safer growing inside its mother's body. It is only possible because of the placenta, a temporary organ that attaches to the uterus and allows nutrients and oxygen to pass from mother to baby, and carbon dioxide and waste to travel in the other direction, without provoking a devastating response from the mother's immune system. There is nothing like this interface between the placenta and womb anywhere else in our bodies. When geneticists looked at the gene responsible for creating it, they realized that it was almost identical to those used by retroviruses to produce the proteins that attach to cells they are infecting without triggering an immune response.[24] The scientists concluded that a crucial function of the placenta didn't emerge gradually as a result of evolution by natural selection but was suddenly acquired when a retrovirus inserted its DNA into our ancestor's genome. If one of our distant ancestors hadn't been infected by a virus hundreds of millions of years ago, humans would reproduce by laying eggs.

Redrawing the Tree of Life

Humans evolved on a planet that was already inhabited by vast numbers of bacteria and viruses. They were only able to survive and thrive by developing the ability to defend themselves against potentially harmful microbes. In fact, infectious diseases have killed so many people throughout history that they are one of the strongest forces shaping human evolution. In the parts of human cells that interact with viruses, it has been estimated that viruses account for 30 percent of all genetic mutations since our species' divergence from chimpanzees.[25] The Black Death—caused by *Yersinia pestis*—killed up to 60 percent of the population and many of those who survived did so because they had specific genes that boosted their immune response.[26] Since the adoption of settled agriculture in sub-Saharan Africa between 5,000 and 4,000 years ago, malaria has killed so many people that it is the "strongest known force for evolutionary selection in the recent history of the human genome."[27] It is therefore not the strongest or most intelligent members of our species who were most likely to survive long enough to pass on their DNA to the next generation; rather, it was humans who had the most effective immune system to cope with the onslaught of infectious diseases, or those who had mutations that made their cells unusable to microbes. Lots of these mutations not only conferred resistance to pathogens but also had a negative impact on cell function. This suggests that humans' struggle for existence was a fight against microbes rather than alpha males and apex predators.

Our bodies are absolutely teeming with microscopic life. Each of us hosts an estimated 40 trillion bacteria—meaning they slightly outnumber human cells.[28] Viruses? At least ten times that figure. In total, the human microbiome—all the microbes living in our body—weighs around the same as our brain, between one and two kilos.[29] The vast majority of these bacteria and viruses don't make us ill. In fact, they have evolved with our ancestors for millions of years, forming close and interdependent relationships with one another. In other words, humans have outsourced some essential tasks to microbes. This is because bacteria can adapt more quickly to new situations than humans. While our cells carry between 20,000 and 25,000 genes, the microbiome contains around 500 times more than that.[30] The enormous number of genes, together with the fact that they reproduce far more quickly than more complex life and are able to transfer genes "horizontally" from one species to another, allows bacteria to evolve much faster than humans. Cooperation between microbes and humans is most evident in the gut, where there is a plentiful supply of proteins, fats and carbohydrates for bacteria to feast on and, in return, they help out with essential processes such as the digestion of food and the production of vitamins and minerals. Viruses keep us healthy too, especially phages that kill harmful bacteria inside our bodies.

There is now growing evidence that the gut microbiome has an important impact on the human brain. We've long sensed this connection, of course. A variety of idioms in the English language seem to link our brains and bellies: you can have a gut feeling or gut instinct about something; butterflies, knots or a pit in your stomach; find a situation gut-wrenching; or ruminate on a problem. A recent editorial in Nature noted that "Just ten years ago, the idea that microorganisms in the human gut could influence the brain was often dismissed as wild . . . Not any more." The study that inspired the editors to write this piece analyzed bacteria in the feces of more than 2,000 Belgians.[31] Of over 500 strains of bacteria they tested, more than 90 percent were able to produce neurotransmitters like dopamine and serotonin that play a key role in regulating human moods. As this ability is unique to bacteria that live in the bodies of animals, it seems that these microbes have evolved over millions of years to create chemical messengers which allow them to communicate with and influence their hosts. The evolutionary reason why bacteria produce chemicals that improve our moods may be that it makes us more likely to be gregarious and therefore provide them with opportunitites to colonize other hosts.

The researchers then compared the microbiomes of volunteers who had been diagnosed with depression with those who had not, finding two types of bacteria—*Coprococcus* and *Dialister*—that were common in the guts of healthy participants but absent in those who suffered depression. Both of these bacteria produce substances known to have antidepressive properties. This is not conclusive evidence of a link between the gut microbiome and the mind, but it is a pretty good start—especially when added to the large amount of research on the link between brain and gut bacteria in "germ-free" mice and rats.[32] It has raised hopes that fecal transplants from people with healthy microbiomes will one day provide a more effective treatment for depression than Prozac or therapy.

The implications of all this are stupefying. Not only did we evolve from bacteria and acquire vital segments of our genome from viruses. It is now clear that our bodies and even our brains are only able to function in the way they do because of the vital contributions of microbes that evolved alongside—and inside—our ancestors. The discovery that the microscopic bacteria in our guts are able to influence our feelings and behavior in indiscernible but important ways suggests that humans are not even fully in control of their own minds. But if bacteria and viruses are such a fundamental part of who we are on an individual level, what role do they play on a collective level? Or, put another way, how have microbes impacted the evolution of human societies and politics? How have they influenced history?

History from Below, Not from Above

One advancement after another in the natural sciences has revealed how insignificant and impotent our species is in the grand scheme of things. And yet humans have been slow to respond to these developments. Most of us still retain an anthropocentric worldview—one in which our species holds dominion over nature, despite all the evidence to the contrary. Our planet is still understood as little more than a stage on which humans act out their parts. This is apparent in the way that most people understand history.

Traditionally, charismatic, brave, visionary individuals—almost all of them males—were seen as the driving force of history. As the Scottish historian-philosopher Thomas Carlyle wrote in the mid-nineteenth century, "the history of the world is but the biography of great men."[33] This theory was blamed for encouraging the rise of totalitarian dictators such as Hitler and Stalin, and has been out of fashion among professional historians since the mid-twentieth century. Despite this, many of Carlyle's heroes are still worshipped: literally in the case of Jesus, Muhammad, and—kind of—Martin Luther; and figuratively with national heroes like Alexander the Great,* Washington, Napoleon and Charlemagne, "the founder of Europe." The twentieth century has provided a new cast of Great Men or—more often—villains: Lenin, Stalin, Churchill, Roosevelt, Hitler, Mao, de Gaulle, and so on. Some of these modern heroes are even women, in the case of Eva Peron or Margaret Thatcher. The history section of your local library and the history documentaries showing on TV are undoubtedly dominated by this cast of characters.[34]

The main alternative to the Great Men theory of history is what Lucien Febvre, the French historian, referred to in the early 1930s as "*histoire vue d'en bas et non d'en haut*," or "history from below and not from above."[35] This approach focuses on the masses of ordinary men and women, often fighting against exploitation and oppression. In this view, it is the cumulative impact of all their struggles that drives progressive social, political and economic transformations. E. P. Thompson's *The Making of the English Working Class* (1963) and Howard Zinn's *A People's History of the United States* (1980) are classic examples of this genre. The idea of history from below is much more inclusive than the worship of a few heroic individuals, but still it focuses on humans as the driving force of history.

This book sets out an alternative way of looking at the world that

---

* Both Greece and Northern Macedonia claim Alexander as a national hero. The question of whether he was a bona fide Greek or a Slav—and therefore worthy of worship in Northern Macedonia—is subject to a highly charged disagreement between the two countries.

incorporates the scientific developments outlined in this chapter: not just Freud's general point that humans have a far less significant place in the world than we used to think, but also the realization that microbes play a much more important role than we would have believed just a few years ago. In medicine, pathogenesis refers to the origins and development (*genesis or γένεσις*) of a disease (*pathos* or πάθος), with a particular focus on the way that pathogens infect our cells and the effect this has on our bodies. In the pages that follow, we will explore how viruses, bacteria and other microbes impact aggregations of bodies—that is, the body politic, body economic and body social. This is history from deep below. Rather than thousands or millions of "little" humans working together to change the world, we will explore the role that billions or trillions of microscopic viruses and bacteria have played in history.

Almost five decades after it was first published, William McNeill's *Plagues and Peoples* (1976) remains the most well-read and important book on the impact of epidemics on society, politics and economics. But so much has changed in the intervening years that it is now necessary to take a new look at the topic. Indeed, McNeill conceded in the opening pages that "exact information is lacking wherewith to create a history of human infections." Back then, the main evidence was eyewitness accounts of people who had lived through pandemics. These provide an invaluable insight into the past but are sporadic at best, as well as heavily biased toward recent history and literate societies. In fact, there were so many gaps in the historical record that *Plagues and Peoples* relies as much on its author's imagination as it does facts to piece together a coherent and convincing account of the narrative.

Around the same time that *Plagues and Peoples* was written, archeologists and anthropologists were trying to analyze ancient skeletons for signs of infectious disease. Unfortunately, they were only able to draw very limited conclusions because the vast majority of pathogens don't leave any visible mark on our bones. In many cases, the only way to really understand anything about the health of an individual was to estimate their height. At the time it must have seemed like we knew everything we were ever going to know about the interaction between infectious diseases and history. But over the past few years, advances in DNA analysis have revolutionized our understanding of pathogens and the past. Ancient skeletons have started to reveal extraordinary secrets—and lots of them. This book pulls together this ground-breaking research, much of which has been published in pay-walled scientific journals and is not widely read outside of academia, and places it in the context of research from other disciplines, including archeology, history, anthropology, economics and sociology.

Outbreaks of infectious diseases have destroyed millions of lives and decimated whole civilizations, but the devastation has created opportunities for new societies and ideas to emerge and thrive. In this way, pathogens have been the protagonists in many of the most important social, political and economic transformations in history: the transition from a planet inhabited by multiple species of human to one in which *Homo sapiens* reigned supreme; the replacement of nomadic hunter-gatherer society with sedentary agriculture; the demise of the great empires of antiquity; the transformations of Christianity and Islam from small sects in Palestine and the Hijaz to world religions; the shift from feudalism to capitalism; the devastation wrought by European colonialism; the Agricultural and Industrial Revolutions; and the creation of the modern welfare state. By the time we have finished, I hope to have changed the way you think about history and our species' role in it—to convince you that the modern world has been shaped by microbes as much as by women and men.

Chapter 1
Paleolithic Plagues

History makes no sense without prehistory, and
prehistory makes no sense without biology.
—E. O. WILSON

Rediscovering Middle-earth

The idea of a world inhabited by multiple human and humanoid species will be familiar to readers of fantasy literature. Take, for example, the Fellowship that accompanies Frodo Baggins on his journey to dispose of the One Ring in the fires of Mount Doom. Aragorn and Boromir are Men, a term used to denote both male and female humans. Frodo, Sam, Merry and Pippin are Hobbits, closely related to Men but roughly half as tall and with oversize, furry feet. Then there is Legolas, a slender and pointy-eared Elf with a superhuman sense of sight and hearing. And Gimli is a Dwarf, belonging to the short, thickset warrior-like people who live in the mountains of Middle-earth.

J.R.R. Tolkien did not create this legendarium from scratch. His fantasy world was strongly influenced by the Germanic mythology that he studied in his day job, as a professor of Anglo-Saxon at Oxford University. This is why Tolkien claimed to have discovered rather than invented Middle-earth.[1] Over the last two decades, researchers have uncovered an array of evidence that has transformed our knowledge of the world that early humans inhabited. New archeological discoveries, combined with advances in the technology used to analyze the DNA retrieved from ancient skeletons, clearly demonstrate that for most of the time *Homo sapiens* has been around—from about 300,000 to 50,000 years ago—the planet resembled Tolkien's Middle-earth or a Norse saga more than the world we occupy today. Although our ancestors didn't live alongside Hobbits, Elves and Dwarves, they shared the earth with a rich cast of human species.

Geneticists estimate that our last common ancestor with chimpanzees dates to between 6 and 8 million years ago.[2] Just over 3 million years ago, protohumans were habitually walking on two legs but the size of their brains and bodies had hardly changed—as demonstrated by "Lucy," the female skeleton discovered in Ethiopia in 1974 by archeologists as they listened to the Beatles' song "Lucy in the Sky with Diamonds." *Homo erectus*, or "upright man," appears in the fossil record about 2 million years ago. With relatively long legs, short arms and a large head, *Homo erectus* is the earliest example of a species that looks recognizably human. They were the first species of humans to migrate out of Africa, and within a relatively short period of time they managed to spread across much of the Old World. Their remains have been found near the southern tip of Africa, in the Caucuses, northern China and Java.

Our own species evolved from *Homo erectus*. The first known skeletal remains with the modern anatomical features typical of *Homo sapiens* are the fossilized bones of five people who died some 100 kilometers from Marrakesh about 315,000 years ago.[3] For most of the time since then, they remained more or less exclusively in Africa—although our ancestors' remains have been found everywhere from Morocco to the Cape. *Homo sapiens* wasn't the only species of humans living in the continent, however. There is both archeological and genetic evidence that we coexisted in Africa with a variety of other species of humans.[4]

Neanderthals also evolved from *Homo erectus*. They diverged from our own species between three-quarters and half a million years ago, when a group of archaic humans migrated out of Africa and ended up in Europe. *Homo neanderthalensis* retained so-called archaic features—that is, lower braincases, heavier brows and less prominent chins—all of which distinguish them from us anatomically modern humans. Neanderthals were also taller, heavier, stronger and had slightly bigger brains than *Homo sapiens*. Their fair skin helped them absorb sunlight—which is crucial for making vitamin D—and their large, frequently blue eyes enabled them to see in the dark European winter. Neanderthals eventually spread out over much of Western Eurasia; their remains have been found from Gibraltar in the west to the Altai Mountains in Siberia in the east.

Over the last two decades, scientists have discovered several more species of humans that were alive at the same time as *Homo sapiens*. Denisovans split from Neanderthals not long after they'd ventured out of Africa and went on to occupy the eastern part of Eurasia. The only physical traces of this species are a few bone fragments uncovered in caves in the Altai Mountains and on the Tibetan plateau. Anatomically, Denisovans would have looked similar to Neanderthals although they appear to have had much bigger teeth, and they carried a number of gene mutations, including one that affected red blood cells and allowed them to live comfortably at high altitudes.[5] *Homo floresiensis* lived on the Indonesian island of Flores. They are colloquially referred to as Hobbits on account of their height—they stood just over a meter tall—and disproportionately long feet.[6] One theory suggests that *Homo floresiensis* is descended from *Homo erectus*, who arrived there about a million years ago and then became isolated by deep waters.* *Homo luzonensis* is another extinct, small-bodied human species that was discovered in 2019 on the island of Luzon, in the Philippines. Their curved fingers and toe bones suggest that they retained the climbing abilities of our prehuman ancestors.[7]

So for the first quarter of a million years, *Homo sapiens* lived in Africa alongside other species of humans, and yet more species of human inhabited Europe and Asia. Then, between 50,000 and 40,000 years ago, something astonishing happened. Within a few thousand years, *Homo sapiens* burst out of Africa and quickly spread across the world— from western Europe all the way to Australia. At the same time, all other species of human vanished from the face of the earth.[8] The most recent trace of *Homo luzonensis* and *Homo floresiensis* is from 50,000

---

* Flores was also home to a now extinct species of dwarf elephant that was not much taller than the diminutive humans that once lived there. The Hobbits and mini-elephants shrank in a process called "insular dwarfism": where resources are limited, smaller bodies are positively selected for because they offer a survival advantage in that they need fewer calories.

years ago.[9] The last evidence of Denisovans dates to between 49,000
and 43,000 years ago, although they may have held out in isolated parts
of New Guinea for longer.[10] Neanderthals appear to have survived
until between 41,000 and 39,000 years ago.[11] The expansion of *Homo
sapiens* and disappearance of other species fundamentally transformed
the planet and laid the foundations for the world we inhabit today.
Why this happened is one of the biggest mysteries of human prehistory.

The Explosive Awakening of the Modern Human Soul

In late December 1994, three spelunkers were searching for caves in
the limestone cliffs above the River Ardèche in southeast France. In a
small recess not far from a hiking trail, one of them felt a draft of cool
air—a telltale sign of a cavity. After clearing away some debris and
crawling along a narrow passage, the group arrived at a ledge looking
down on to a vast, dark chamber. They descended 10 meters to the
cave floor down a chain ladder and began to explore. Then, when the
light from their headlamps hit the cave wall, one of them shouted:
"They were here!"

The three colleagues had just rediscovered one of the most remarkable examples of prehistoric art: beautiful depictions of mammoths,
lionesses, aurochs, bison, ibex, horses and woolly rhinoceroses that use
the irregularities of the limestone to conjure a sense of movement and
three-dimensionality. Judith Thurman, writing in the *New Yorker* after
visiting Chauvet, described a "bestiary of such vitality and finesse that,
by the flicker of torchlight, the animals seem to surge from the walls,
and move across them like figures in a magic-lantern show."[12]

The oldest Chauvet cave paintings were created between 37,000
and 33,500 years ago, just a few millennia after *Homo sapiens* first arrived in western Europe and Neanderthals disappeared.[13] This period
of prehistory appears to have been one of extraordinary creative flourishing.[14] The cave paintings of animals and hands at Altamira in northern Spain date to the same period. The earliest examples of art carved
from mammoth ivory were produced around the same time in what is
now southern Germany. The Venus of Hohle Fels, a statuette with bal-

looning breasts and an elaborately carved vulva, is the first undisputed depiction of a human being.[15] The *Löwenmensch* of Hohlenstein-Stadel is a 30-centimeter-high figurine with the head of a lion and an upright, partly human body. It is the oldest known representation of a creature that does not exist in the real world.[16] In addition, several flutes carved from mammoth ivory and animal bone that date to around 40,000 years ago have been discovered in German caves, including Hohle Fels. This is the earliest evidence of humans playing music.[17]

In terms of scale and technical skill, the only example of prehistoric art comparable to Chauvet is at Lascaux, about 350 kilometers to the west.[18] But this Paleolithic masterpiece is "just" 17,000 years old—that is, as close in time to the present day as to Chauvet.[19] Lascaux was inadvertently rediscovered by amateurs in 1940, when a group of school friends stumbled upon the paintings when they were looking for a legendary underground secret passage to the nearby château. When Picasso visited he is supposed to have remarked to his guide, "They've invented everything."[20] The anecdote underlines the sophistication of the humans who created these masterpieces and how similar their preoccupations and aesthetic tastes were to those of modern humans.

Prior to 40,000 years ago, evidence of human creativity amounts to a few hand stencils, some perforated, colored shells that would have been used as jewelry, and iron-rich rocks that were probably processed to produce ocher pigment—most likely to paint walls, shells or bodies. But there was nothing to suggest that *Homo sapiens* had the imagination or technical ability to produce the Chauvet cave paintings, the *Löwenmensch* and the Venus of Hohle Fels. It is astonishing that they were all created within a few thousand years and a few hundred kilometers of one another. In Werner Herzog's documentary film about Chauvet, *Cave of Forgotten Dreams* (2010), he says of the appearance of prehistoric art in what is now France and Germany: "It was not a primitive beginning or a slow evolution. It rather burst onto the scene like a sudden explosive event. It is as if the modern human soul had awakened here."

The ingenuity that is evident in Paleolithic European cave art plays a key role in the most popular explanation for *Homo sapiens'* rise to world dominance. Our species is said to have triumphed over all others because it was uniquely capable of what paleoanthropologists—

researchers concerned with the origins and development of early humans—call "symbolic behavior." In other words, *Homo sapiens* had the unique capacity to use language and art to express and exchange ideas. The ability to think and behave in complex ways allowed us to plan, cooperate and out-compete the bigger, stronger Neanderthals, as well as other humans who did not possess these skills.[21] This theory is based on a particular view of nature, seeing *Homo sapiens* as engaged in a struggle for survival with other species from the same genus. According to this argument, we came out on top because we were more intelligent.

It isn't difficult to understand why many people find this idea appealing. It allowed humanity to regain the privileged position that it lost when Darwin's theory of evolution by natural selection made it clear that we were just another species of animals. We might be apes, but at least we are exceptionally brainy apes. The most famous recent advocate of this theory is the Israeli historian Yuval Noah Harari in his bestselling book *Sapiens* (2014). Harari argues that "Homo sapiens conquered the world thanks above all to its unique language . . . that allows us to ingest, store and communicate a prodigious amount of information about the surrounding world." This explanation is by no means unique to Harari, however; it is widely accepted among scholars who study the topic. The assumption that we are uniquely clever is apparent in the name we have given our species—*Homo sapiens,* of course, literally means wise man. Symbolic behavior is seen as so vital to the essence of modern humans that several influential academics have referred to us as the "symbolic species" or "*Homo symbolicus.*"[22]

Archeologists and anthropologists have identified a variety of characteristics that they say are evidence of complex symbolic behavior, and therefore distinguish modern *Homo sapiens* from cognitively inferior human species.[23] Some of these can be observed in the archeological record, including burying one's dead, wearing jewelry, using ocher for decoration and producing art. The clearest example of symbolic behavior is the mind-blowingly impressive and well-preserved prehistoric art that appeared in western Europe between 40,000 and 30,000 years ago, which Harari and others see as conclusive evidence of *Homo sapiens'* cognitive superiority.

There is, however, an obvious problem with the argument that *Homo sapiens'* capacity for symbolic behavior allowed them to break out of Africa and vanquish all other species of humans: *Homo sapiens* have been around for at least 300,000 years as an anatomically distinct species, but their apparent cognitive superiority only kicked in between 40,000 and 50,000 years ago, when they surged out of Africa and vanquished all other human species. A quarter of a million years seems like a long time to wait for a breakthrough. The theory makes even less sense when we consider that, from a historical perspective, migrating out of Africa was not remarkable. *Homo erectus* managed it about 2 million years ago, and so did the Neanderthals' ancestors about half a million years ago. Both species are supposed to be inferior to our own.

Proponents of the idea that *Homo sapiens'* superior intelligence enabled their rise to world dominance try to overcome this problem with some logical gymnastics, arguing that they evolved their exceptional cognitive abilities a long time after they developed the anatomical characteristics which distinguish them from other species. Harari and many other scholars argue that modern humans underwent a "cognitive revolution" between 70,000 and 30,000 years ago that transformed the way they thought and behaved. These newly acquired abilities gave *Homo sapiens* a competitive edge and explain their rise to dominance.

The idea of the cognitive revolution is conveniently Eurocentric. It locates modern-day France and Germany as the site of the metamorphosis of human behavior and identifies the first *Homo sapiens* capable of symbolic thought as those who left Africa and then turned left when they reached the Levant. This isn't surprising. The discoveries of Lascaux in 1940, Chauvet in 1994 and the Venus of Hohle Fels in 2008, as well as the reconstruction of the *Löwenmensch* in the 1980s, dazzled several generations of scholars who grew up believing that "white" people originating in Europe were inherently superior to "non-white" people from elsewhere. The notion of a cognitive revolution can be seen as the prehistoric version of British art historian Kenneth Clark's thesis in *Civilisation*, the remarkably popular but dated 1969 BBC television series, which argues that civilization was the product of the artistic and cultural achievements of France, Italy and Germany from the Middle Ages to the twentieth century.

Rethinking the Cognitive Revolution

Stanley Kubrick's *2001: A Space Odyssey* (1968) begins not at the turn of the twenty-first century but with a scene entitled "The Dawn of Man," set at an unspecified time prior to the emergence of *Homo sapiens*. As the sun rises over an immense and desolate Namibian Desert, a band of ape-like creatures wake to find an alien-made black monolith. Richard Strauss's "Thus Spoke Zarathustra" kicks in, then one of the animals picks up a bone and starts hitting things with it. He beats a tapir to death, then joins some club-wielding buddies to attack a rival band, killing the alpha male and chasing the rest away from a prized watering hole. Ecstatic, one of the apes throws their bone spinning into the air. The camera follows it upward, setting the scene for the most famous match cut in film history, as the viewer is transported thousands—perhaps even millions—of years forward in time to a shot of a space station orbiting the earth. The implication is that the black monolith miraculously kick-starts the process of technological development. The adoption of basic tools like a bone club allowed our ancestors to consume more meat, which aided brain development and set in motion a process of invention and innovation that ultimately enabled humans to conquer the planet and even outer space.

The idea that a slab of black marble was responsible for human progress is obviously preposterous. It is almost as fanciful to suggest that a cognitive revolution occurred sometime between 70,000 and 30,000 years ago. For a start, there is no satisfactory explanation as to how and why. Harari suggests that it may have been the result of a gene mutation that improved *Homo sapiens'* ability to communicate. However, there isn't clear evidence that the anatomy of our brains changed around this time.[24]

Another suggestion is that eating fish rich in omega-3 fatty acids encouraged brain tissue development and improved cognitive function. Until recently it was believed that only *Homo sapiens* ate seafood, but a study published in *Science* in 2020 showed that Neanderthals living 86,000 to 106,000 years ago near Lisbon harvested and ate mussels, crustaceans and fish; they would therefore have benefited from the same nutrients as *Homo sapiens*. It is likely that Neanderthals across coastal Europe had a diet rich in seafood, but the evidence has been destroyed by the rise in sea levels since the end of the last Ice Age.[25]

A further challenge to the notion of a cognitive revolution is recent evidence that *Homo sapiens* were capable of symbolic behavior a long time before modern humans spread out of Africa. Most striking is a recent study based on excavations at a dried-up lake bed in Olorgesailie, Kenya.[26] Archeologists found lumps of rock that appeared to have been processed to create pigments over 300,000 years ago: manganese ore, ground down to produce black or dark-brown coloring, and iron-rich minerals that were used to make ocher. The ocher rocks did not come from the nearest source, which suggests that they were transported from farther afield because of their particularly bright hue. So, just as *Homo sapiens* were emerging as a distinct species, they were going to great efforts to get their hands on pigments in order to decorate themselves or paint things. The repercussions of this discovery are seismic: *Homo sapiens* didn't go through a distinct cognitive revolution; rather, modern human behavior arose at the same time as anatomically modern humans.

But if *Homo sapiens* were already capable of symbolic behavior— and were therefore superior to all other species of humans—300,000 years ago, why did it take them a quarter of a million years to break out of Africa and spread across the world? The answer is simple. A plethora of recent discoveries point to the fact that *Homo sapiens* weren't, in fact, smarter than other species of human.

In 1856 Johann Carl Fuhlrott, a schoolteacher, discovered the bones of a hitherto unknown species of human in a cave in the Neander Valley, western Germany. Following the publication of *On the Origin of Species* just three years later, there was a fierce debate about where the new specimen fit into the Tree of Life. Had *Homo sapiens* evolved from this strange humanoid or did it belong on an altogether separate branch? Conservative paleontologists working in cahoots with the Catholic Church made a concerted effort to emphasize the differences between the two species. By portraying Neanderthals as only very distantly related to *Homo sapiens*, they hoped to retain our status as a separate and exceptional species. When the first complete skeleton of a Neanderthal was discovered by three Catholic priests in 1908 in La Chapelle-aux-Saints in southern France—about 300 kilometers west

of Chauvet—the Church made sure it ended up in the hands of someone who shared their worldview, Marcellin Boule, director of the Laboratory of Paleontology at Muséum d'Histoire Naturelle in Paris,
reconstructed the specimen so that it looked much more simian than
human, with its forward-jutting head, slouching shoulders, hunched
spine, bent knees and even opposable toes. Boule's work was flawed,
but it had a profound impact on scientific understanding of Neanderthals for the next half-century and it still informs the popular stereotype of the ape-like cave man.[27]

The supposed differences between *Homo sapiens* and Neanderthals
extended to cognitive ability. Boule suggested that there was a link
between the Neanderthal's physical and mental attributes, arguing
that its "brutish" and "clumsy" posture indicated a lifestyle characterized by "functions of a purely vegetative or bestial kind."[28] William
King, the geologist who insisted Neanderthals were a separate species
and coined their name, was confident that they were incapable of
"moral and theistic conceptions."[29] At the end of the nineteenth century Ernst Haeckel, a German zoologist, Social Darwinist, promoter of
scientific racism, and strong influence on Nazi ideology, proposed calling Neanderthals *"Homo stupidus"* to distinguish them from *Homo
sapiens*.[30] Although no one uses this term anymore, the public's understanding has not really moved on and the received wisdom still holds
that we are superior. One dictionary definition of Neanderthal is
an "uncivilized, unintelligent, or uncouth man," which neatly sums up
the way in which the species name is used negatively in colloquial English.

Over the past couple of decades, however, it has become increasingly clear that Neanderthals were capable of all sorts of sophisticated
behaviors that until recently were only associated with *Homo sapiens*.
There is archeological evidence that Neanderthals manufactured stone
tools requiring cognitive skill and dexterity,[31] made fire on demand,[32]
sailed from mainland Europe to Crete and the Ionian Islands,[33] produced glue from the bark of the birch tree,[34] and appear to have treated
maladies with medicinal plants that had anesthetic and antibiotic
properties: traces of DNA from poplar trees, which contain salicylic
acid—the naturally occurring inspiration for the synthetic aspirin, and
Penicillium mold, the source of penicillin—have been found in the

calcified plaque of Neanderthals.[35] In 1989, archeologists found a Neanderthal hyoid, the delicate U-shaped bone that anchors ligaments and muscles in the throat and is key to human speech. This indicates that they would have been able to talk, albeit in a very high-pitched tone.[36] While we don't know anything about Neanderthal language, the fact that there wasn't a big behavioral gap between them and *Homo sapiens* is a strong indication that it would have had a similar level of complexity.[37]

We also know that Neanderthals buried their dead. In the 1950s and 1960s, the American archeologist Ralph Solecki and his team uncovered the remains of ten Neanderthals in Shanidar Cave, northern Iraq. At least some of these bodies had been deliberately buried. One skeleton is referred to as the "flower burial" because the clumps of pollen found close to it were believed to indicate that he was laid to rest on a bed of wildflowers, including yarrow, groundsels, grape hyacinth and St. Barnaby's thistle. The image of Neanderthals picking wildflowers to line the grave of a loved one really brings home how similar they were to us. Solecki claimed that his discovery revealed "that the universality of mankind and the love of beauty go beyond the boundary of our own species."[38] However, recent research suggests that burrowing rodents— the Persian jird—might have been responsible for introducing the wildflower pollen into the grave at a later date.[39]

Another Shanidar skeleton belonged to a male who may have been in his mid-forties when he died around 45,000 years ago. The man had suffered from severe disabilities for much of his life: he was blind in one eye as a result of a crushing blow to his head at a young age; his right arm was withered, and had possibly been amputated; he had fractured a metatarsal on his right foot, which had healed; and he was profoundly deaf.[40] This find is astonishing because it suggests that the band of Neanderthals living in Shanidar were willing and able to look after a very vulnerable member of their community. Such expressions of compassion are widely understood to be one of the key characteristics of a civilized society; indeed, for the anthropologist Margaret Mead, human civilization began when we started to care for the weak and sick.[41]

Over the past few years, archeologists have discovered many artifacts that indicate Neanderthals' symbolic behavior, including ocher-stained seashells with holes that would have been used for jewelry 115,000 years ago.[42] They predate by tens of thousands of years the earliest known examples of similar behavior among *Homo sapiens*. Evidence from Maastricht in the Netherlands indicates that Neanderthals were using red ocher that had been produced from rocks located 40 kilometers away a quarter of a million years ago. This is only slightly more recently than the remarkable find in Olorgesailie, showing that *Homo sapiens* did the same 300,000 years ago.[43] We also know that 176,000 years ago, 330 meters into Bruniquel Cave in southwest France, a group of Neanderthals broke off 400 stalagmites weighing a total of two tons to construct a stone circle, presumably used for a ceremonial purpose.[44]

Most incredible of all, recent research demonstrates that Neanderthals were the first human species to create cave art, the *sine qua non* of symbolic behavior. In Spain there are a number of caves decorated with prehistoric art, including red and black geometric shapes, hand stencils and hand prints. In 2018, researchers used uranium-thorium dating to estimate the age of the thin crusts of minerals that have formed on top of the paintings.[45] The paintings turned out to be at least 65,000 years old—making them the earliest known examples of cave art anywhere in the world. This was 10,000 years before the first indication that *Homo sapiens* lived in western Europe, meaning that these Paleolithic doodles must have been made by Neanderthals.[46] The results fundamentally challenged the notion that *Homo sapiens* was uniquely capable of sophisticated thought.

Recently, Chris Stringer, Head of Human Evolution at the Natural History Museum in London, and his collaborators concluded: "While there are certainly biological differences between Neanderthals and *H. sapiens*, the behavioural gap has narrowed to a point where there seems to be little difference between the two."[47] Bearing in mind the overwhelming lack of evidence, you might be wondering why anyone still thinks that there is a significant cognitive gap between Neanderthals and *Homo sapiens*. The answer seems to be blind prejudice. One recent academic article argues that it is the result of a "modern human superiority complex," while an anonymous archeologist quoted in the *New York Times* refers to "modern human supremacists."[48] It is true that Neanderthals did not produce anything comparable to the striking beauty and sophistication of the Chauvet cave paintings or the *Löwen-mensch* figurine—but neither did *Homo sapiens* until after the Neanderthals disappeared.

The remarkable artistic accomplishments that seemingly emerged from nowhere between 40,000 and 30,000 years ago in western Europe may have occurred when Neanderthals and *Homo sapiens* began to mix and exchange ideas after being separated for several hundred thousand years.[49] While the hypothesis that Neanderthals inspired *Homo sapiens'* creative explosion is speculative, it is certainly plausible. The American geneticist David Reich cites evidence that Neanderthals borrowed tool-making technology from *Homo sapiens*.[50] And there are other instances in history where the interaction of two distinct cultures resulted in an explosion of creativity. One obvious example is jazz, which originated among African American communities in New Orleans in the late nineteenth and early twentieth centuries and combines musical traditions that were brought by enslaved people from West Africa—such as syncopated rhythm and improvisation—with harmonies and instruments from European classical music.

Clearly, the hypothesis that Neanderthals and *Homo sapiens* exchanged painting tips is impossible to verify or refute. But we know for sure that the two species met on multiple occasions, and over the last two decades we have begun to understand something about the substance of these interactions.

Poison and Antidote

In fiction, there are various examples of humans reproducing with humanoids. Their offspring often inherit superpowers from the non-human parent. Hrólfr Kraki's saga features Skuld, a princess with magic powers, who is born after the Danish King Helgi rapes an Elf woman. In Tolkien's legendarium, Arwen is part-Elf, part-Man, which makes her immortal. *Star Trek*'s Spock is half-human, half-Vulcan. From the Vulcan side of his family, he retained the ability to merge his mind with another person's just by touching his fingertips to their temples. Outside of fantasy novels, ancient mythology and sci-fi, the idea of hu-

mans procreating with other humanoid species seems preposterous—
perverted even.* But over the last ten years, it has become apparent
that *Homo sapiens* reproduced with other species. These liaisons allowed their descendants to acquire a variety of traits that weren't exactly superpowers but helped them adapt to new challenges as they
migrated out of Africa.

About a decade ago, researchers managed to extract DNA from Neanderthal bones and sequence the genome.[51] When they compared
their findings to the *Homo sapiens* genome, they realized that anyone
alive today whose ancestors are Europeans, Asians or Native Americans has inherited about 2 percent of their genes from Neanderthals.[52]
While this might not sound like much, we don't all have the same bits
of Neanderthal DNA and when we pool all these gene variants they
account for about 40 percent of the Neanderthal genome[53]—providing
incontrovertible evidence that the two species not only met, but had
sex and reproduced. Neanderthal males coupled up with *Homo sapiens*
females and vice versa.[54] Interbreeding happened over tens of thousands of years, but the most active period of mating was between about
50,000 and 60,000 years ago.[55]

Ancient DNA even provides some tantalizing clues about what
these interspecies trysts would have been like. When scientists looked
at the calcified plaque of a 48,000-year-old Neanderthal's teeth, they
found the DNA of a strain of archaea called *Methanobrevibacter oralis*
that is present in the mouths of humans today and is associated with
gum disease.[56] After comparing the Neanderthal sample with a modern strain, it became clear that the microbes' last common ancestor
lived about 120,000 years ago. As that is several hundred thousand
years after Neanderthals and *Homo sapiens* diverged, the germ must
have been transmitted between the two species. The most likely way
this happened was through kissing or perhaps sharing food. This suggests that the liaisons between Neanderthals and *Homo sapiens* were

* Tales of interspecies reproduction are much more salacious and disconcerting in
Greek mythology. Helen of Troy hatched from an egg after Zeus transformed himself into
a swan and had sex with—or, in some versions of the story, raped—Leda, wife of the king
of Sparta. The half-man half-bull Minotaur was born after Pasiphaë—the wife of Minos,
king of Crete—asked Daedalus to build a hollow model of a cow from wood so she could
climb into it and have sex with a bull that had become her obsession.

consensual—in other words, more like the love story of Arwen and Aragorn than King Helgi's attack on Skuld's Elfish mother.

The Neanderthal gene variants retained in the *Homo sapiens* genome are not random. Over the hundreds of thousands of years that Neanderthals and their ancestors lived in Europe they adapted to the climate, flora, fauna and pathogens through the excruciatingly slow process of evolution first described by Charles Darwin. At the same time, *Homo sapiens* evolved to better cope with the various challenges that they encountered in Africa. This is how *Homo sapiens* and Neanderthals became two separate species.

Ice Age Europe would have been a forbidding environment for *Homo sapiens*, having evolved in Africa. Fragments of a 210,000-year-old *Homo sapiens'* skull have been discovered in a cave on the Mani Peninsula in southern Greece; this very early foray was not permanent, and Neanderthals occupied the same site forty millennia later.[57] Similarly, *Homo sapiens* remains dating to between 100,000 and 200,000 years ago have been found at various sites in Israel, while Neanderthal bones from between 48,000 and 60,000 years ago have also been uncovered in the same area.[58] This demonstrates that *Homo sapiens'* early incursions out of Africa into the Eastern Mediterranean did not develop into a permanent move. Instead, *Homo sapiens* advanced and then retreated, and Neanderthals expanded into areas that they once occupied. It is more evidence—if the reader needs it—that *Homo sapiens* were not innately superior to Neanderthals.

After they reproduced, *Homo sapiens* retained certain Neanderthal gene variants which helped them to survive as they migrated northward. Geneticists call this "adaptive introgression"—and it is the closest that humans can get to the process of horizontal gene transfer, which allows different species of bacteria to exchange DNA in order to adjust to new environmental challenges. Modern humans retain Neanderthal gene variants that influence skin pigmentation and hair cells—important adaptations for a species that had evolved for hundreds of thousands of years in sunny Africa but was now beginning to migrate into cold, dark Europe.[59] *Homo sapiens* also acquired immune-related Neanderthal genes that helped them adjust to the new disease environment that they encountered.

From about 200,000 years ago, nomadic groups of *Homo sapiens* and

Neanderthal hunter-gatherers encountered one another as they pushed out of their respective homelands into the Eastern Mediterranean. When the two species began to interact, they had already been exposed to different pathogens for hundreds of millennia. They had evolved at least partial immunity to diseases that were endemic in their own species, but they would have been extremely vulnerable to the bacteria and viruses spread by the other species. Pathogens that caused relatively innocuous symptoms in Homo sapiens could be deadly to Neanderthals, and vice versa. As a result, infectious diseases created an "invisible barrier": it was impossible for Homo sapiens to migrate out of Africa because sooner or later they would encounter Neanderthals and their pathogens and get ill, and the same was true when Neanderthals pushed southward.[60] For early humans, the Eastern Mediterranean region must have seemed like a cursed realm, the Paleolithic equivalent of Tolkien's Mordor.*

Without vaccines, our immune systems are the only defense against infectious diseases. Homo sapiens could have overcome the invisible barrier created by Neanderthal diseases through Darwinian evolution. Sooner or later, genetic mutations would have occurred that allowed Homo sapiens' immune systems to mount an effective response to Neanderthal pathogens. Because people with these gene variants were more likely to survive, over time they spread widely through the population. But Homo sapiens took a much quicker route to immunity—by interbreeding. Reproducing with another closely related species is an unintentional kind of biohacking: it immediately endows a species with gene variants that are already adapted to the new environment. Introgressed Neanderthal DNA was crucial in helping Homo sapiens to adapt to the new pathogens that they encountered as they migrated out of Africa. This process has been called the "poison-antidote model" of adaptive introgression: Neanderthals gave Homo sapiens a "poison" by exposing them to a novel pathogen, but also the "antidote" in the form of introgressed gene variants that confer resistance to the patho-

---

* To understand the potential impact of contact between Homo sapiens and Neanderthals, consider that Native Americans and Europeans had been separated for about 17,000 years before renewed contact literally decimated the indigenous population of the Americas in the sixteenth century. Modern humans and Neanderthals were separated for at least thirty times longer.

gen.[61] As a result, many of the Neanderthal gene variants that remain in our genome relate specifically to our immune response.[62]

We even know something about the type of pathogens that *Homo sapiens* encountered when they interacted with Neanderthals. Neanderthal gene variants most likely to be retained by Europeans today are those which code for proteins that interact with RNA viruses, particularly HIV and flu, and were first acquired about 50,000 years ago.[63] This is strong evidence that *Homo sapiens* encountered similar diseases when they mixed with Neanderthals in the Eastern Mediterranean. As Neanderthals didn't manage to survive, it is less clear what *Homo sapiens* diseases they struggled with. From a theoretical perspective, RNA viruses are the most likely candidates as they tend to be less accurate than DNA ones when copying their genetic code; as a result, mutations occur much more frequently and there is a greater likelihood that an RNA virus will adapt and jump the species barrier. This explains why so many contemporary diseases are caused by RNA viruses—not just flu and HIV-AIDS but also measles, polio, Ebola, SARS and, of course, Covid-19.[64]

Neanderthals weren't the only human species to crossbreed with *Homo sapiens*. The same process occurred when modern humans interacted with Denisovans, who lived in Eastern Eurasia. Despite the faint physical trace that they have left behind—just a handful of bone fragments—their gene variants remain present in the genomes of billions of people alive today. Denisovan DNA comprises less than 1 percent of East and South Asians' genomes, but between 3 and 6 percent of New Guineans'.[65] And just like the Neanderthal-*Homo sapiens* poison-antidote model, many introgressed Denisovan gene variants carried are involved in immune-related processes, suggesting that these genes facilitated *Homo sapiens'* adaptation to pathogens that they encountered as they pushed into Eastern Eurasia.[66]

Beyond the immune system, introgressed Denisovan gene variants account for much of the remarkable physical diversity of modern humans, allowing them to live in a variety of extreme habitats. Tibetans carry a Denisovan gene mutation that affects red blood cells, making it possible to live comfortably on a 13,000-feet- or 4,000-meter-high plateau where the air contains 40 percent less oxygen than at sea level.[67] Another gene variant that increases the size of the spleen is carried by the Sama-Bajau, nomadic people who live on flotillas of houseboats in the seas off the Philippines, Malaysia and Indonesia.[68] The spleen stores oxygen-carrying red blood cells, and when humans hold their breath it expels these cells to boost oxygen levels; this helps to explain how Sama-Bajau are able to dive to depths of over 230 feet or 70 meters with nothing more than a set of weights and a pair of wooden goggles. The Inuit of northern Canada and parts of Greenland and Alaska have retained Denisovan genes that influence the storage of fats, which helps them to thrive in an exceptionally cold climate.[69] These capabilities may not make the cut for a fantasy novel, but they are nonetheless extraordinary. When you think about it, however, the immune system might well be the most remarkable superpower of all.

Paleolithic Viruses and the Ascent of Modern Humans

The poison-antidote model is not a one-way process. Neanderthals would have also developed resistance to infectious diseases carried by *Homo sapiens* through adaptive introgression. The genome of a Neanderthal man who lived roughly 100,000 years ago in the Altai Mountains contains *Homo sapiens* gene variants that enhance the immune response to viral infections.[70] But if adaptive introgression helped both species to build up immunity to each other's diseases, why did *Homo sapiens* prevail and Neanderthals disappear? To answer this question we need to consider how climate impacts the prevalence of infectious disease.

The Last Glacial Period—which lasted from around 110,000 to 12,000 years ago—covered much of North Eurasia in ice and made it difficult for Neanderthals to survive. Estimates for their population size vary from 5,000 to 70,000—tiny when one considers that they were spread across a region that stretched from the Atlantic Ocean to Siberia.[71] It shouldn't come as a surprise that there is evidence of long-term inbreeding. DNA analysis of a female Neanderthal who was alive over 50,000 years ago in the Altai Mountains demonstrates that her parents were half-siblings and that mating between close relatives had been common among her recent ancestors.[72] The impact of the glacial period would have been far less catastrophic in Africa, where *Homo sapiens* still lived. Food would have remained abundant and the fall in temperature made the climate more favorable. There were between 120,000 and 325,000 modern humans when they began to venture out of Africa,[73] and their genome had four times greater diversity.[74] *Homo sapiens* would therefore have been more resilient to infectious diseases carried by Neanderthals.

The climate also affected the two species' ability to survive each other's pathogens in another way. The closer one gets to the equator, the hotter it is, because more of the sun's energy reaches the earth. Vegetation in the form of trees and plants tends to be more abundant, which in turn supports dense and varied animal life. The clearest example of this is tropical rainforests, which cover just over 5 percent of the earth's surface but are home to half the world's animals.[75] They teem with buzzing insects, howling monkeys, singing birds, and the occasional big cat on the prowl. All these animals support a vast array of microbes, some of which cause infectious diseases. The vast majority of pathogens that are capable of infecting humans are zoonotic—that is, they originate in animals and then jump the species barrier to infect us. So the greater variety of life in tropical regions means that there are many more deadly pathogens there than in temperate zones. *Homo sapiens*, whose ancestors had lived in Africa for millions of years, carried a far greater disease load than Neanderthals, who had inhabited Europe for hundreds of thousands of years. As a result, *Homo sapiens* would have developed resistance to Neanderthal viruses and bacteria before Neanderthals became tolerant to *Homo sapiens'* pathogens.[76]

When *Homo sapiens* gained immunity to Neanderthal diseases between 50,000 and 40,000 years ago, they were finally able to migrate northward out of Africa into areas inhabited by Neanderthals without getting horribly ill. The curse that had made the Eastern Mediterranean all but uninhabitable for tens of thousands of years was lifted. Our ancestors traveled deep into Eurasia, where they encountered Neanderthal and Denisovan communities that had never been exposed to African pathogens and hadn't had the opportunity to build up any tolerance. Within a relatively short period of time all other human species died out and were replaced by the newly ubiquitous *Homo sapiens*. The world would never be the same again. It ceased to resemble Middle-earth, with its rich cast of human species, and quickly became the *Homo sapiens*–dominated planet that we still inhabit today.

Chapter 2
Neolithic Plagues

> *Epidemiologically, this was perhaps the most lethal*
> *period in human history.*
>
> —JAMES SCOTT

Stonehenge: Built by Immigrants

When I drive from London to see my parents in southwest England, the A303 takes me across the bleak, almost treeless Salisbury Plain. About halfway through the journey, the traffic slows as drivers turn to gawk at the neatly arranged megaliths standing on the horizon about 150 meters from the road. Since as long as there have been written records, people have been fascinated by Stonehenge. The first person to write about it was the twelfth-century historian Henry of Huntingdon. He observed that "no one can work out how the stones were so skilfully lifted up to such a height or why they were erected there." His contemporary, Geoffrey of Monmouth, suggested it was built by the wizard Merlin, with the help of giants. Since then, everyone from William Wordsworth to Spinal Tap, the fictional heavy metal band, has wondered who built Stonehenge and why.* It is only in the past

---

* At the end of the eighteenth century, Wordsworth described Stonehenge as being "So proud to hint yet keep Thy secrets." One of the songs in the 1984 mockumentary suggests that the monument was built by a "strange race of people, the Druids," but that "No one knows who they were or what they were doing."

couple of decades that archeologists have begun to provide some partial answers.

The first stage of construction took place about 5,000 years ago. It involved creating a circular earth bank and ditch that now form the foundation of Stonehenge. Then, around 500 years later, the stones were transported and raised. The "bluestones," which weigh between 2 and 5 tons, came from Preseli Hills in west Wales, over 140 miles away.[1] The larger sarsen stones weigh up to 25 tons and were brought from about 15 miles to the north.[2] In a time before wheels and domesticated horses, this was a remarkable feat. We do not know why the Neolithic inhabitants of the British Isles went to all this trouble, but there are plenty of clues that point to Stonehenge being a site of great social and religious significance: it would have taken tens of millions of man-hours to quarry, shape, transport and erect the stones;[3] at summer solstice the sun rises directly in the middle of the two tallest sarsen stones; there are a large number of cremated remains buried in the vicinity; and people traveled there from as far afield as Scotland and west Wales, bringing pigs with them to eat at a feast site nearby.[4]

Stonehenge is one of the wonders of the British Isles. In the pantheon of Great British icons, it is up there with the late queen or fish-and-chips. But who actually constructed it? Just by looking at the megaliths, we can see that the builders had a sophisticated understanding of both astronomy and engineering. And the scale of the project suggests that they must have belonged to a society that was large, prosperous and organized. But until recently, we didn't have much more detail than that. Then, in 2019, scientists published a study that extracted and analyzed DNA from ancient skeletons belonging to seventy-three prehistoric Britons.[5] It revealed that—just as the Windsors are actually the House of Saxe-Coburg and Gotha, and battered cod was introduced to the country by Jewish refugees in the sixteenth century—the provenance of Stonehenge is complicated.

Stonehenge wasn't built by the earliest people to permanently inhabit the British Isles. It was constructed by farmers who originated in Anatolia and arrived in northwestern Europe about 6,000 years ago and almost completely replaced the genetically distinct hunter-gatherer population who had lived there since the end of the Ice Age. The irony of this was obvious. Three years before the study was made public, the

British electorate had voted to leave the European Union. Anger at uncontrolled immigration from Eastern Europe, plus the fear that Turkish people might soon be able to move to the UK without a visa, were seen as major factors in the outcome of the referendum. Conceptual artist Jeremy Deller responded to the study's release by mocking up a fake road sign that read "Stonehenge: Built by immigrants" in the colors and typography of a conventional British road sign.

The DNA analysis also demonstrated that Stonehenge's longevity contrasted starkly with the fate of the people who transported and arranged the giant stones. Presumably Britain's first farmers had gone to all this trouble because they wanted to create a structure that would be used and admired by future generations. But very quickly Stonehenge become a monument to a disappeared people. Within a century or two of the great sarsen stones being put in place the monument builders' ancestors were replaced by another new, genetically and culturally distinct group that forms the basis of the current population of the United Kingdom. So even those white British people who claim to be the indigenous population are not directly related to the builders of Stonehenge.

While the tale of Stonehenge is specific to the small corner of the world that I inhabit, it illustrates a more general phenomenon. Prehistory was punctuated by massive waves of migration that resulted in a new population moving into a region and almost completely wiping out the previous inhabitants. Nearly always, the migrants were unwittingly aided by an invisible but devastating weapon of mass destruction: infectious diseases to which they were to some extent immune but to which original communities had little or no resistance. In addition to novel pathogens, Neolithic immigrants brought new genes, new languages and new ideas such as farming and metallurgy. In this way, plagues that occurred thousands of years ago played a crucial role in shaping the world we now inhabit.

The Worst Decision in Human History?

For the first 2 million years after humans evolved as a distinct genus and the first 300,000 years of *Homo sapiens'* existence as a species, everyone everywhere sustained themselves by hunting and gathering. Until recently, it was widely accepted that all hunter-gatherers lived in small egalitarian bands, often not much bigger than their extended family; and that these groups were almost exclusively nomadic, traveling vast distances dictated by animal migrations and the seasonal availability of plants.[6] This romanticized idea was based on nineteenth- and twentieth-century anthropologists' observations of foraging societies, including the San Bushmen of the Kalahari Desert or aborigines in the Australian Outback. But it is wrong to infer that such communities simply provide a window into the distant past. While many of our prehistoric ancestors may have lived this way, there were also plenty of exceptions.

As the authors of The Dawn of Everything, David Graeber and David Wengrow, point out, the latest archeological research reveals sporadic but very definite evidence that foragers behaved in all sorts of ways that are normally associated with agricultural societies.[7] In the wetlands of Mesopotamia, where food was plentiful, the population settled down in semi-permanent hamlets prior to taking up agriculture.[8] The foraging people that Europeans encountered when they reached the Canadian northwest coast spent their winters in large villages. The 11,000-year-old, richly decorated stone temples of Göbekli Tepe in what is now southeast Turkey demonstrate that hunter-gatherers were capable of building monumental architecture. There are other examples of this phenomenon, including the massive earthworks at Poverty Point, Louisiana, that were created by Native Americans about 3,600 years ago.

As we saw in the previous chapter, infectious diseases weren't totally absent from hunter-gatherer societies, but they were far less common: the foraging lifestyle discouraged their emergence and spread. With the exceptions of dogs, hunter-gatherers didn't domesticate animals, which limited the opportunity for pathogens to jump from one species to another. Although foraging societies didn't only live in isolated, mobile bands, and some groups seem to have come together periodically in large congregations, the world's population was relatively small. Before the widespread adoption of settled agriculture, the planet probably had about 5 million inhabitants—less than one-thousandth of today's total.[9] Such a sparsely populated world provided limited opportunities for pathogens to spread when they did emerge. It is fair to assume that hunter-gatherers were on the whole a relatively healthy lot. A study based on observations of foraging communities over the last fifty years or so estimated the average lifespan of hunter-gatherers to be around seventy-two years.[10] Remarkably, this figure is only one year less than the global life expectancy today according to World Bank data.

The so-called Neolithic Revolution—or the First Agricultural Revolution—began 12,000 years ago in the Fertile Crescent. It coincided almost exactly with the end of the last Ice Age and the beginning of the Holocene—the period of relatively warm, stable climate that made agriculture possible. But this doesn't mark a point in time when everyone in the Middle East suddenly gave up hunting and gathering to instead cultivate crops and rear animals. Rather, it was the start of a long-drawn-out process. The first people to try to grow plants and breed docile animals probably weren't motivated by the desire to produce more food: it was already available in abundance in the Fertile Crescent—hence the name—and the change in climate would have been a boon for foragers as well as farmers. Rather, farming likely began as a series of playful experiments or as a way to spend longer each year in a semi-permanent settlement rather than on the move.[11]

Over many centuries, the results of multiple flirtations with farming were exchanged between villages in the Middle East. After about three millennia, the Neolithic Revolution had concluded—although Graeber and Wengrow argue that the process was too long, and too meandering to be referred to as a revolution at all. Whatever you call it, by 9,000 years ago, more or less everyone in the region had adopted a "Neolithic package" that provided them with most of their calories: this included emmer wheat, einkorn and barley, and sheep, goats, pigs and cattle. Over the next few thousand years, and independent of developments in the Near East, similar transformations happened elsewhere: in China the population domesticated rice, soybeans and different types of pigs; and in India millet, mung beans, another variety of rice and humped zebu cattle.[12] Settled agriculture spread slowly but surely across Eurasia, and by 2000 BCE farming supported large cities from the Mediterranean all the way to the Far East.[13] Farming also emerged in the Peruvian Andes, Mesoamerica and West Africa, where it foreshadowed the rise of early cities and states; and in the Amazon, the eastern woodlands of North America, and the central highlands New Guinea, where it did not.

Was the Neolithic Revolution good or bad for humanity? In what American political scientist and anthropologist James Scott calls the "standard civilizational narrative"—which is advocated by everyone from Thomas Hobbes to Marx—the adoption of settled agriculture is assumed to be an "epoch-making leap in mankind's well-being: more leisure, better nutrition, longer life expectancy, and, at long last, a settled life that promoted the household arts and the development of civilization."[14] The alternative to the standard civilizational narrative sees prehistoric hunter-gatherers as the real-world equivalent of Adam and Eve in the Garden of Eden.[15] Humans lived in a milieu of happy abundance until we decided to take up farming. This may have had the benefit of allowing us to produce more food, but it also led to the emergence of despotism, inequality, poverty and back-breaking, mind-numbing work. Jean-Jacques Rousseau is perhaps the most notable champion of the "Fall of Man" theory, and more recently Jared Diamond argued that the adoption of settled agriculture was the "worst mistake in the history of the human race."[16]

Graeber and Wengrow argue that both of these grand theories oversimplify the argument. They assume that the adoption of settled agriculture—in particular cereal-farming and grain storage—led to the emergence of hierarchies and states. In the standard civilizational narrative this is the best thing that ever happened to our species; for Rousseau and Diamond it is the worst. But the link between farming and civilization is far from straightforward. The earliest examples of complex states don't appear until six millennia after the Neolithic Revolution first began in the Middle East, and they didn't develop at all in some places where farming emerged. "To say that cereal-farming was responsible for the rise of such states is a little like saying that the development of calculus in medieval Persia is responsible for the invention of the atom bomb." Thankfully, the impact of settled agriculture on infectious diseases is more straightforward to analyze.

The First Epidemiological Revolution

By growing calorie-rich cereals, farming societies were able to feed many more mouths on the same amount of land: Diamond suggests 100 times more.[17] A recent study demonstrated that our planet is capable of supporting no more than 10 million hunter-gatherers.[18] By 1800 CE, the world's population had grown to about 900 million with only very basic technology, so this estimate is pretty much spot on.[19] The earth now supports nearly 8 billion people, albeit precariously.

Population growth was five times faster after the adoption of agriculture.[20] The demographic boom was driven by an abrupt rise in fertility rates: women began to have babies much more frequently.[21] Whereas hunter-gatherers had a child roughly every four years, women in early agricultural societies gave birth on average every two years.[22] A recent study of the Palanan Agta people in the Philippines demonstrates that, even in the twenty-first century, nomadic hunter-gatherer women have markedly fewer children than those who have adopted sedentary agriculture.[23] Farming allows women's bodies to recover faster from the strain of childrearing because they get to eat calorie-rich cereals and dairy products rather than low-calorie game, seafood and plants, and expend much less energy on carrying their infants. The Neolithic diet also made it possible to wean children off breast milk faster. In my own experience, when we began to give our daughter solid foods, the first things we tried included Weetabix mixed in milk and creamy porridge. I can't imagine it would have gone as well if we'd used venison and walnuts.

The Neolithic Revolution didn't result in an inexorable population boom. Between 500 and 1,000 years after a community adopted settled agriculture we tend to see a marked increase in deaths, causing population growth to level off and, in some cases, go into reverse.[24] What caused this sharp rise in mortality? Part of the answer related to diet. Hunter-gatherers would have eaten a wide array of seasonal seeds, nuts, fruits and vegetables. In the 1960s, the American anthropologist Richard Borshay Lee observed that foragers in the Kalahari Desert ate more than 100 types of plant.[25] In contrast, Neolithic farmers tended to grow only one or two cereals. In good years, this would provide them with enough food to see them through lean winter months, seeds to plant for next year's crop, and grain to pay their taxes. There was a lot of room for things to go wrong, however.

Disease or adverse weather could wipe out the harvest. Stored surplus could be stolen by raiders, eaten by pests, or destroyed by mold. Consequently, settled agriculturalists were much more likely to starve than hunter-gatherers. The American anthropologist Marshall Sahlins sardonically refers to the adoption of agriculture as the "Neolithic Great Leap Forward"—an allusion to the Chinese Communist Party's Second Five Year Plan (1958–1962), which contributed to the greatest famine in history and tens of millions of deaths. Even when the harvest didn't fail or the grain stores survived the winter months, the Neolithic diet was lacking in protein and vitamins. As a result, almost everywhere that humans adopted settled agriculture, early farmers were less healthy than hunter-gatherers. Their skeletons were shorter and more likely to show signs of anemia due to iron deficiency and enamel defects as a result of lack of vitamins A, C and D, calcium and phosphorus.[26]

Malnourishment weakens the immune system, which was a problem because humans' exposure to pathogens increased markedly after the adoption of agriculture. There were some infectious diseases in hunter-gatherer societies, but epidemics cannot take hold in small, scattered, nomadic hunter-gatherer groups as virulently as they do in densely populated, well-connected farming societies. James Scott refers to Neolithic villages as "multispecies resettlement camps."[27] For the first time in history, humans lived in close proximity to a variety of animals—domesticated ones as well as parasites like rats. This aided the emergence of new zoonotic infectious diseases, which jump from animals to humans. The increasingly crowded and unsanitary living conditions encouraged the spread of pathogens from person to person or via infected water. Even today in the Philippines, those Agta who have adopted sedentary agriculture have higher levels of viral and parasitic worm infections than those who still practice the traditional nomadic hunter-gatherer life.[28]

An array of DNA evidence is now vindicating one of William McNeill's key arguments: that the adoption of settled agriculture, coupled with population growth and increased trade, created a golden age for viruses, microbes and other animals. Many of the infectious diseases that afflict contemporary humans are caused by Neolithic pathogens.[29] Hepatitis B has been circulating in the European population for something close to 7,000 years.[30] The plague—specifically *Yersinia pestis*—is believed to have emerged in farming settlements in southeast Europe about 6,000 years ago.[31] Tuberculosis appears about the same time, although we can't be sure where.[32] Measles diverged from rinderpest, a disease that affects cattle, in the first millennium BCE.[33]

Even where there is no genomic evidence, the archeological record supports the argument that an epidemiological revolution followed hot on the heels of the Neolithic Revolution. The origins of smallpox are unknown, but it is closely related to cowpox. Three mummies, including the young Pharaoh Rameses V, were found to be covered in a rash that resembles smallpox. The oldest of these remains dates back to the sixteenth century BCE.[34] Polio appears to have emerged around the same time: Ancient Egyptian artwork depicted otherwise healthy-looking people with withered limbs, and young children who walked with the assistance of a cane.[35]

The spread of mosquito-borne diseases was aided by the adoption of agriculture in West Africa.[36] The *Anopheles gambiae* mosquito, which transmits the most lethal form of falciparum malaria, cannot breed in very shaded water. They wouldn't have been able to reproduce in the dense tropical rainforests that covered much of the region, so the emergence of slash-and-burn agriculture was a boon for both the mosquitoes and the plasmodium that causes malaria. The genome of the parasite that causes falciparum malaria reveals that although it first began infecting humans long before the Neolithic Revolution, there has been a sudden and marked increase in the population size in the last few thousand years.[37] The *Aedes aegypti* mosquito that spreads yellow fever also benefited greatly from recent human activity because it likes to reproduce in containers full of stagnant water. This had led the American historian John McNeill to suggest that they are, in fact, a domesticated insect.[38]

This tidal wave of infectious diseases killed so many people that it left a scar on our DNA. A recent study analyzed the evolution of the more than 1,500 genes that play a role in humans' innate immune system, revealing that most adaptations—where a favorable new gene mutation quickly spreads throughout the population—occurred in the last 6,000 to 13,000 years, which roughly corresponds to the period when humans took up settled agriculture.[39] In farming societies big and well connected enough to maintain a chain of infection, the infectious diseases that emerged after the Neolithic Revolution would have quickly become endemic childhood afflictions. Anyone who had reached adulthood would have been exposed to these pathogens, survived and developed some level of immunity. Consequently, archeologists who study the skeletons in prehistoric cemeteries across the world have noted that about 1,000 years after the adoption of settled farming the proportion of child and adolescent skeletons increased markedly.[40]

Cheddar Man

The oldest complete human skeleton found in Britain was uncovered in 1903 by two workmen digging a drainage trench in a cave in Cheddar Gorge, not far from where I grew up in southwest England. Since then this 9,000-year-old specimen has become famous, being named "Cheddar Man" and put on display at the Natural History Museum in London. The bones belonged to one of the first permanent inhabitants of the British Isles. During the last Ice Age, continental Europe and what is now southern England were connected by a land bridge. This extremity of northwestern Eurasia was too cold to inhabit on a permanent basis, but bands of nomadic hunter-gatherers would visit in the summer in search of food.[41] Then, about 12,000 years ago, increasing temperatures made the region fit for year-round habitation and a couple of millennia later rising sea levels created Great Britain, the ninth-largest island in the world.

We know from archeological sites in the British Isles that Cheddar Man and his kin were highly skilled hunters who carved antlers to make harpoons for fishing, used bows and arrows, and kept dogs to assist with hunting and protect them from predators. About five years ago, researchers from the Natural History Museum and University College London managed to extract and analyze Cheddar Man's DNA.

The results revealed that he belonged to a genetically distinct group of people who migrated to Europe from the Middle East as the glaciers retreated. Scientists who study ancient DNA refer to this population group as Western Hunter-gatherers.[42] They inhabited much of the continent and their remains have been found in what is now Spain, Luxembourg and Hungary. The study also managed to determine Cheddar Man's physical appearance. As it turns out, the first Briton looked about as far as one can imagine from the stereotype of a fair-haired, pale-skinned "English Rose." He had dark skin, curly black locks and blue-green eyes.[43] David Lammy, a prominent Black Labor MP, responded to the news by tweeting: "I just wish I knew about you when I was growing up and people asked me where I was 'really' from."

This research challenged the widely held assumption that the British Isles have always been inhabited by white people. Before the advent of ancient DNA analysis, it made sense to assume that *Homo sapiens* had quickly evolved lighter skin as they spread northward out of Africa into Europe about 40,000 years ago. Paleolithic Europeans had no need for dark skin to protect them from the harsh African sun, whereas a lighter complexion would have allowed their bodies to absorb more sunlight and produce larger quantities of vitamin D. The fact that dark-skinned hunter-gatherers were able to live in the British Isles indicates that they could get sufficient vitamin D from other sources: their diet was extremely rich in fish and meat. It was only after the Neolithic Revolution, when early farmers survived on a much less nutritious diet, that lighter skin conferred a survival advantage.[44]

Far from being trailblazers, the people of northern Europe—and Britain in particular—were slow to adopt settled agriculture. Farming did not emerge there independently. Rather, it spread into the Aegean from Anatolia between 8,000 and 9,000 years ago, and then moved northward up the Danube and westward along the Mediterranean coast.[45] Agriculture reached southern France between 7,700 and 7,800 years ago and Iberia shortly afterward. There is evidence of cultivation in the Paris basin about 500 years later. It did not begin in the British Isles and northern Europe until about 6,000 years ago. A thousand years later, most of the continent was inhabited by farmers. Until recently it wasn't clear how agriculture spread. Did Cheddar Man's descendants see their neighbors growing crops and rearing animals and decide to copy them? Or were they murdered by early farming communities who wanted to cultivate the land they had roamed for thousands of years? Studies of ancient DNA have resolved this mystery once and for all.

Ötzi the Iceman

In the summer of 1991, two German tourists walking in the Ötztal Alps close to the Austrian-Italian border made a grim discovery. Peeking out of the melting glacial ice was a human torso, its skin covered in tattoos. The freeze-dried corpse was so well preserved that the walkers assumed it belonged to an unfortunate fellow hiker who had lost their way in bad weather. But when the body was recovered, it became clear that it was very, very old. Ötzi the Iceman, as he became known, had died about 5,300 years ago.

Scientists have studied Ötzi in extraordinary detail over the past three decades.[46] We know he died in his mid-forties after being hit in the shoulder with an arrow. He was wearing a coat made from sheepskin and goatskin. His last meal included einkorn wheat. And he was afflicted by various debilitating health problems: he suffered from Lyme disease; his clothes were infested with fleas; parasitic worm eggs were found in his intestines; and his hips, shoulders, knees and spine showed signs of significant wear. The state of Ötzi's health, his clothes and diet all suggest that he was a farmer rather than a forager.

DNA confirmed that Ötzi did not belong to the dark-skinned, black-haired Western Hunter-gatherers such as Cheddar Man who dominated western Europe prior to the Neolithic Revolution. Rather, he was from another genetically distinct population that geneticists refer to as Neolithic European Farmers.[47] They looked similar to the population that currently lives around the Mediterranean, with olive skin and dark hair. Ötzi's ancestors separated from Western Hunter-gatherers around 43,000 years ago. Prior to the adoption of settled agriculture they lived in Anatolia. As farming spread northward and westward out of what is now modern Turkey around 8,000 to 9,000 years ago, the genetic makeup of Europe's population changed. Western Hunter-gatherers such as Cheddar Man were to a large extent replaced by Neolithic European Farmers like Ötzi. This phenomenon was starkest in the British Isles: the DNA of human remains buried before the uptake of farming 6,000 years ago shows that the population were 100 percent Western Hunter-gatherers. But after the adoption of agriculture, the newcomers account for between 70 percent and 80 percent of the DNA in skeletons.[48]

It isn't entirely clear why Western Hunter-gatherers were so swiftly and decisively replaced, but we can try to piece together the clues. As settled agriculture can support a far larger population—perhaps including specialized warriors who do not need to be directly involved in food production—it's plausible that Neolithic European Farmers conquered the continent and killed the majority of its indigenous people. Even though hunter-gatherers were considerably bigger and healthier, they would have had little chance against the much greater numbers of farmers. There is, however, nothing to suggest that the spread of agriculture was accompanied by the kind of massive violent conflict that would explain such a dramatic turnover in population.[49] The archeological record is so sparse that we can't definitively say it didn't happen, but studies of ancient DNA hint at another possibility.

If Neolithic European Farmers had swept across the continent in a blaze of violence, then we would expect that the invaders would have been mostly men. But analyses of DNA from people alive around this time demonstrate that roughly equal numbers of males and females migrated westward.[50] The fact that the couples and probably whole families moved en masse to set up farms suggests that there was little or no resistance from Western Hunter-gatherers. It is inconceivable that the indigenous foragers would have allowed their land to be stolen and their way of life destroyed. So if farming wasn't spread by conquest, how did it happen?

The most likely answer is that the farmers were unwittingly aided by pathogens that emerged after the Neolithic Revolution. Over the several millennia since the Neolithic Revolution began in the Fertile Crescent, pathogens would have jumped from animals to farming communities. Initially infectious diseases would have killed lots of them, but over time they would have developed resistance to such diseases through both acquired and genetic immunity. In contrast, the hunter-gatherers that the Neolithic European Farmers encountered as they migrated westward through Europe would have been almost defenseless against these viruses and bacteria. The scene was set for what the American historian Alfred Crosby refers to as a "virgin soil epidemic."[51]

To get an idea of what might have unfolded when Europe's hunter-gatherers first came into contact with new pathogens, we can look at what happened to previously uncontacted communities in the Amazon over the last century or so. Let's consider the example of the 6,000- to 8,000-strong Cayapo tribe in South America, who accepted a single missionary in 1903. This contact precipitated the destruction of the tribe: by 1918 there were 500 survivors, by 1927 just twenty-five, and by 1950 only two or three people who could trace their descent to the Cayapo.[52] A more recent example comes from 1983, when Peruvian loggers kidnapped four young men from the isolated Nahua tribe and took them to the nearest town, where they introduced them to beer among other things. When the young men returned to the Amazon rainforest they were carrying influenza, whooping cough and other diseases. Despite receiving medical care, between half and two-thirds of the population quickly died.[53] Decades later, the Nahua's numbers had still not returned to the pre-contact level.

Western Hunter-gatherers would surely have been struck by similarly catastrophic epidemics once they began to interact with Neolithic European Farmers. So when large numbers of farmers swept westward across the continent between 9,000 and 6,000 years ago, they would have encountered a population already shattered by infectious diseases. With the arrival of settled agriculture, the population of Europe boomed as women had more children and the men exploited the land more productively than the foraging population. This can be seen in the increased number of artifacts found at archeological sites as well as the type of pollen uncovered, which shows that woodland was being cleared and the area of land under cultivation was growing.[54]

Stonehenge was built by the olive-skinned, dark-haired descendants of Ötzi who had brought farming to the British Isles. But within a few hundred years of transporting and raising the massive stones into place, the Neolithic European Farmers were replaced by a second and final great wave of migration which came from the east and spread across Europe.[55] The Amesbury Archer was one of these new immigrants. Found a couple of miles from Stonehenge in 2002 when builders were digging foundations for a new school, his grave contained more artifacts than any other burial in Britain up to this point. These included sixteen flint arrowheads, metalworking tools, three copper blades and a pair of gold hair ornaments—the first gold ever found in the British Isles. He was also buried next to bell-shaped drinking vessels, the latest pottery fashion that had spread northward out of the Iberian Peninsula.[56] Analysis of the oxygen isotope in his enamel demonstrates that he was a first-generation immigrant who grew up in or near modern-day Switzerland. In the first few centuries after the arrival of this new genetically distinct group in the British Isles ancestry proportions were variable, but by 2000 BCE the newcomers accounted for about 90 percent of the DNA of ancient skeletons.[57] In other words, the British Isles experienced an almost total population turnover in a matter of centuries.

Who were these new migrants, and what happened to the people they replaced?

The Final Steppe

The grasslands of the Eurasian Steppe stretch about 8,000 kilometers from Hungary and Romania in the west to Mongolia and northeast China in the east. For thousands of years after the Neolithic Revolution, this vast region remained largely untouched by farming because there was too little rain to support agriculture and too few bodies of water to sustain herds of animals. Then, about 5,000 years ago, the western part of the Steppe—as far east as the Altai Mountains—exploded into life as a culturally and genetically distinct population, whom archeologists refer to as Yamnaya and geneticists call Western Steppe Herders, took advantage of two monumental innovations. With the invention of the wheel, oxen could be hitched up to wagons and used to carry water a long way from the rivers. This made large tracts of the Steppe accessible to nomadic herders for the first time. And the domestication of horses allowed one person to control many more animals than was possible on foot, so the size of herds increased markedly.[58]

The main archeological relics left by the Steppe Herders are graves marked by earthen mounds several meters tall, known as kurgans, that are dotted across the Steppe of Western Eurasia. These sometimes contained horses and wagons, underlining their importance. They were also buried alongside cutting-edge bronze implements of various sorts. DNA analysis shows that the Steppe Herders were fair-skinned, light-haired and tall. Unlike the earlier inhabitants of Europe, many Steppe Herders were lactose-tolerant.[59] But recent research demonstrates that the continent's original farmers consumed dairy products despite not having the gene for lactose-tolerance, and that their inability to absorb the nutrients was a major survival disadvantage during famines and epidemics.[60]

Until the emergence of ancient DNA analysis in the last couple of decades, the most accurate way to identify distinct prehistoric communities was by the pottery that they were buried with. In the late nineteenth century, archeologists noted that something remarkable happened about 4,900 years ago: a new style of pottery distinguished by its cordlike patterns emerged, replacing a patchwork of localized styles across a massive area that ranged from the Rhine in the west to beyond the Volga in the east—adjacent to the Western Eurasian Steppe. Archeologists had no idea how and why this pan-European Corded Ware culture emerged. But in the last few years, ancient DNA analysis has resolved the quandary.

The DNA in skeletons buried next to Corded Ware pottery overwhelmingly belonged to Steppe Herders. By dating the age of these skeletons, we know that between 4,800 and 4,900 years ago the Steppe Herders began to migrate across northern Europe and very quickly they more or less replaced the pre-existing farming communities.[61] Archeologists found it hard to understand how a small group of shepherds who roamed over a vast area on the edge of Europe were able to make such a marked demographic dent on an already densely populated farming community.[62] They reasoned that, compared to the established population, the number of incomers would have simply been too small to make a noticeable difference. But the genetic evidence shows otherwise.

In contrast to the spread of Neolithic European Farmers a few millennia before, ancient DNA analysis suggests that the Steppe Herders may have used violence as they surged across the continent. Ninety percent of the migrants were male, which indicates that the westward spread of Western Steppe Herders could have involved an invasion led by warriors with the aid of cutting-edge bronze weapons, horses and wagons.[63] But while military superiority over the Stone Age farmers might have allowed invaders to conquer and rule northern Europe, it still doesn't account for such a striking turnover of population in so short a period of time. David Reich compared the impact of Western Steppe Herders on the European DNA to more recent historical invasions.[64] It looks nothing like what happened when the Mughals and then the British conquered much of South Asia and then ruled the subcontinent for several centuries. The effects of these invasions on the region's politics, economy, language and culture remain abundantly clear. But still they left almost no perceptible mark on the genome of modern India. Rather, the impact of the migration of Steppe Herders looks much more similar to the European colonialization of the Americas after 1492. In the decades after the Spanish arrived they managed to conquer vast and sophisticated empires, sometimes with just a few dozen men, as Old World pathogens raced ahead of them and literally decimated the Native American population.

Could diseases have helped a relatively small community of shepherds to replace a well-established farming society in northern Europe in the first half of the fifth millennium BCE? Although we don't yet have a smoking gun, there is strong circumstantial evidence that indicates this might have been the case. The population in the region did not keep on growing inexorably after agriculture was adopted. In the northwest of the continent the initial period of growth occurred between around 6,000 and 5,500 years ago, but then the population crashed; by 5,000 years ago it was up to 60 percent less than it had been at its height.[65] It remained low for another half-millennium. In Britain the population continued to raise livestock, but many people seemed to have abandoned cereal cultivation and instead reverted to foraging.[66] Interestingly, it was between 5,000 and 4,500 years ago—when the population was at its lowest point—that the Neolithic European Farmers went to all the trouble of building Stonehenge. Was the construction of this great monument an ultimately futile effort to appease their gods and arrest the decline of their community?

The Neolithic Black Death

About two decades ago, archeologists managed to extract the DNA of about eighty people who had died within a short period and been buried together in Frälsegården, western Sweden, around 4,900 years ago.[67] The remains belonged to farmers who inhabited the northernmost parts of Europe. They lived in small settlements consisting of dispersed farmsteads, so it is remarkable to find a mass grave with that number of people. When the sample was analyzed in a laboratory, it became clear that the ancestry of the people in the tomb was about half Neolithic European Farmers and half the pre-existing hunter-gatherer population. But their cause of death remained unknown.

The process of extracting ancient human DNA also picks up genetic material from microorganisms that were in the bloodstream at the time of death. Initially, researchers overlooked this vast amount of information. But in the last couple of years they have started to analyze the DNA of microbes found in the dental pulp of ancient teeth—which tend to be better preserved than bones because they are protected by enamel. This research is beginning to revolutionize our understanding of Neolithic plagues.

When scientists looked again at the DNA that had been collected from the ancient skeletons buried in the Frälsegården tomb they detected traces of *Yersinia pestis*—making this the oldest evidence of plague bacteria ever found.[68] The researchers concluded that an epidemic must have swept through southern Sweden almost 5,000 years ago, killing large numbers of people, including those buried in the mass grave. The significance of this discovery extends well beyond Scandinavia, however. Scientists have used similar methods to identify plague DNA in ancient but slightly younger skeletons across Eurasia, from modern-day Germany to Siberia.[69] By comparing the genomes of these different strains of bacteria it's possible to calculate how long ago they diverged from one another. It turns out that all the various samples of *Yersinia pestis* were related to a common ancestor that was circulating about 5,700 years ago.

It is highly likely that the sharp fall in the population that occurred in Britain and the rest of western Europe about 5,000 years ago was caused by a "Neolithic Black Death." But this devastating epidemic differed from the fourteenth-century Black Death in one crucial respect. *Yersinia pestis* did not evolve into a flea-borne bubonic plague until the beginning of the first millennium BCE.[70] Prior to that it would have been transmitted by sneezing and coughing and infected the lungs. According to the World Health Organization (WHO), pneumonic plague kills almost all infected people if it is left untreated, compared to between 30 and 60 percent for bubonic plague. It was, however, easier to avoid inhaling plague bacteria than getting bitten by infected fleas which traveled on the black rats that were ubiquitous in medieval Europe.

Scientists now have a pretty good idea of where plague first emerged as a disease capable of infecting humans.[71] Some of the earliest towns were founded about 6,000 years ago and are located between the modern cities of Kyiv and Odessa in Ukraine.[72] Archeologists have identified fifteen Cucuteni-Trypillia "mega-settlements" of over one square kilometer—equivalent to about 200 football pitches. The largest was three times this size, making it slightly bigger than the City of London and a bit smaller than New York's Central Park.[73] These towns were home to as many as 15,000 inhabitants, who lived in wattle and daub houses built on stone foundations and arranged in concentric circles with a large gap in the middle.[74] Archeologists have speculated that this open space might have been used to host ceremonies, assemblies or farm animals.[75]

The unprecedented size of the Cucuteni-Trypillia mega-settlements was possible because of the remarkable fertility of the black soil in the region. The inhabitants fed themselves through a combination of small-scale crop agriculture, orchard cultivation and animal husbandry, complemented by hunting. This brought them into close proximity with both domesticated livestock and parasitic species. In terms of population densities and close contact with animals, the living conditions were unprecedented. They were, to borrow James Scott's tongue-in-cheek label, multispecies resettlement camps par excellence. This, combined with their location at the meeting point of southeast Europe and the Eurasian Steppe and the dates they were inhabited, makes the mega-settlements a likely candidate for the location where plague first emerged as a disease capable of infecting humans.*

From Cucuteni-Trypillia mega-settlements of southeastern Europe, the plague would have spread throughout Eurasia—even to remote locations like Scandinavia—via long-distance trade networks. After the adoption of settled agriculture, links emerged between far-flung populations as craftspeople produced more goods and the newly wealthy ruling elite had the resources to buy them. The most remarkable evidence of long-distance trade around this time is jewelry containing lapis lazuli that was mined in Badakhshan (in what is now northeastern Afghanistan) and found 5,000 kilometers away, in a 5,500-year-old archeological site in Egypt.[76] Some scholars have argued that the increased connectivity between distant parts of the Old World amounted to nothing less than prehistoric globalization.[77] These networks facilitated the spread of infectious diseases across the Eurasian land mass—just like air travel and tourism helped the spread of Covid-19 from Wuhan to the rest of the world.

Could the plague have been the cause of the population crash between 5,500 and 5,000 years ago? Did *Yersinia pestis* contribute to the decline of the first farming people who built Stonehenge? No trace of the ancient plague bacteria has ever been found in the British Isles, so we cannot say for sure. But we know that plague was present in other out-of-the-way parts of Europe, and that there was contact between people living on either side of the Channel.[78] The fact that Britain was

---

* This might help to explain another peculiarity of Cucuteni-Trypillia culture. Every sixty to 150 years, the towns appear to have been burned to the ground and then new buildings constructed on top of the ruins. No one knows why. One possibility is that this was a response to infectious disease outbreaks. Then, about 5,400 years ago, the mega-settlements were abandoned forever—and the people who used to live there moved to smaller villages in the vicinity. Again, archeologists do not know why this happened. Could it be that one final devastating epidemic convinced the inhabitants to permanently abandon this experiment in urban living?

an island may have protected it from pathogens for a while, but its isolation ultimately made the early farming population more vulnerable to infectious diseases from the continent. In 2300 BCE, when the Amesbury Archer and his shepherding mates arrived in Britain from the continent, they would have found a relatively empty land and limited resistance from the Neolithic European Farmers.

A Continent of Immigrants

The influx of the Steppe Herders in the third millennium BCE was the last great migration movement in Europe. Although various groups of immigrants have continued to enrich the gene pool in the intervening years, with the Steppe Herders' arrival all the components of the modern European genome were present. People of European ancestry are a mixture of three genetically distinct population groups (plus, in some cases, trace amounts of other DNA).[79] First, Western Hunter-gatherers, such as Cheddar Man, who had dark skin and hair and light eyes.[80] Second, olive-skinned, dark-haired Neolithic European Farmers like Ötzi the Ice Man who migrated into Europe from Anatolia approximately 9,000 years ago, bringing farming with them, and arriving in Britain three millennia later. And third, the Steppe Herders: tall, fair-haired, light-skinned shepherds who migrated westward from the Eurasian Steppe about 5,000 years ago and adopted farming when they settled in Europe. The implications of this are momentous: contemporary Europeans are neither genetically "pure" nor are they the region's indigenous people. Even white Europeans are mongrel immigrants.[81]

The proportions of these three ancestral components vary within Europe and help to explain the physical variations between populations now living in different parts of the continent. Hunter-gatherers contribute a small amount of DNA to the genome of all modern Europeans. The Neolithic Farmers account for a large proportion of southern European genomes, including in Greece, Spain and Italy. Sardinia appears to have avoided the influx of Steppe Herders, with between 80 percent and 90 percent of Sardinian DNA deriving from Neolithic

European Farmers.[82] The population of the mountainous Basque region in northeast Spain and southwest France are also strongly related to the people who first introduced settled agriculture to Europe.[83] Steppe Herder DNA is the largest source of ancestry in northern Europe, comprising about half of the genome of modern Norwegians and slightly less for other northern Europeans, including those from the British Isles.

The Steppe Herders that swept across Europe after the Neolithic Black Death are also the most likely source of all Indo-European languages, which are now spoken by just under half of the world's population.[84] English, German, Latin and related languages, Greek, Russian, Farsi, Hindi and so on, all descend from one common ancestral language. At some point in the distant past, Proto-Indo-European must have been spoken by a relatively small population somewhere in Eurasia who then spread across Europe and South Asia, bringing their language with them. Over time, Proto-Indo-European diverged into distinct but related languages spoken by geographically separate populations.

For the past two and a half centuries, since the link between Indo-European languages was first noticed, academics have wondered about their original source. Recent ancient DNA discoveries have finally helped to clear this up. All Indo-European languages share similar vocabulary for words related to wagons, including axle pole, harness and wheel. This is very strong evidence that the population responsible for Proto-Indo-European must have migrated into Europe after wheeled vehicles started appearing in the archeological record between 6,000 and 5,000 years ago.[85] As the first great migration of Neolithic European Farmers from Anatolia into Western Eurasia began 9,000 years ago, it couldn't have been the source of Indo-European languages.* The westward migration of Steppe Herders, on the other hand, began 5,000 years ago and introduced the wheel and wagon into Europe. Their DNA is found in significant amounts among people who speak

---

* We can hazard an educated guess as to what language Europe's first farmers spoke. As the Basque people have a high proportion of Neolithic Farmer ancestry and their language has no relation to any other, it is likely to be the last surviving descendant of the tongue spoken by Neolithic Farmers.

Indo-European languages—not just in Europe but also in Central and South Asia.[86] This makes the Steppe Herders the most likely source of languages now spoken by several billion people.

It is remarkable to think that the impact of the migration of a small number of shepherds out of the Western Eurasian Steppe 5,000 years ago, which was most likely made possible by a devastating plague pandemic, can literally still be seen and heard today across the world.

Chapter 3
Ancient Plagues

*Religion is the sigh of the oppressed creature, the heart
of a heartless world, and the soul of soulless conditions.*
—Karl Marx

As Flies to Wanton Boys

Homer's *Iliad* begins with a plague. The story is set toward the end of
the Achaean army's siege of Troy. In the opening lines, the Greek
invaders raid a nearby town and take two beautiful Trojan maidens
captive. Chryseis becomes the property of Agamemnon, the king of
Mycenae and commander of the Achaean army, while Briseis is claimed
by the great warrior Achilles. When Chryseis' father—a priest—turns
up at the Achaean camp to plead for her return, Agamemnon refuses
the offer of a ransom and taunts him cruelly. Disconsolate, Chryseis'
father implores Apollo to punish the Greek king, and he responds by
striding down from Mount Olympus to fire arrows of plague into the
Greek encampment. After nine days of disease and death, Agamemnon concedes that Apollo must be appeased. Chryseis is returned to
her father and the plague ceases, but in order to save face the Greek
king takes Briseis from Achilles. This sets off a devastating feud that
plays out over the rest of the epic poem.

The account of the Trojan War that Homer describes in the *Iliad*
had been retold and embellished for hundreds of years before being
written down in the eighth century BCE, making it among the earliest

works of Western literature. The fact that infectious diseases played such an important role in the narrative points to the devastating impact that epidemics had on society at this time. More than this, the *Iliad* provides an insight into how people living several thousand years ago comprehended the world. The Greek belief system was dominated by anthropomorphic deities who frequently interfered in the lives of mortal humans and epidemics were understood to be a tool of divine retribution wielded by Apollo. As Susan Sontag puts it: outbreaks of infectious disease were seen as "collective calamities, and judgments on a community."[1]

A devastating outbreak of infectious disease also played a prominent role in one of the earliest efforts to write history, Thucydides' account of the on-off twenty-seven-year war between Athens and Sparta in the second half of the fifth century BCE. His *History of the Peloponnesian War* describes how, when the Spartans attacked Attica in 430 BCE, the Athenians followed a defensive strategy devised by Pericles, the most prominent general and statesman of the day. The rural population of Attica abandoned the countryside to the invading force and retreated behind Athens' city walls. This made sense from a military perspective: the Spartans had a superior army, so the Athenians wanted to avoid fighting them in battle. They would simply wait until the enemy lost patience and returned home, then use their naval dominance to win the war. From a public health perspective, however, this strategy was a disaster. With the influx of several hundred thousand people from the countryside, the population of Athens doubled or even quadrupled.[2] The city became crowded and unsanitary. It wasn't long before a devastating outbreak of infectious disease struck, returning in several waves between 430 and 426 BCE.

The epidemic was interpreted by conservative Athenians, who were steeped in Homeric myth, as evidence that the gods—and Apollo specifically—favored Sparta. Thucydides records in a matter-of-fact way that the Spartans had visited the Oracle of Delphi before waging war and were told that if they attacked Athens with all their might, Apollo would support them and they would win the conflict. An older prophecy, recalled by many Athenians, predicted that war with Sparta would be accompanied by a plague. Despite relaying his compatriots' superstitions, Thucydides is much less willing than Homer or Herodotus to believe stories of meddling deities who communicated with mortal humans through oracles. This skepticism wasn't unique to Thucydides but was part of an intellectual movement in fifth-century Athens that is sometimes referred to as the Greek Enlightenment. For example, his contemporary Hippocrates broke with the view that angry gods were responsible for disease outbreaks and instead argued that physicians should observe a patient's symptoms, diagnose what is wrong with them and take an appropriate course of action. And of course Socrates was sentenced to death for impiety and corrupting the Athenian youth.

There is no conclusive evidence regarding the identity of the pathogen that devastated fifth-century-BCE Athens. Efforts to recover bacteria or virus DNA from the remains of ancient humans have so far proved futile.[3] Our best clue is Thucydides' account of symptoms, which included a sore throat, heavy cough, diarrhea, burning fever, painful rash, unquenchable thirst and insomnia. He was certainly well placed to describe the malady, having caught it and recovered. Researchers have even analyzed Sophocles' depiction of the epidemic that struck Thebes at the beginning of *Oedipus Rex* for clues because the play was written just after the Plague of Athens occurred, and the fictional epidemic is assumed to have been inspired by the real one. Based on the available sources, typhus and smallpox are seen as the most likely candidates.[4]

Thucydides claims that an "untold number" of Athenians died from the plague. He describes how the "dead and dying lay on top of one another, and half-dead men tumbled in the streets and around all the springs in their craving for water." Modern estimates suggest that around a quarter of the population perished—that is, somewhere in the region of 75,000 to 100,000 dead in just over three years.[5] In the late 1990s, construction workers building a new subway stop just outside the old city gates in preparation for the millennium Olympic Games made a grim discovery that appeared to confirm Thucydides' description. They chanced upon a mass grave that dated to the exact years of the plague, and when archeologists investigated further they noted that upper layers of corpses had been thrown in far more haphazardly than those at the bottom, pointing to "a sense of mounting panic in the city."[6] Crucially, the Spartans don't appear to have been impacted at all by the epidemic because they remained a safe distance from Athens and retreated when they saw the funeral pyres burning. As a result, the plague undermined Athens' capacity to fight against the Spartans and had a profound impact on the course and outcome of the Peloponnesian War.

Thucydides traces the origins of the conflict between Athens and Sparta to 479 BCE, when an alliance of Hellenic city-states defeated an invading Persian army led by Xerxes. Landlocked Sparta had been the dominant political force in Hellenic civilization for over a century; but when the Greco-Persian Wars ended it withdrew from involvement in Pan-Hellenic political life and the coastal city-state of Athens became the leading power. The Delian League, a naval alliance of islands and coastal *poleis*, was formed to protect Greeks from another Persian attack, but it gradually became a tool of Athenian imperialism: in 454 BCE the league's treasury was transferred from Delos to Athens and military contributions gave way to monetary tributes. City-states that tried to secede from the Delian League had their walls torn down and were forced to remain in the alliance under much worse conditions. In *Histories*, Herodotus expresses his concern that Athens is turning into the kind of aggressive imperial power that it had helped to defeat in the Greco–Persian wars. Thucydides argues that Athens' emerging superpower status in the Aegean made conflict with the erstwhile regional hegemon, Sparta, unavoidable: "it was the rise of Athens and the fear that this instilled in Sparta that made war inevitable."

The two city-states were remarkably different. In Athens, the middle decades of the fifth century BCE were a period of extraordinary cultural, intellectual and political flourishing that has few parallels in history. Many of the people and ideas that we associate with Ancient Greece come from this time. Socrates has had a massive influence on philosophy in his own right, but also through his student Plato, and Plato's student Aristotle. Thucydides was born in Athens and Herodotus migrated there. The plays of Sophocles and several of his contemporaries are still performed today. Hippocrates is referred to as the father of Western medicine because he pioneered clinical observation and the systematic classification of diseases that form the basis of modern medicine. Athenian democracy thrived in these years. Almost every week, citizens would meet on the Pnyx—the hill next to the

Acropolis—to discuss and vote on important political issues.* Pericles was the most influential politician in the city-state—so much so that the period is often referred to as the Age of Pericles. It was also a time of massive publicly funded construction projects, including the rebuilding of the temple dedicated to Athena on the Acropolis. The marble sculptures that once adorned its walls are now in the British Museum, but the Parthenon still looms over the Greek capital as a symbol of the flawed brilliance of fifth-century-BCE Athens.

Sparta—or *Lacedaemon*, as the Ancient Greeks referred to it—was very different. The Spartans had little or no interest in literature or the arts and did not leave written records, which is unsurprising when you consider that the etymology of "laconic" is someone from Lacedaemon. Even Athenian writers who were sympathetic of Sparta describe it as a brutal, militarized, hierarchical society.[7] Its citizens formed a warrior caste that prized toughness and devotion to the state above everything else. Weak male infants were left to die at the base of Mount Taygetus. At the age of seven Spartan boys entered the *agōgē*, a boarding establishment for military training, staying there until they were twenty. Adult men then served in the army for forty years. This system was necessary in order to violently subjugate the helots (state-owned serfs), who formed the majority of the population. Every year the Spartan rulers formally declared war on the helots, so their subjects could kill them without running the risk of divine punishment.

Thucydides argues that the Plague of Athens had a critical impact on the outcome of the conflict with Sparta. Referring to the outbreak, he notes: "Nothing did the Athenians so much harm as this, or so reduced their strength for war." Approximately a quarter to one-third of the army died between 430 and 426 BCE, but the plague stunted Athens' military power for decades because there were fewer boys to grow into adult soldiers and fewer women to give birth to boys.[8] The plague killed Pericles in 429 BCE and Thucydides viewed this as a turning point. I am generally skeptical of the "Great Men" school of history, but in this specific case Thucydides may have had a point. Pericles'

---

* While Athenian participatory democracy was remarkable, we must not overlook the fact that by our standards the system was seriously flawed because women, immigrants and slaves could not vote or stand for office.

successors pursued a much more offensive and less successful strategy. This was most apparent in 415 BCE, when Athens sent a massive expeditionary force on a disastrous foray to attack the Spartan allies in Syracuse, Sicily—a move that was so catastrophic that it has been compared to Napoleon's and Hitler's invasions of Russia. The Athenians expected a quick victory but suffered a drawn-out, humiliating rout that destroyed their army and navy. This made Sparta's eventual victory in 404 BCE inevitable.

The question of what would have happened if Athens had defeated Sparta and cemented its position as the dominant power in Hellas is one of the great "what-ifs" of ancient history. The Peloponnesian War was a clash between two very different states and societies: democratic, cosmopolitan, culturally and intellectually dynamic Athens on the one hand and conservative, inward-looking, militaristic, oligarchic Sparta on the other. The English historian Arnold J. Toynbee argues that defeat killed off the first iteration of Western civilization just as it was getting started.[9] But the Spartans had expended so much effort winning the on-off twenty-seven-year war that they were in no position to consolidate their control over the other city-states after their victory.

The next half-century was punctuated by sporadic warfare between competing city-states until the middle of the 300s BCE, when Philip of Macedon—which is located at the very northern limits of Greek civilization—took advantage of this power vacuum to conquer most of the Hellenic world.* The exploits of his son, Alexander the Great, were even more astonishing. He inherited his father's throne at the age of twenty, in 336 BCE. Soon after, this "drunken juvenile thug"—in the words of the British classicist Mary Beard—began a series of military campaigns which saw him first consolidate his rule over the Greek world and then attack the great Persians. When Alexander died at the age of thirty-two, he had managed to conquer all the land between Greece and what is now India, as well as Egypt. The vast empire was

---

* Ancient Greek sources sometimes describe the Macedonians as Greek and at other times as Barbarians. In the fifth century BCE there was some debate about whether they were Greek enough to take part in the Olympic Games. In the end the authorities acquiesced. The following century, one of Philip's horses apparently won the Olympic flat race on the day that Alexander was born. Nevertheless, the Macedonians' ethnic identity remains unclear.

divided among his generals, who carved out their own Hellenistic dynasties from the spoils, including the Ptolemies in Egypt and the Seleucids, whose territory ranged from Asia Minor to what is now Afghanistan.

During the Golden Age of Athens, what was then the Roman Republic was a small city-state in the Italian Peninsula. But it slowly expanded control over neighboring areas and then kept on growing. By 220 BCE Rome controlled all of the Italian Peninsula. It conquered most of Greece in 146 BCE, and the Hellenistic kingdoms followed. A much-reduced Seleucid Empire was swallowed by the Romans in 63 BCE; Cleopatra was the last Ptolemaic ruler of Egypt before it became a Roman province in 30 BCE. But Greek civilization lived on. As the Roman poet Horace points out, "conquered Greece took captive her conqueror," by which he meant that the philhellenic Romans adopted Greek culture and their gods, including Apollo. In fact, one of the most famous Roman origin myths is Virgil's *Aeneid*, which explicitly links Rome to the Ancient Greeks. Aeneas, who features elsewhere in Greek mythology, including the *Iliad*, is one of the few Trojans to survive the fall of Troy. He flees the Aegean and, after a fling with Dido in North Africa, settles down in western Italy to found the dynasty that eventually gives rise to Romulus and Remus. But in reality the influx of Greek-speakers into Rome came later. Studies of DNA extracted from ancient skeletons demonstrate that as the Roman Empire expanded, the vast majority of people living in the imperial capital were no longer of European ancestry. Rather, they were the descendants of vast numbers of slaves and citizens who poured into the city from the prosperous eastern provinces in the last one and a half centuries BCE.[10]

By the turn of the millennium, about one-quarter of the world's population lived in areas controlled by Rome.[11] The Roman Empire covered the whole of the Mediterranean shoreline and much of the hinterland in three continents. The territory stretched from northern Britain, along the Rhine and Danube, all the way to the Euphrates in the east, skirting the Sahara in the south and reaching the Iberian Peninsula in the west. The Romans believed that the military victories that drove this remarkable territorial expansion were due to their collective piety, which brought them the favor of the gods. But within a few hundred years polytheistic paganism had disappeared, to be replaced by two monotheistic sects that emerged in the Middle East. Followers of these new religions were convinced that it was the righteousness of their beliefs that explains their rapid growth. But, as we shall see, infectious diseases played a vital role in both the demise of the Greco-Roman gods and the rise of two new religions: Christianity and Islam.

What Have the Romans Ever Done for Us?

In a scene from *Monty Python's Life of Brian*, the leader of the People's Front of Judaea—played by John Cleese—tries to drum up support for an attack on Pontius Pilate's palace by screaming that "they've taken everything we have" and then posing the rhetorical question: "What have they ever given us in return?" The literal-minded members of the PFJ respond by reeling off a list of improvements made by the Roman conquerors, to which their exasperated leader responds: "All right, but apart from the sanitation, the medicine, education, wine, public order, irrigation, roads, a fresh-water system and public health, what have the Romans ever done for us?" To this question, someone in the audience pipes up with "Peace."

This joke reflects the great admiration that many people, particularly in Europe and its colonial offshoots, have for the Romans—a sentiment famously expressed by the eighteenth-century English historian Edward Gibbon, who described the Roman Empire around this time as the "most happy and prosperous" society in history. There is, however, something unsettling about a group of white, Oxford- and Cambridge-educated men extolling the virtues of colonialism, albeit for comedic effect. The implication—that Roman imperialism imposed a superior culture on the warring, uneducated and dirty people of the Middle East—echoes the common claim that the British Empire brought civilization (in the form of railways, the English language, capitalism, etc.) to the societies it conquered, and is also apparent in justifications for more recent neo-colonial interventions, such as the invasions of Iraq and Afghanistan.

And yet it's undeniable that the century and a half after the crucifixion of Christ (and Brian) was a time of unprecedented stability and affluence, a period known as the *pax Romana*. The expansion of the empire ground to a halt. The half-million-strong army fought several wars on its borders—most notably against the great Parthian Empire based in Iran. It also had to put down some rebellions within the empire, including in Judaea, where the population rose up on several occasions. But by the standards of what went before and after, this was a remarkably calm period. It allowed the Mediterranean elites who dominated the upper echelons of imperial politics to focus on governing their vast territories. The state collected taxes across the empire that added up to a staggering 5 percent of its total economic output.[12] Among other things, this money was used to pay the army, provide free grain to several hundred thousand inhabitants of Rome, build infrastructure, and fund pagan temples and priests.

The Romans also managed to clear the Mediterranean of pirates who had terrorized traders and travelers for centuries. It was now possible to move in relative safety via the sea and a vast network of roads from one end of the empire to the other. This allowed merchants to take full advantage of the fact that the empire was a free-trade zone with a single currency and common legal system that ranged well beyond the limits of the present-day European Union. Silver mined in northwest Europe, wine and olive oil from the south, timber from southern Russia and northern Anatolia, dried fruits from Syria, marble from the Aegean coast and grain from North Africa and the Danube Valley were all transported across the empire.[13]

Trade networks extended across much of the known world. The thousands of exotic animals—including leopards, lions, elephants and rhinos—that were transported to provide brutal entertainment in the empire's amphitheaters illustrate the close links with sub-Saharan Africa. At the very beginning of the first millennium CE there was a sufficiently large community of Roman traders in the southern Indian town of Muziris to support a temple dedicated to Augustus. Ptolemy's *Geography*, which illustrates Roman knowledge of the world in the mid-second century CE, includes the Malay Peninsula and the South China Sea. In 166 CE, Chinese chroniclers report the arrival of Romans at the imperial court. This marked the first evidence of direct contact between the two great empires at either end of the Eurasian land mass, which between them controlled about two-thirds of the population of the Old World.[14]

The *pax Romana* was a time of unprecedented prosperity. The number of public buildings constructed across the empire, the dates of shipwrecks found in the Mediterranean, and information on wages and prices gleaned from papyrus documents preserved in the arid Egyptian climate all point to this.[15] One study has analyzed the amount of lead pollution in an ice core drilled in central Greenland— a good proxy for economic activity in the ancient world because it was mostly produced in the process of smelting lead ores to extract silver, which was used to make the Romans' standard silver coin, the *denarius*.[16] Lead pollution—which rose at times of peace and prosperity and fell during periods of economic and political instability—increased fourfold during the *pax Romana*. At the same time, the Roman Empire became increasingly populous and urban. The population went from about 60 million to 75 million. Rome grew to a city of more than a million residents. The next metropolis to reach this size was London— and that wasn't until almost two millennia later, at the beginning of the nineteenth century. A handful of other towns—including Antioch, Alexandria and Carthage—had several hundred thousand inhabitants and one in five people across the empire lived in urban areas.[17]

So far, so good: but what about *Monty Python*'s claim that the Romans brought fresh water, sanitation, public health and medicine to the areas they conquered? On the face of it, they have a point. The Romans piped water into their cities from surrounding areas via aqueducts. Some of these systems were over 100 kilometers long and parts are still visible today—most notably, the Pont du Gard near Nîmes in southern France. Rome itself was served by eleven aqueducts that transported over half a million cubic meters of water into the heart of the imperial capital every day—that is, about 500 liters per person.[18] The aqueducts provided water for drinking, bathing and public fountains. Even now, the water in the Trevi Fountain is supplied by an aqueduct dating from the first century CE. The water supply made living in a city the size of Rome possible—a point Pliny the Elder understood when he wrote: "there is nothing to be found more worthy of our admiration throughout the whole universe."

Regular bathing was, of course, an important part of life for Romans of all classes. Public baths were not just places to wash off dirt, but venues where people met and socialized. Rome had several hundred of them. The biggest, the Baths of Diocletian, could accommodate 3,000 people. They were constructed throughout the empire, from Bath in southwest England—yes, that's where the town gets its name—to Hammam Essalihine in Algeria, where visitors can still soak in the 2,000-year-old baths. Roman cities also boasted magnificent public toilets, with tightly spaced seats for dozens of people to sit side by side. There was an extensive network of drains under the imperial capital. This included the Cloaca Maxima, which was, according to Pliny the Elder, high and wide enough to allow the passage of a wagon loaded with hay. This drain was even protected by its own goddess, Cloacina.

It might come as a surprise, therefore, that Roman towns and cities two millennia ago were filthy, stinking and disease-ridden. The Romans didn't understand how pathogens made people unwell—not even Galen, the preeminent doctor in the empire.[19] So despite the majestic civil engineering achievements, even the rudiments of public health were absent from Roman society. Today, for example, we know that washing one's hands regularly, particularly after using the toilet and before touching food, is one of the most basic and effective ways to stop diseases spreading. But despite having plenty of flowing water, such personal hygiene measures simply weren't part of the Romans' routine. It was a similar story as far as community sanitation was concerned. Rome's elaborate sewage system was built to drain standing water from low-lying areas rather than remove human waste. The American historian Ann Koloski-Ostrow paints a lucid picture of streets "cluttered with dung, vomit, pee, shit, garbage, filthy water, rotting vegetables, animal skins and guts, and other refuse from various shops that lined the sidewalks."[20]

One and a half millennia after they were last used, Rome's communal toilets look impressive—even if the lack of privacy might seem strange. Back then, though, you would have been well advised to stay away. These weren't flush toilets that neatly whisked away human waste. In the summer especially, the smell would have been almost unbearable. Gases such as hydrogen sulfide or methane built up in the sewers and, when ignited by the heat or a naked flame, blasted fire and human waste out of the seat openings.* *Tersoria,* the shared sponges on sticks that the Romans used to wipe their bottoms, were another oddity that highlighted the lack of basic hygiene.[21]

Many homes had private toilets, which were often located in the kitchen. The majority of loos weren't connected to public sewers because, before the invention of the U-bend, rats and all sorts of other creatures would have run amok in people's houses. One apocryphal tale from the Roman author Aelian describes how a giant octopus swam from the sea into the sewer and entered the house of a wealthy merchant in the Bay of Naples through the toilet, then proceeded to eat all the pickled fish in his pantry.[22] Instead, most private toilets emptied into a cesspit located below the house. When loos were situated upstairs, human waste was carried to the basement by terra-cotta pipes that leaked at the joints.[23] The contents of the cesspits were periodically removed and spread on fields or in gardens. This organic fertilizer increased the yield, but as it was not composted it also aided the spread of pathogens. Researchers have examined microbes in human feces before and after they were colonized by Romans for signs of microbes, concluding that the introduction of toilets didn't improve health.[24]

Even the lauded baths were more of a danger than a benefit to public health. In Rome's bigger institutions thousands upon thousands of people soaked in the same water every day. Bathers didn't use soap, preferring to cover themselves in olive oil and then scrape it off with an instrument called a *strigil.* Contemporary writers complained about the water being dirty and contaminated with human excrement. In other words, Roman baths created an ideal environment for waterborne diseases to spread.

Given the problems with sanitation, it should come as no surprise that waterborne diarrheal diseases killed large numbers of people every year in Rome and other large cities. The American historian Kyle

---

* Even today this can happen. For example, one person died and seven others were injured when a pit latrine exploded in 2016 in Shaanxi Province, China.

Harper looked at the dates on about 5,000 ancient Christian grave-stones in Rome to find out at what time of year the city's inhabitants died and at what age.[25] Just as in modern Europe, there was a surge in deaths in the cold winter months, when respiratory diseases like flu kill the elderly. But Ancient Rome experienced a much more notable jump in mortality among children and young adults in the hot summer months, a pattern we do not see today. The spike is almost definitely the result of gastrointestinal bugs that enter the body via water or food contaminated with feces. This happens more often in the summer be-cause the bugs reproduce at a faster rate in warm weather. They dis-proportionately affected infants and new arrivals from the countryside who hadn't yet developed immunity. Malaria also thrived in Rome and was probably the second-biggest killer. It was particularly prevalent in the autumn months, when the rains ended the dry, hot summer and the Pontine Marshes once again became an ideal breeding ground for mosquitoes.[26]

Although endemic pathogens killed large numbers of Romans, they also had a surprising benefit: diarrheal disease and malaria created what amounted to a protective force field around the imperial capital. Anyone who had survived until adulthood would have acquired immu-nity but people who came from outside, including those who wanted to conquer the city, were at high risk of getting sick or dying if they stayed too long. Malaria had prevented attacks on the imperial capital since at least the late third century BCE, when Hannibal managed to cross the Alps with 60,000 troops, 12,000 horses and 37 war elephants. The Carthaginian army routed the Romans on several occasions. It was malaria, which killed Hannibal's wife, son and many of his sol-diers, that brought the invasion to an end and saved Rome.[27]

But infectious diseases only worked in Rome's favor for so long. The *pax Romana* produced conditions that were ideal for the emer-gence of epidemic infectious diseases. The growth of long-distance trade with sub-Saharan Africa, India and China increased the risk that Romans would come into contact with novel pathogens—and the well-connected, highly urbanized Roman Empire created a perfect breed-ing ground for fast-spreading new diseases. It was only a matter of time before an outbreak brought this unprecedented period of peace and prosperity to a sudden halt.

Germs Are Deadlier than Germans

In Ancient Greece, societies that didn't follow classical Hellenic customs and speak Greek were referred to as Barbarians (βάρβαρος) because their unintelligible languages apparently sounded like "barbarbar." In the Romans' appropriation of all things Greek, they adopted the term to denote the supposedly less civilized groups living on and beyond the empire's borders. It encompassed the various Germanic tribes to the north, Celts in Britain, the Huns in eastern Europe, the Arabs in the Middle East and the Berbers in North Africa. Barbarian invasions played a crucial role in the transformation of the Roman Empire, from the vast, integrated, prosperous and peaceful polity of the *pax Romana* into something very different and in many respects diminished.[28]

Until recently, infectious diseases were largely ignored in mainstream accounts of the decline or transformation of the Roman Empire. But in his recent book *The Fate of Rome*, Kyle Harper gathers a large amount of evidence to show that a series of pandemics caused immense damage and played a crucial role in weakening the Roman Empire, not just in absolute terms but also relative to the neighboring "Barbarians." This is because, although the term "Barbarian" is problematic in that it lumps together an incredibly diverse set of communities into one indistinguishable and supposedly inferior mass, all these groups tended to have one thing in common: they lived in much less-populated and less-connected societies than the Romans. As a result, pandemics tended to cause far more devastation to the Romans than to Barbarian societies. The differential impact of infectious diseases is a key factor in the political dynamics of the Roman Empire from the mid-second century CE until the fall of Constantinople to the Ottomans in 1453.

The first pandemic to have a major impact on the Roman Empire was the Antonine Plague—named after the dynasty in power when the outbreak hit. It appeared in the southeast of the empire in 165 CE, which suggests that the pathogen arrived via the Indian Ocean and originated in southern Africa, India or China.[29] The plague reached the city of Rome the following year, and then spread throughout the empire. As it moved inexorably toward the imperial capital, Galen fled, returning only when he was summoned by the joint emperors Marcus

Aurelius and his adoptive brother, Lucius Verus, in 168 CE. Historians and epidemiologists have since tried to identify the pathogen from Galen's description of the symptoms, which include a black rash that covered the whole body. The most likely candidate is smallpox. Galen's discussion of the causes and cures of the disease reveals the poor state of Roman medicine. He believed that it was caused by an excess of the humor called black bile, and suggested treatments including mountain cows' milk, dirt from Armenia, and boys' urine.[30]

Most Romans understood this devastating outbreak of infectious disease as an act of divine anger. Six centuries earlier, the Greeks had blamed the Plague of Athens on Apollo's displeasure at their warmongering. Similarly, the Romans believed that the Antonine Plague was a consequence of Apollo's displeasure after legionnaires campaigning in the east stole a statue of him from a temple in Seleucia—a Hellenistic outpost on the Tigris and former capital of the Seleucid Empire—and brought it back to Rome in 165. Evidence of Roman attempts to appease Apollo have been uncovered across the empire, from a pewter amulet found in London in 1989 that beseeches the gods to "send away the discordant clatter of raging plague," to a statue of Apollo the "averter of evil" erected in 165 in Hierapolis, modern-day Turkey.[31]

The Antonine Plague was devastating. Estimates for the total deaths vary widely, from 2 percent to one-third of the empire's population. Kyle Harper settles on 10 percent—between 7 and 8 million people. Epidemics returned periodically over the next twenty-five years. This caused massive disruption to Roman society and brought the *pax Romana* to an abrupt end. The economy appears to have collapsed.[32] In the province of Egypt the proportion of silver in coinage fell markedly in the 160s and then no coins were produced in Alexandria in the 170s. There were similar halts in provincial coin production in Palestine and Syria around this time. Traces of lead in Greenland ice demonstrate that silver-mining declined markedly almost immediately after the Antonine Plague and remained low for over 500 years.[33]

The mighty Roman army was severely weakened by the epidemic. Contemporary reports describe the plague raging among the troops in Aquileia, northern Italy in 168 and then devastating the whole of the military in 172. Soldiers appear to have died at a rate between 50 to 100 percent higher than the general population.[34] Marcus Aurelius was forced to take the unusual step of recruiting slaves and gladiators into his army to make up the numbers.[35] In contrast, the epidemic doesn't appear to have had anywhere near the same impact on Germanic tribes in northern Europe—a result of their societies being much less densely populated and well connected. Barbarian armies took advantage of the opportunity afforded by the epidemic, invading deep into Roman territory, besieging Aquileia and almost reaching Athens.

The crisis that followed the Antonine Plague eventually subsided. While the empire would never again enjoy the swaggering confidence of the *pax Romana*, order was restored and Rome regained control of its vast territory. Then, in the middle of the third century, the Roman Empire was gripped by another epidemic that caused even more upheaval. The chronicles describe the outbreak as coming from Ethiopia and hitting Egypt in 249. It reached Rome in 251, wracked the whole empire, and lasted for fifteen years. Dionysius, Bishop of Alexandria, describes the plague as being so devastating that people would have been happy to lose only their first-born sons—as the Old Testament claims happened to the Egyptians during the time of Moses. Dionysius' report from Alexandria, which is based on the number of people on the city's grain dole, estimates that the population fell from about 500,000 to 190,000. Even accounting for exaggeration and people fleeing to the countryside, the scale of death was clearly enormous.[36]

Once again, the gods were invoked to stop the death and devastation. The Roman state minted coins that featured the image of "Apollo the Healer." Unlike the Plague of Athens or the Antonine Plague, there was no Thucydides or Galen to document the symptoms. Instead, we have to rely on the surviving sermons of Cyprian, the Bishop of Carthage, who gave his name to the pandemic. On the basis of his description of high fever, vomiting, diarrhea and sometimes bleeding from the ears, eyes, nose and mouth, Harper believes the epidemic was most likely caused by a viral hemorrhagic fever similar to Ebola. Even today, if patients are treated in modern medical facilities with the latest drugs, Ebola still kills half the people who contract it. Assuming this was the case, the Plague of Cyprian would have been a particularly gory and deadly pandemic—even by the standards of this book.

The pandemic caused the Roman frontiers to disintegrate: "germs were the first, invisible wave of attack in the great invasions," according to Harper. Germanic tribes once more crossed the Danube. At the Battle of Abritus in 251 they killed the Emperor Decius and his son, and destroyed his army. In the mid-250s, the defensive lines on the Rhine fell too. Looting raids pierced deep into Roman territory, reaching as far as the Iberian Peninsula, the Aegean, and in 260 the outskirts of Rome. The situation was equally perilous on the eastern frontier, where the much more aggressive Sasanians had taken over from the Parthians. The Sasanians attacked in the east specifically because they knew that the Roman army had been depleted by disease. They crossed the Euphrates in 252 and overran Syria and Asia Minor. In 260 they surrounded the Roman army and captured Emperor Valerian. Some historical accounts claim that Shapur I, the Persian leader, used his Roman counterpart as a living footstool, before flaying him and keeping the stuffed skin as a trophy.[37]

The Roman Empire also suffered from internal strife as one usurper after the other seized the throne. In the 260s, the empire broke apart. In the west, Gaul, Germania, Britannia and, for a time, Hispania split off to form the Gallic Empire. A few years later the provinces in the Middle East and North Africa, as well as large parts of Asia Minor, came under the control of the Palmyrene Queen Zenobia. The political implosion was accompanied by an economic catastrophe. The Greenland ice core data show that silver mining and processing in Europe hit its lowest point for over 1,000 years in the middle of the third century.[38] Rome's monetary system collapsed. The ancient denominations, including *denarii*, were melted down and ceased to exist. The newer *antoninianus* continued in circulation but was repeatedly debased: it contained about two grams of silver per coin in the first half of the third century but by 270 this had fallen to almost zero.[39]

The Roman Empire managed to piece itself back together following what came to be known as the Crisis of the Third Century. From 268, emperors ensured the loyalty of the military by paying soldiers a gold bonus on accession and then every five years after that. The territories that had seceded were reconquered in the 270s. For the next century, the Roman Empire experienced a new era of political and economic stability, but it had changed indelibly. The walls built around Rome in the 270s reflect its newly felt vulnerability; they were the first major defenses to be constructed in the city since the late fourth century

BCE. The great imperial capital no longer felt it was unconquerable. But Rome was becoming less and less important to the empire. For the previous 500 years, Roman politics had been dominated by moneyed Mediterranean aristocracy. From this point onward the vast majority of emperors were soldiers from the Danube frontier; over the next three and a half centuries, three-quarters of Roman emperors came from a region that accounted for 2 percent of Roman territory. As the descendants of legionnaires who had settled on the northern frontier centuries earlier, the new rulers identified as Romans. But they spent most of their time in the north and hardly ever visited Rome—so seldom, in fact, that the city ceased to be the empire's administrative capital. The military rulers instead governed from Milan and Ravenna in northern Italy, or Nicomedia in what is now Turkey.[40]

Even though the Roman Empire managed to survive the Plague of Cyprian and the Crisis of the Third Century, the damage had been done. Rome plunged into a long, debilitating and transformational crisis. But the plague's most lasting impact was not political. It was religious. The pandemic turned a tiny and obscure Jewish sect on the periphery of the empire into a major world religion, one that today has 2.3 billion adherents and accounts for almost a third of the world's population.[41]

The Resurrection of Christ

Christianity was virtually invisible for the first two centuries after Jesus' death. The New Testament informs us that Christ had 120 followers on the morning of his ascension to heaven, and this reached 3,000 by the end of the day as the result of Peter's preaching. But this exponential growth didn't continue. The Jewish community in Palestine failed to convert en masse to Christianity, and the Church instead turned to recruiting gentiles. By the beginning of the third century, there were perhaps 100,000 followers scattered across the empire.[42] This amounts to about 0.15 percent of the population, around the same as the proportion of Sikhs in the U.S. today and considerably smaller than those in the UK (0.7 percent).[43]

Despite the small numbers, Roman emperors brutally persecuted adherents to Christianity. The first, empire-wide attacks came during the reign of Marcus Aurelius (161–80). One of the most notorious incidents occurred in 177 at the Amphithéâtre des Trois-Gaules in present-day Lyons where, in front of a roaring crowd, the followers of the Jesus sect were stretched on the rack, cooked on a red-hot iron chair and ripped apart by lions. Persecution then eased off, but resumed once again in the middle of the third century. In 250, Emperor Decius decreed that everyone in the empire except Jews must make a sacrifice to the Roman gods in the presence of a magistrate.* Those who completed the task were issued with a certificate. In Egypt they were made of papyrus and many examples have survived. This was an effective way of identifying believers in Jesus, as they were not allowed to worship other deities. Prominent members of the Christian community—including Pope Fabian—were then executed for not making an offering to the pagan gods. It wasn't a coincidence that the two high points of repression coincided with the Antonine and Cyprianic Plagues. Pagans believed that the presence of a new religion was displeasing the Roman gods or driving them away, and therefore Christianity was responsible for the widespread death and disruption.[44]

The oppression of the Church did not have the desired effect, however. In the middle of the third century, Christianity suddenly appears to have become a mass phenomenon. Evidence of its growth can be found in Rome's catacombs. Only a handful of Christian burial chambers there date from the late second and early third centuries, but the numbers rise massively in the third quarter of the third century.[45] It is also apparent that Christian first names became increasingly popular in parts of the empire. For example, between 15 percent and 20 percent of the population of Egypt appear to have been Christian at around the start of the fourth century. In 312, Emperor Constantine converted to Christianity. Persecution ended and the Roman state began to support his new religion. For example, Sunday became the day of rest and public money was provided to build places of worship, including the Church of the Resurrection in Jerusalem and St. Peter's Basilica in

---

* This is because Judaism was an ancient religion that didn't proselytize, so wasn't seen as a threat to the pagan gods, and Decius was keen to avoid another revolt in Judaea.

Rome. Constantine's successors continued to support Christianity and in 380 it became the official faith of the Roman Empire. At the same time, paganism suffered a startling collapse. Temple-building came to a halt in the mid-third century CE and the state no longer updated the register of temple personnel and property after 259.[46] It was as if the Greco-Roman gods, who had played a dominant role in people's lives across a vast region dating back to at least the time of Homer, simply packed up and left.

How do we explain the sudden transformation of Christianity from a marginal Jewish sect to a popular religion? The American sociologist Rodney Stark argues that infectious diseases are a crucial part of the story. The Christian faith skyrocketed because it provided a more appealing and assuring guide to life and death than paganism during the devastating pandemics that struck the Roman Empire in the second and third centuries CE. In fact, he goes as far as to say that if it wasn't for the Antonine and Cyprianic Plagues, "Christianity might never have become so dominant a faith."[47]

One major point of difference between the old and new faith was the issue of what happens when we die. Jesus promised everlasting life in paradise, whereas "pagans believed in an unattractive existence in the underworld." Then there was the question of why pandemics occur: the Greco-Roman gods were capricious, angry, indifferent to human suffering and sometimes downright cruel. Remember, the Romans believed that Apollo conjured up a plague that killed 7 million people to punish the transgressions of a few light-fingered legionnaires in the middle of the second century. In this belief system, the best way to save oneself from Apollo's wrath was to try to deflect his anger by making a sacrifice or some other form of offering. In contrast, Jesus' message that hardship brought redemption was much more reassuring in the face of the recurring devastation of plagues. It offered hope and meaning by explicitly promising a better life in the next world for those who were suffering on earth.

Christianity provided another more tangible benefit over paganism. Traditional Roman society was not uncharitable—in its heyday, the state doled out free wheat and later bread to 200,000 people in the imperial capital, for example—but their deities did not reward altruism. So when plagues were raging, people of means—including Galen—

took flight, and those who remained tried to avoid contact with the sick. Observing the pagans, Bishop Dionysius of Alexandria noted: "their dearest they fled from, or cast them half dead into the road." Christianity was different. Believers were expected to show their love for God through acts of kindness to each other. As a result, followers of Jesus tried to guarantee entry into heaven with good deeds in their earthly lives. Dionysius describes how Christians looked after the ill during the Plague of Cyprian: "Heedless of danger, they took charge of the sick, attending to their every need." Christians would have been able to reduce mortality by up to two-thirds just with basic nursing, such as providing food and water.[48] The fact that so many more Christians survived, and that Christians managed to save pagans abandoned by their families, would have provided the best recruitment material any religion could ask for: miracles.

Gibbon argues that as the Christian Church grew, it weakened the empire from within by encouraging the brightest and bravest Romans to reject civic duty and instead dedicate their lives to God—"the last remains of military spirit were buried in the cloister." Although this reflects his staunchly pro-Enlightenment, anti-Church standpoint, there does appear to be something to this explanation for the decline of the Western Empire. By the end of the fourth century, the total number of priests, monks and so on was half the size of the army, so Christianity was a considerable drain on manpower. And around this time it seems that the Roman state was struggling to find army recruits—for example, they had to lower the minimum height for entrants and enlist an increasing number of Barbarian units.[49]

At the beginning of the fifth century, when large numbers of Goths were pushed out of the Steppe by the Huns and then the Huns themselves surged westward, the once-great empire was unable to withstand the pressure.[50] In 410, the Gothic leader Alaric led a three-day-long sack of Rome—the first time this had happened in 800 years. Although malaria didn't stop Alaric from entering the great city, it did prevent him from basking in the glory of his achievement: the disease killed him soon afterward.[51] In the middle of the fifth century Attila the Hun rampaged across Roman territory. In 452 CE, his army razed Aquileia. The whole of the Italian Peninsula was defenseless, but after his army was struck down by a devastating disease—most likely malaria—Attila was forced to retreat to the high and dry Hungarian Steppe. It is not clear why the defensive shield that repelled invading armies for centuries finally cracked, but in 476 Romulus Augustulus was deposed by Odoacer, a soldier who led a federation of Germanic tribes and became King of Italy. This is traditionally seen as the end of the Western Roman Empire.

Long after the Roman Empire ceased to exist in the west, it continued to thrive in the wealthy eastern provinces. Constantinople became the imperial capital in 324 and its population grew tenfold, from 30,000 to 300,000.[52] By the mid-sixth century it had reached about half a million and was bigger than Rome. Just as in the old imperial capital, infectious diseases created a defensive force field around the new one. In 447, an earthquake destroyed Constantinople's defenses and left it exposed. The Huns closed in on the city but were sent packing by gastrointestinal bugs. According to one chronicler, "He who was skillful in shooting with the bow, sickness of the bowels overthrew him—the riders of the steed slumbered and slept and the cruel army was silenced."[53] Constantinople became a nexus of commerce, finance and industry, brimming with people and goods from all over the known world. Egyptian grain that once had been earmarked for Rome was redirected there. So many ships traveled between Alexandria and the new capital that it was said that they created an artificial strip of dry land between the two great cities. In addition to food, the boats carried rats and fleas that brought another devastating, world-altering pandemic.

No God but God

Dante Alighieri's *Divine Comedy* is the most famous literary representation of the Christian afterlife. In his journey through Hell, Purgatory and Heaven, Dante the Pilgrim comes across many of the characters that we have encountered in this chapter. He is guided through the Inferno by the Roman poet Virgil. In the First Circle of Hell we meet the good and great of Greco-Roman civilization, who as pagans are not able to enter Heaven. In the Seventh Circle of Hell, which is reserved for murderers and tyrants, Attila the Hun and Alexander the Great are forced to stand up to their eyebrows in a river of boiling blood for the rest of eternity. Dante then climbs Mount Purgatory and ascends into *Paradiso*, where he meets a variety of virtuous Christians who have earned their place in Heaven through their good deeds on earth. Among these is Justinian, ruler of the Eastern Roman Empire from 527 to 565, who is portrayed as a defender of the Christian faith and the man who brought the city of Rome back under the control of the Roman Empire.

On the face of it, Dante's positive depiction of Justinian seems justified. In Constantinople he carried out a massive building program that included the Hagia Sophia, a masterpiece of early Christian architecture that still dominates central Istanbul today, albeit now as a mosque. In 532, Justinian agreed to the "Perpetual Peace" with his most dangerous enemy, the Persians. It lasted until 540. But this bought him enough time to reconquer many of the empire's former western provinces, which were controlled by Germanic invaders. His Byzantine army defeated the Vandals in North Africa in 533–34. They set their sights on the Ostrogoth-controlled Italian Peninsula, quickly seizing Sicily and Naples. They captured Rome in 536 and Ravenna in 540. In 552, the Byzantines took southern Spain from the Visigoths. As the provinces were absorbed back into the empire, its military and financial strength grew. For a time, it looked as though the *renovatio imperii* was going to succeed and the Romans would once again rule the whole of the Mediterranean world.

But after this initial flurry of victories, the natural world seemed to conspire to undermine Justinian's efforts. Beginning in 536, several massive volcanic eruptions in Iceland spewed ash into the atmosphere. Eyewitnesses in Constantinople reported eighteen months of darkened skies and unseasonable weather. The following decade was the coldest of the previous 2,000 years, as the temperature fell by 1.5 to 2.5 degrees Celsius.[54] In 541, a deadly infectious disease appeared in Pelusium, which sits at the eastern edge of the Nile Delta. From there it spread to Alexandria and then to Constantinople, where Justinian became ill but managed to survive. The first pandemic lasted until 544 and affected the whole Roman world and beyond. Recurrent waves ravaged Europe and Asia for the next two centuries.

Unlike the other devastating pandemics that had hit the Greco-

Roman world in the previous 1,000 years, which can only be tentatively identified based on sketchy accounts, we can be pretty sure that the Plague of Justinian was bubonic plague. This has long been suspected based on eyewitness descriptions of symptoms, in particular the characteristic swollen and painful lymph nodes or "buboes." But the diagnosis has recently been confirmed by traces of *Yersinia pestis* DNA in mid-sixth-century skeletons dug up in southern Germany, Cambridge in the British Isles, central and southern France and Valencia in Spain.[55]

The bacteria that caused the Plague of Justinian had genetically mutated sometime between the Bronze Age and the fifth century.[56] This adaptation allowed *Yersinia pestis* to survive in fleas. In fact, it made the fleas feel especially hungry so they were more likely to sink their teeth—or more precisely their mouths—into someone or something. Consequently, the bacteria no longer had to be passed from person to person via infected droplets and could now be mainlined into the bloodstream when these insects bit. These fleas were most notably transported by black rats, which first arrived in Europe from South East Asia in the second century BCE and became increasingly ubiquitous as a result of the Roman proclivity for moving and storing vast amounts of grain to feed the population.[57] Within ten days or so the rat populations in an area would all die from plague, and then the fleas would move on to humans.[58]

From plague bacteria's perspective, humans and black rats are second-rate hosts because of their tendency to die quickly after the pathogen enters their bodies. Some other species, most notably great gerbils and marmots, both of which live in mountainous areas of Central Asia, have partial resistance to *Yersinia pestis*. Their bodies provide an environment where the bacteria can reproduce without killing the host. This means that while plague epidemics quickly burned out in human and rat populations, the pathogens could survive for centuries or even millennia in gerbils and marmots, before once again spilling out into the rat and then human populations when conditions allowed.

William McNeill notes how nomadic people living on the Steppe "had mythic explanations to justify epidemiologically sound rules for dealing with the risk of bubonic infection from marmots." This included taboos on trapping or touching the animals. Such measures were not always successful at stopping the spread of the plague. Ancient DNA analysis has identified a nomadic Hun who died from a strain of *Yersinia pestis*, similar to the one that caused the Plague of Justinian, in the Tian Shan Mountains of Central Asia in the second century BCE.[59] (This does not seem to have led to a big outbreak, presumably because the Hun's nomadic lifestyle meant that the disease killed them before they came into contact with others.)

When the climate got markedly colder in the 430s, gerbils and marmots were forced to venture beyond their traditional habitat in search of food. Sooner or later they would have come into contact with black rats and infected fleas jumped from one species to the other. Once this had happened it was inevitable that *Yersinia pestis* would spread throughout North Africa and Western Eurasia.[60]

The arrival of plague was a hammer blow to Justinian's revitalized empire. The Byzantine writer Procopius, who witnessed the first wave of the epidemic, describes how "the whole human race came near to being annihilated." He claims that 10,000 people died every day in Constantinople at its height. This might well have been an exaggeration, but the message is clear: the outbreak was devastating. The picture is confirmed by the other notable eyewitness, John of Ephesus, a Christian bishop who was in Alexandria when the plague first hit in 541 and then traveled overland through the Levant and Asia Minor to Constantinople. He observes that many settlements "were left totally without inhabitants," with herds of farm animals turning feral and crops left to rot in the fields. John estimated that between 250,000 and 300,000 people died in Constantinople out of a total population of half a million.[61]

As the plague swept through Europe, the Eastern Roman Empire struggled to find enough men to join its army. This was in part a result of the depleted population, but also because the collapse of the tax base forced Justinian to cancel the gold bonus that had been paid regularly to assure the loyalty of legionnaires for the past 200 years. Before the plague, the total size of the Byzantine army was about 350,000 and it was not uncommon to send 25,000–30,000 soldiers onto the battlefield at one time. A few decades after the plague first struck, the army totaled 150,000 and had difficulty mustering 10,000 soldiers to fight.[62] From the 560s onward, the Eastern Roman Empire once again began to lose the western provinces, which it had only just regained, to Barbarian invaders. The Lombards reduced the areas under Roman control in Italy, Slavs and Avars pushed into the Balkans, Visigoths conquered the Roman province of Hispania and Berbers captured much of the countryside in North Africa.

The Greco-Romans, along with the Persians, had been the major powers in Western Eurasia since the Spartan-led Hellenic League successfully defeated Xerxes' invasion more than 1,000 years earlier. Various iterations of these two great empires had fought each other on several occasions since then, but neither side had ever been capable of delivering a knockout blow.[63] The start of the seventh century was a particularly violent time in their relationship. Initially, the Sasanians, who now controlled Persia, were successful against the plague-weakened Byzantines. They conquered Jerusalem in 614, along with much of the Middle East, and took the relic of the True Cross—that is, the cross that Jesus was supposedly crucified on—as a trophy; between 618 and 621 they gained Alexandria and the province of Egypt, which provided Constantinople with most of its grain. The Sasanians even besieged the imperial capital in 626 but failed to capture it. Then, in 627, the tide turned: the Sasanians were badly hit by an epidemic which is said to have killed half the population, including the emperor Sheroe, who gave his name to the plague.[64] In the next couple of years the Byzantines reclaimed Jerusalem and the cross, then reconquered Alexandria and the rest of Egypt.

As wave after wave of disease struck Eastern Romans and Persians, the two empires became ever weaker. All the while, the Prophet Muhammad looked on with interest from Medina.[65] He saw in the wars between the Christian Eastern Romans and Zoroastrian Sasanians a reflection of his own struggle to spread a monotheistic faith among the polytheistic pagans of the Arabian Peninsula. The history of the Kaaba, the small cubic building located in Mecca, illustrates just how much Muhammad transformed the region. In pre-Islamic Arabia it contained a cosmopolitan roster of 360 deities, including a version of the goddess that Egyptians called Isis, the Greeks Aphrodite and Romans Venus; Jesus and the Virgin Mary; and Hubal, the Syrian god of the moon.[66] By the time of his death in 632 Muhammad had succeeded in converting the region to Islam, uniting for the first time its disparate tribes, who continued to visit Kaaba in order to worship the one true God. But in the next couple of decades the reach of this new faith expanded far beyond the Arabian Peninsula.

In the 630s and 640s, Muslim Arab armies swept across the wealthy and densely populated Roman provinces in the Middle East and North Africa. The holy city of Jerusalem was captured in 637. Alexandria, the great center of Greek culture, fell in 641. These territories would never be regained by the rulers in Constantinople, although they continued to control a much-reduced Byzantine Empire until 1453. The Arabs also expanded eastward into Mesopotamia and Persia. By the early 650s the Sasanians were totally defeated and the Persian Empire ceased to exist. Within a few decades, the Rashidun Caliphate controlled an area that stretched from what is now Algeria to Pakistan, and the Black Sea to the Indian Ocean. Over the next 100 years, the Islamic Empire grew even more under the Umayyad Caliphate. Ibn Khaldun, the fourteenth-century Arab historian, believed the expansion was miraculous and it's not hard to see why. But is there a more prosaic explanation?

Muhammad's ideas were important in uniting the disparate peoples of the Arabian Peninsula. At a time when plague, as well as war and climate change, appear to have convinced many people that the end of the world was imminent, Islam's key message—"worship the one God, for the Hour is at hand"—would have been appealing.[67] But religious doctrine cannot explain the explosive emergence of the Arabian Empire, because most inhabitants of the conquered Roman provinces and Sasanian territories didn't immediately convert to Islam. For this reason, the British writer Tim Mackintosh Smith describes the early Caliphates as rising like a soufflé.[68] Christian, Jewish and Zoroastrian communities were allowed to maintain their own traditions as long as they paid taxes and respected the political authority of the new conquerors. In fact, most subjects of the caliphate continued to follow Christianity and Zoroastrianism for several centuries.[69] Syria-Palestine didn't become Muslim majority until the twelfth century, and Egypt not until the fourteenth. In fact, large parts of the population in Upper Egypt, the mountains of the Levant and northern Mesopotamia remained Christian until well into the twentieth century.

The creation of the Arabian Empire was the result of a series of astonishing military victories against the plague-devastated Byzantines and Sasanians. In the south and west of the Arabian Peninsula many inhabitants—including Muhammad—lived in permanent settlements. But a large proportion of the population were nomadic Bedouins. On the origins of the word "Arab," Mackintosh Smith points out that "for more of known history than not, the word has tended to mean tribal groups who live beyond the reach of settled society . . . it is certainly what they were during most of the second AD millennium."[70] Consequently, the region was much less prone to a disease that was spread by flea-carrying rats, and the Roman and Persian Empires were weakened not only in absolute terms but also relative to the newly Muslim and united Arabs.

When the Muslim armies operated in the newly conquered areas they began to suffer terribly from outbreaks of the plague too. The first major outbreak to hit the Arab Empire was the Plague of Amwas in 638–39, which killed large numbers of people in Syria—both the invaders and the local population. The subsequent disruption contributed to the decline of the Rashidun Caliphate and, after a decade of infighting, the rise of the Umayyad dynasty in 661. But the Arab commanders learned that when an epidemic struck it was safest to remove their troops from the city to isolated highland or desert locations until the danger had passed. Similarly, the Umayyad Caliphs would retreat to the desert palaces and live like Bedouins during plague season.[71]

The spread of Arab Muslim armies throughout much of the Old World was extraordinary. Less than 100 years after Muhammad's death, the Umayyad Caliphate presided over an empire that reached from the Atlantic to northern India and China's western border. It controlled the vast territories that Alexander the Great had conquered in Asia—without the alcohol and brutal violence—as well as more than half of the Roman Empire. This is the point in time when a large part of the Old World took its modern form. Although the Muslim rulers in Spain were finally defeated in 1492, the new civilization that came into being in the seventh and eighth centuries has survived in some form until the present day. Without the lethal effects of *Yersinia pestis*, it is almost impossible to imagine that Islam would have blossomed from a sect with a small group of followers in the Hijaz to a major religion practiced by almost a quarter of the world's population, or that Arabic would have gone from being the language of a few desert tribes to one that is now spoken by almost half a billion people across North Africa and the Middle East.[72]

The Arab armies' expansion played an important role in forging the modern world well beyond the areas they conquered. Since the days of the *pax Romana*, the Mediterranean had been the main route along which people, goods, ideas and germs flowed from the much more advanced east to northwestern Europe. With the devastation of the Eastern Roman Empire, this artery was severed. The renowned Belgian historian Henri Pirenne famously argued that without Muhammad, Charlemagne would be inconceivable.[73] The political vacuum in northwestern Europe ultimately led to the emergence of a new order that was dominated by a patchwork of small kingdoms, feudal lords and thriving city-states but was at the same time unified by its Christian identity, in opposition to its Muslim neighbors to the south and east.[74]

Chapter 4
Medieval Plagues

Then the plague struck. And it devastated Europe.
But in spite of the havoc it wrought, it did a service to
the West. It guaranteed that in the generations after
1348 Europe would not simply continue the pattern
of society and culture of the thirteenth century.
—David Herlihy

Silence in Heaven

Ingmar Bergman's *The Seventh Seal* (1957) tells the story of a knight and his squire who return home to Sweden after ten years' fighting in the Holy Land to find their country devastated by the Black Death. At the beginning of the movie, in one of the most iconic images in film history, the protagonist is confronted by the black-hooded, white-faced personification of Death who has come for him. But Antonius Block isn't ready to die, so in order to forestall the inevitable he challenges his assailant to a game of chess. Death accepts and the game continues at various locations during Block's eventful journey through the plague-ravaged countryside to his castle.

Over the next ninety minutes, the audience witness one shocking scene after another: in a church, Block tries to confess his innermost secrets, including the chess move that will save his life, but after talking for some time he realizes that it is not a priest but Death on the other side of the screen; a young woman accused of having sex with the devil is burned at the stake; a wretched procession of masochistic flagellants pass by, shrieking as they are whipped; and the preacher who a decade earlier had exhorted Block to join the crusade is caught robbing corpses and threatening to rape a young mute woman. Eventually Death wins the game of chess and announces that when he next meets Block, it will be for the last time. The knight manages to reach his castle. As he eats with his entourage, his wife reads the passage from the *Book of Revelation* that gives the film its name: "When He broke open the seventh seal, there was silence in heaven for about half an hour." Then Death interrupts and leads them away.

There are plenty of historical inaccuracies in *The Seventh Seal*, and it is as much a meditation on Bergman's own loss of faith as anything else. Nevertheless, the film lucidly captures some key features of the Black Death, such as the breakdown of social norms and the ever-present threat posed by the plague—which Block's chess match not so subtly alludes to. It is not a coincidence that the film was made in the 1950s, a decade that was haunted by the devastation of the Second World War and the Holocaust, as well as the widespread fear that the Cold War would descend into a nuclear apocalypse. For Bergman, the outbreak of plague that hit Europe in the middle of the fourteenth century provided an obvious metaphor for the climate of existential angst and foreboding he was living through. Others made this link too. The American historian Barbara Tuchman not only describes the 1300s as a "violent, tormented, bewildered, suffering and disintegrating age" in which there was "no sense of an assured future," she also argues that it was a "distant mirror" to our own troubled times.[1]

Despite the parallels between the fourteenth century and the present, there are—to state the obvious—massive differences. Following the decline of the Roman Empire in western Europe, a feudal society emerged in which lords and knights ruled over the countryside from their castles. This system discouraged technological innovation, so there had been little or no improvement in living standards since Roman times for the masses who toiled away in the fields. The Catholic Church not only taught followers to unquestionably accept its doctrine but brutally punished anyone who stepped out of line. And in the minds of medieval Europeans, the beating heart of Christian civilization was still very much to the south and east, in Constantinople and—in the popular imagination at least—Jerusalem. When various popes urged Christians to take up arms and reconquer the Holy Land, tens of thousands of men, women and children responded enthusiastically.

To people living in the early 1300s, it would have seemed as if society was going to carry on very much like this until the end of time.[2] But if we fast-forward 700 years, politically, socially and economically, Europe is incomparably different. Stagnant feudalism has been replaced by a capitalist system that is characterized by the incessant search for profits and seemingly inexorable growth. The vast majority of people now live in towns and cities. In much of the region, the power of the Catholic Church has waned in the face of challenges from Protestantism and more recently secularism. The permanent loss not just of Jerusalem but also of Constantinople and most of what used to be the Eastern Roman Empire, coupled with the colonization of the Americas and the status of the U.S. as the leader of the Western world, has seen the soul of Europe shift evermore northward and westward.

How do we account for the decline of medieval Europe and the emergence of the modern world? The Black Death played a crucial role, triggering a series of events that—over several centuries—resulted in this transformation. It was, as one historian put it, "the great watershed in medieval history" that ensured "the Middle Ages would be the middle, not the final, phase in western development."[3]

Winter Is Coming

The period between about 1000 and 1300 is referred to as the High Middle Ages by historians and the Medieval Warm Period by meteorologists. The longer and warmer summer increased agricultural yields and the population boomed. Feudal societies absorbed the growing population, but they achieved this by bringing more land under cultivation rather than increasing agricultural productivity. Forests were felled. Marshland was drained. People moved into uplands that had previously not been suitable for farming. Lords colonized new regions on the edge of the continent: for example, Germanic Junkers pushed eastward across the Elbe and Polish Szlachta expanded into the Eurasian Steppe in what is now Ukraine. As the general population grew, so did towns and cities. Urban artisans and merchants organized themselves into guilds that satisfied growing demand from feudal lords for weapons and luxury goods, especially textiles. It was in this period that many of the great Gothic cathedrals were built—Notre-Dame, for example, was started in 1163. The oldest university in Europe was founded in Bologna in 1088. Universities emerged in Oxford and Paris around this time too. But because agriculture hadn't become more productive, the urban population increased in absolute numbers but it didn't grow as a proportion of the total population.

Then, at the end of the thirteenth century, the world entered the so-called Little Ice Age. This started with a volcanic eruption on the island of Lombok in what is now Indonesia, the most powerful explosion for 7,000 years.[4] The vast amounts of ash pumped into the atmosphere blocked out the sun. Summers became cooler and shorter, and winters longer and harsher. 1315 appears to have been a particularly bad year. It rained almost constantly throughout the summer. Crops rotted in the ground. Harvests failed. When Edward II stopped at St. Albans on 10 August, he was unable to find bread to feed his entourage. According to one chronicler, the grape harvest was so poor that "there was no wine in the whole kingdom of France."[5] Another noted that the poor ate dogs, cats, bird droppings and even their own children.[6] The so-called Great Famine continued until 1317 and killed about a tenth of the population of northwest Europe.[7] Over the next few decades, the climate became colder and the harvest failed on several more occasions.

For two centuries after the Plague of Justinian (541–49), *Yersinia pestis* caused repeated epidemics in Europe, the Middle East and North Africa. Then there is no record of a plague outbreak for more than 500 years.[8] But the bacteria hadn't disappeared entirely. They continued to survive among gerbils and marmots in the mountains of Central Asia. When the climate changed, these wild rodents emerged from their isolated habitats once again, and the stage was set for the first major outbreak of plague in half a millennium.

The spread of plague across the Eurasian landmass was aided by favorable geopolitical conditions. By the thirteenth century, Genghis

Khan and his heirs had built one of the largest empires in history. It covered not just China but also most of Central Asia and what is now Russia, Iran and Iraq. The pathogen's journey across the Eurasian landmass was assisted by the stability that the Mongols brought to the continent. During the so-called *pax Mongolica*, the Far East was linked to the Black Sea by a network of relatively safe and well-maintained routes that made up the Silk Road. It was around this time that Marco Polo set off from Venice for Xanadu, hoping to develop trading links and convert Kublai Khan, Genghis's grandson, to Christianity. Polo would have shared the roads with all sorts of other travelers, including messengers capable of covering 160 kilometers a day, slow-moving caravans transporting their wares, and armies marching back and forth.[9]

The earliest genetic evidence of fourteenth-century plague comes from *Yersinia pestis* bacteria in the teeth of seven individuals who died in the late 1330s in Kyrgyzstan, Central Asia.[10] Surviving historical accounts show that China was hit by a series of epidemics in 1331–34, 1344–46, and then throughout the 1350s.[11] According to imperial records, these were devastating. An outbreak in the northeast province of Hebei in 1331 is reported to have killed 90 percent of its inhabitants. The Chinese population collapsed, falling from about 125 million at the beginning of the fourteenth century to 65 million at the end— although war and floods also contributed to the death toll.[12] We cannot be sure which pathogen caused these epidemics because official accounts do not describe the symptoms, but both the timing and high mortality point to *Yersinia pestis*. William McNeill suggests that the plague was a key factor in the political instability that struck China in the mid-fourteenth century. This culminated in the fall of the Great Yuan—Genghis Khan's descendants—and the emergence of the Ming dynasty, which seized control in 1368.

In the 1340s, *Yersinia pestis* made its way along the Silk Road to Europe.[13] The plague is believed to have re-entered the continent via Kaffa (now Feodosia), a trading station on the Black Sea that Genovese merchants had bought in the late thirteenth century from the khanate of the Golden Horde—part of the Mongol Empire that dominated the Western Eurasian Steppe. As the location of the region's biggest slave market, where Genovese traders bought humans captured in the region north of the Black Sea and trafficked them to Europe, the Middle

East and North Africa, Kaffa was one of the key links between Mongol territory and the Mediterranean. Supposedly, Italian merchants contracted plague in the autumn of 1346 when Mongol soldiers besieged Kaffa and catapulted the corpses of plague victims over the city walls. This story is apocryphal, but that hasn't stopped some scholars identifying it as the first instance of biological warfare.[14] When the winter ended the Genovese fled westward on their ships and brought the plague with them. The Black Death reached Constantinople in the summer of 1347 and from there it was transported to all the great port cities of the Mediterranean, from where it spread throughout Europe, as well as the Middle East and North Africa.

In spring 1348, the plague devastated the Italian Peninsula. One of the most famous eyewitness accounts of the Black Death can be found in the introduction to Giovanni Boccaccio's *Decameron*, the Florentine writer's collection of 100 bawdy short tales told by ten well-to-do young women and men holed up in a rural villa to escape the pestilence. The raconteurs' entertaining fortnight in the Tuscan countryside stands in stark contrast to the shocking scenes taking place within the walls of the crowded city they had escaped. Boccaccio describes how his home city was overcome by the stench of death, with people dropping dead in the streets and bodies left to rot in houses. To capture the scale of the tragedy, he describes over 100,000 inhabitants dying in a matter of weeks—more people than he imagined lived in Florence before the plague hit. Agnolo di Tura, a chronicler from nearby Siena, describes how he had to bury all five of his children with his own hands. Most of the deceased weren't treated with such dignity. Another eyewitness in Florence wrote of throwing bodies into a mass grave, covering them with earth, adding more bodies and then earth, "as one makes lasagne with layers of pasta and cheese."[15]

Not long afterward, the Black Death reached Avignon in southern France, where the popes were exiled for most of the fourteenth century. Bodies had to be discarded into the River Rhône until huge new graveyards were dug and consecrated. On the advice of Guy de Chauliac, the papal physician, Clement VI retreated to his chamber, saw nobody, and spent all day and night between two great fires—no mean feat in the Provençal spring and summer.[16] He survived because the flames inadvertently kept the rats at bay. By June, the Black Death had reached Paris, the Low Countries and England. From there it spread throughout northern Europe. It seemed like the world was coming to an end: a Franciscan monk in Kilkenny, Ireland, who died in the plague, left blank pages in his chronicle and a message in case "any child of Adam may escape this pestilence and continue the work thus commenced."[17] Below this, someone added a postscript dated 1349: "it seems that the author died here."

Petrarch, Boccaccio's friend and fellow Renaissance poet, remarked that the situation was so abysmal that future generations "will look upon our testimony as a fable." But this isn't the case. The devastation has been corroborated by scholars who have painstakingly combed through medieval censuses, tax records and manorial registers in order to estimate accurately how many people died. Their findings corroborate eyewitness accounts of widespread death. The Norwegian historian Ole Benedictow estimates that roughly 60 percent of the population of Europe—that is about 50 million out of 80 million people—died from the plague between 1346 and 1353.[18] Analysis of an ice core drilled in the Swiss Alps reveals that lead pollution disappeared from the air in these years.[19] No silver mining occurred during the Black Death. The economy appears to have simply ground to a halt.

Most people seemed to blame the carnage going on around them in more or less the same way that the Ancient Greeks and Romans had done. The Black Death was widely understood to be a form of divine punishment, although it wasn't clear what for.[20] The medical faculty of the University of Paris, the most prestigious learning institution in Europe, argued that the devastation was the result of a malign conjunction of Saturn, Jupiter and Mars that occurred at 1 p.m. on 20 March 1345. This accorded with the idea that the plague was the will of God, as stars were believed to be the instruments through which His will became reality on earth. The misalignment of the planets was thought to have caused the release of noxious gases—possibly after an earthquake—which then rolled across Europe from the east. This understanding is apparent in the work of Shakespeare, who has Timon of Athens curse Alcibiades as he hands him some gold: "Be as a planetary plague, when Jove [Jupiter] / Will o'er some high-viced city hang his poison / In the sick air."[21] There was, however, an equally preposterous but much darker explanation for the source of the Black Death.

The Blame Game

In 1998, archeologists in Erfurt, a small town in central Germany, discovered a haul of treasure weighing almost 30 kilos hidden in the wall of a cellar. It consisted of more than 3,000 silver coins, fourteen silver ingots, intricately decorated silver cups, and over 700 pieces of gold and silver jewelry. The most beautiful item is a gold wedding ring in the shape of a miniature Gothic tower with Mazel Tov inscribed in Hebrew on the roof. The trove also includes what has been described as the only surviving medieval cosmetic set, complete with ear cleaners, tweezers and a perfume bottle that has retained a discernible scent.

The Erfurt Treasure was found in the house where Kalman von Wiehe, a Jewish merchant, lived with his family in the middle of the fourteenth century. It is likely that he hid the valuables in his basement shortly before 21 March 1349, when the town's Jewish quarter was attacked by an angry mob. Presumably, von Wiehe hoped to retrieve the valuables when things calmed down, but he was murdered alongside Erfurt's entire Jewish community. His worldly possessions remained undiscovered for almost 650 years, by which time his descendants had been chased halfway across the world by violent oppressors and been victims of some of the most shameful events in human history.

The Erfurt massacre was far from an isolated incident. The orgy of violence began in northern Spain and southern France in the spring of 1348, ostensibly because the gentiles believed Jewish communities were the source of the Black Death. In the summer and autumn of 1348, several Jews in the French Alps confessed—albeit after being tortured on the rack—to causing the plague by poisoning wells.[22] Similar rumors spread across the German-speaking world faster than the disease itself—and so did the attacks against Jewish communities. These conspiracy theories appear to have been have widely accepted. The city council in Strasbourg wrote to nearby towns to ask whether the well-poisoning accusations were true. Of the nineteen responses that exist in Strasbourg's municipal archives, just one professes skepticism.[23] This appears to have been taken as a sign to proceed. On Valentine's Day 1349 the city's 2,000 Jews were forcibly marched through the town as baying crowds ripped their clothes off, hoping to find gold sewn into the lining, and were then burned to death.

Eyewitness accounts document a series of horrific attacks. The Jewish community in Mainz, perhaps the biggest and wealthiest in Europe, managed to repel the first attack and killed 200 assailants. But the next day the mob returned with reinforcements and annihilated all 3,000 of them. In Hansa towns in the north, Jews were walled up in their houses and left to starve. The Jewish community in Esslingen in the southwest decided to lock themselves in the synagogue and set it on fire rather than await their fate. As Philip Ziegler wryly notes, "it is a curious and somewhat humiliating reflection on human nature that the European, overwhelmed by what was probably the greatest natural calamity ever to strike his [sic] continent, reacted by seeking to rival the cruelty of nature in the hideousness of his own man-made atrocities."[24]

In 1348, Pope Clement VI issued two papal bulls that pointed to fundamental flaws in the well-poisoning libel: Jews were dying in similar numbers to gentiles in continental Europe and the plague was also devastating England, which had expelled its Jewish community in 1290. The Patriarch condemned those taking part in attacks on Jews as having been "seduced by that liar, the devil" and threatened them with excommunication. But his intervention had limited impact. The most powerful secular leader in Europe, Charles IV, the Holy Roman Emperor and King of Bohemia, encouraged the violence.* He offered the Archbishop of Trier the property of those Jews in Alsace "who have already been or may still be killed" and promised the Margrave of Brandenburg the best three houses in Nuremberg "when there is next a massacre of the Jews."[25] Local political elites took advantage of the situation too. In Cologne, Jewish property was split between the town council and archbishop, and the proceeds were used to beautify the cathedral and build a new town hall. In Augsburg, the man who opened the town gates to assailants from outside—the Bürgermeister, Heinrich Portner—was heavily indebted to Jewish moneylenders.[26] After the massacre, there was no one left alive to collect the money owed.

By the time the violence petered out in 1351, there had been about

* This doesn't seem to have affected Charles IV's reputation in his home country. His name is still plastered across Prague—on Charles University, Charles Bridge, Charles Square, for example.

350 attacks on Europe's Jews.[27] Sixty large and 150 smaller communities were annihilated.[28] Many Jews who managed to survive the double blow of plague and persecution fled to eastern Europe, a region that until then had an insubstantial Jewish population. Casimir the Great of Poland offered the migrants protection in his vast kingdom, which didn't just cover modern-day Poland and Lithuania but also newly colonized lands in what is now Ukraine. Contemporary gossip suggested Casimir was well disposed to these refugees because his favorite mistress was a Jewish women called Esterka. The truth is less romantic: that he was keen to benefit from the refugees' supposed expertise in moneylending and long-distance trade.

The immigrants settled in shtetls, the Jewish market towns that grew up adjacent to the agricultural estates. Over the next few centuries, these provided a relatively safe environment in which their cultural, intellectual and religious life flourished. Toward the end of the eighteenth century, the Polish-Lithuanian Commonwealth was devoured by the Romanov, Habsburg and Prussian empires. About three-quarters of Polish-Lithuanian Jews now found themselves living in Russia. From the outset they faced discrimination and oppression—"pogrom" is a Russian loan word. The metaphor of the Fiddler on the Roof—"trying to scratch out a pleasant simple tune without breaking his neck"—is meant to evoke the precarious situation of Jewish communities in the Pale of Settlement. Sholem Aleichem, whose short stories formed the basis of the Broadway musical, and Marc Chagall, whose paintings inspired the title, are testament to the manner in which Jewish cultural life continued to flourish in the shtetls in the early twentieth century.

The Return of the Plague

If Europe had been hit by just one shattering outbreak of plague in the middle of the fourteenth century, European societies would have recovered and returned to normal within a few generations.[29] Alas, the Black Death was anything but an aberration. The pestilence struck again and again over the next couple of centuries as *Yersinia pestis* was reimported into Europe from the mountains of Central Asia, where it continued to circulate in wild rodent populations.[30] It was the recurrent nature of the plague that made it so destructive and ended up causing such profound social, political and economic change. A second outbreak in 1361 killed perhaps 20 percent of the population, but among young people who hadn't been alive a decade earlier—and therefore hadn't developed immunity—the mortality rate was no different from that of the first epidemic.[31] Petrarch lamented that the initial Black Death was "only the beginning of our mourning." The plague returned every few years for the rest of the fourteenth and all of the fifteenth centuries. Epidemics became less frequent and widespread after 1500, but they continued to take a toll. Records from Italian cities give us a detailed picture of the damage. In 1629–30, plague killed one-third of Venice's population, just less than half of Piacenza's and almost two-thirds of Verona's.[32] Another epidemic in 1656–57 killed half of the inhabitants of Naples and Genoa. The demographic scar left by wave after wave of plague was deep and abiding. The population did not return to its 1300 level until the sixteenth century in Italy and France, the eighteenth century in England, and the nineteenth century in Egypt, which was at the time part of the Ottoman Empire.[33]

The Italian city-states were the first communities to take action to protect themselves from the plague. Starting in the 1370s, all ships wanting to enter Venice had to wait on the nearby island of San Lazzaro until the health magistrates granted the crew permission to disembark. Over time, the waiting period became standardized at forty days—the word quarantine is derived from *quaranta*, the Italian for forty. The length was informed not by scientific observation but by its significance in the Bible.* Despite this, forty days was effective because it was longer than it took for people to develop symptoms. The ships, peoples and goods were held in lazarettos or quarantine stations on islands away from the port city until the period of quarantine was completed. Venice built the first permanent lazaretto in the early fifteenth century. There were still occasional outbreaks, as noted above,

---

* Forty days is, for example, the amount of time that the great flood in Genesis lasted, Moses passed on Mount Sinai while waiting for the Ten Commandments and Jesus fasted in the wilderness.

but quarantine was deemed to be an effective public health intervention and it was adopted throughout western Europe.

The other major anti-contagion policy was to restrict overland movement using a cordon sanitaire. This began in an ad hoc fashion during the Black Death with vigilantes, motivated by fear and suspicion of outsiders, turning away strangers who wanted to enter their city, town or village. Eventually the strategy became regularized, rigorously applying the same logic behind quarantines to land borders. Parts of "Le Mur de la Peste," a wall built during the Great Plague of Marseilles in 1720 to stop people moving between the city and the hinterland, are still visible. The most remarkable example of a cordon sanitaire was constructed on the eastern boundary of the Habsburg Empire, in order to stop the transportation of the disease overland from Ottoman-controlled territory. It operated between 1710 and 1871 along a 1,600-kilometer military border that stretched from the Adriatic to the Transylvanian mountains. During times of high alert, people wanting to pass from east to west were required to stay for forty-eight days in quarantine facilities located at official border crossings. Anyone caught trying to avoid detention risked being sentenced to death by firing squad.[34]

The introduction of regulations such as quarantine and cordons sanitaires in late-medieval societies had significance well beyond public health, because they extended state power into areas of human life that had not previously been subject to political authority. Michel Foucault saw the shift in the focus of states from controlling territory to governing people's bodies as a key feature of the modern world.[35] (During the Covid-19 pandemic, lockdowns and other restrictions on movement were controversial precisely because they so starkly revealed the enormous power of the modern state over our lives.) In public health terms, the combined effort of quarantines and cordons sanitaire had an impact, however. The last major plague epidemics in western Europe were in the first half of the eighteenth century, killing 100,000 people in Marseilles and its surrounding areas in 1720–21 and 48,000 in Messina, Sicily, in 1743.[36] Regular plague outbreaks continued to afflict the Ottoman Empire until the mid-nineteenth century.[37] But Yersinia pestis' biggest impact on Anatolia and the Middle East occurred in the immediate aftermath of the Black Death.

The New Barbarians

Accounts of the Ottomans' final, successful assault on Constantinople in 1453 read like a scene from a swashbuckling action movie. Turkish cannon pounded the city walls. Besieging the capital was an army of 60,000, twice its population. The last Byzantine emperor, another Constantine, had only a few thousand Greek and Italian soldiers under his command but refused to surrender. Those who could not fight packed into the Hagia Sofia and prayed for the Virgin Mary to intercede and save Constantinople—as she is purported to have done in the eighth century when the Umayyad dynasty attacked. When guns finally smashed a hole in the ramparts, the attackers surged through. Constantine and his entourage ran toward them, swords drawn, in a vain attempt to halt the tide. He was never seen again. After three days of plundering, Sultan Mehmed II rode into the new Ottoman capital astride a white horse.

In the previous chapter we saw how, over several centuries, pandemics weakened the Roman Empire and strengthened so-called Barbarian societies on the empire's borders, where conditions were not so favorable to the spread of infectious diseases. By the Middle Ages, the former Barbarians—most notably the various Germanic tribes and the Arabs—lived in densely populated and well-connected polities of their own. Consequently, mortality rates from the Black Death were astonishingly uniform across the continent, and the medieval plague did not upend the power balance on the continent as it had done in antiquity—except in the southeast, which witnessed the remarkable rise of the Ottomans.[38]

Until the eleventh century, the much-diminished Eastern Roman Empire still ruled over Anatolia—what is now modern Turkey—and most of the Balkans from Constantinople. The imperial capital remained an enormous city, with a population of half a million. But over the next couple of hundred years all this changed as a result of the emergence of a formidable new enemy. The Turks were an ethnolinguistic group of nomadic animal herders that appear to have originated in the steppe of Central Asia. They were pushed out of their traditional grazing lands by the Mongol expansion. The Turks converted to Islam in the second half of the 900s and under the Seljuk dynasty conquered vast swathes of the Middle East in the eleventh century—including much of Hellenized, Christian Asia Minor. This transformed the character of a region that for 2,000 years had been a wealthy, intellectually vibrant part of the Greco-Roman world.[39]

By the end of the thirteenth century, the Seljuk Sultanate had disintegrated into a patchwork of small Turkish principalities or *beyliks*. On the frontier with the Byzantine Empire in northwestern Anatolia, small groups of ghazis—supposedly religiously enthused warriors who fought on horseback—made a living by raiding their Christian neighbors, looting property and kidnapping humans to sell as slaves.[40] This was how the Ottoman Empire began: as a nomadic band of ghazis under the leadership of Osman in the late thirteenth and early fourteenth centuries. Success in raiding the Byzantines brought prestige, followers and power, allowing the Ottomans to expand southward and eastward to bring the various *beyliks* of Anatolia under their control.

Little more than a century after Osman's death in 1326, his dynasty had conquered vast swathes of southeast Europe, captured the imperial capital of Constantinople, and extinguished the last vestiges of the ancient Roman Empire. The expansion of the Ottoman Empire caused great unease in northwest Europe and many suspected it was due to God's interference. In 1498, when Albrecht Dürer created prints of the various scenes from the *Book of Revelation*, he styled two of the Four Horsemen of the Apocalypse—War and Plague—as Ottoman janissaries. Around the same time, both Erasmus and Martin Luther were proclaiming that the Turks had been sent by God to punish sinning Christians. But it's not possible to understand the seemingly miraculous Ottoman expansion unless we consider the impact of the Black Death.

When Genovese traders carried *Yersinia pestis* from Kaffa to Constantinople in 1347, the Byzantine state was already weakened and vulnerable after two destructive wars of succession in the 1320s and 1340s. Anatolia was also affected by Black Death, particularly the densely populated, well-connected cities along the coast. But the Ottomans were still nomads. Ibn Battuta, the North African explorer and scholar, traveled extensively across the Muslim world in the fourteenth century. He noted that Osman's successor, Sultan Orhan, who led the Ottomans from about 1323 to 1362, "was always on the move, never staying in the same place for more than a few days."[41] This peripatetic lifestyle would have protected him and his followers from plague. Unlike people who lived in permanent villages and towns, nomads didn't store large amounts of grain or accumulate big piles of food waste, both of which attracted rats. The nomadic Turkish would have suffered fewer plague casualties than their settled Turkish neighbors, the Byzantines and the Slavs in the Balkans.[42]

While the territory controlled by the Ottomans started to grow prior to the Black Death, the most important—and unlikely—conquests occurred afterward. In 1354, the Ottomans seized the fortress of Gallipoli on the western side of the Dardanelles after it had been damaged by an earthquake. This marked the beginning of their expansion into Europe. In the 1360s they captured Adrianople, 240 kilometers west of Constantinople, which became their capital, Edirne. Within a couple of decades, the Ottomans had conquered much of the Balkans. These conquests reduced the size of the area ruled by the Eastern Roman emperor. For almost a century before the fall of Constantinople in 1453 it was an imperial capital without an empire, with the Byzantines controlling only a small territory around the city plus parts of the Peloponnese.

The final capitulation was hardly surprising, but it still caused dismay among Christians. As the Pope put it, the Ottomans had "plucked out one of the two eyes of Christendom"—the other being Rome.[43] Threatening to expand far into Europe's heartlands, the Ottomans besieged Vienna in 1529, which began a century and a half of military tension. They attacked again in 1683 but were defeated by the combined forces of the Polish-Lithuanian Commonwealth and Habsburg-led Holy Roman Empire. By then, however, the emergence of the Ottomans had forever altered the character of Europe.

The Ottoman expansion didn't just occur in Europe. In the early sixteenth century, they conquered much of the Middle East and North Africa—including Jerusalem, Damascus, Mecca and Medina—which had been ruled by the Mamluk Sultanate from their capital of Cairo. The Black Death once again aided the Turks' southern and eastern expansion. Egypt, the Levant and Syria were repeatedly devastated by the plague, as they were densely populated and well connected to Asia. The disruption appears to have been even greater than in Europe: from

1347 to 1517, when Cairo fell to the Ottomans, there were twenty major outbreaks of plague in Egypt compared to seventeen in Europe.[44] The loss of large numbers of peasants in the densely populated Nile Delta undermined the sultanate's tax base. The Mamluk armies were particularly badly affected by the plague, as they didn't recruit soldiers from North Africa and the Middle East but instead purchased them from Genovese slave traders. Having grown up in rural, isolated areas to the north of the Black Sea, Mamluks had lower levels of immunity and died in much larger numbers than the local population. Several outbreaks of plague in the late fifteenth and early sixteenth centuries are reported to have killed at least a third of Mamluk soldiers.[45] When the Mamluk Sultanate was defeated in the 1510s, over a quarter of the population of Anatolia were nomadic, so the plague would have had much less of an impact on the Ottomans.[46]

As the Ottomans expanded they gave up the nomadic existence that had given them such an advantage and began to suffer the ill effects of the plague like the rest of the population; this may be why they never replaced the Balkan population in the way they did in Anatolia.[47] Some communities—most notably the Albanians and Bosnians—converted to Islam in large numbers, but the majority remained Christian. The consequences of this partial conversion of the region 500 years ago played out in the Yugoslavian Wars of the 1990s, when nationalist politicians attempted to carve the remnants of the relatively tolerant, diverse Ottoman Empire into religiously and/or ethnically homogenous states. The Orthodox Christian Bosnian Serb army committed acts of genocide against Muslim Bosnians, most notoriously when they murdered over 8,000 men and boys at Srebrenica. Another legacy is the Muslim-majority Albanian province of Kosovo's ongoing struggle for independence from Serbia.

Without the plague, it is inconceivable that the Ottomans would have been able to quickly establish control over a vast territory that stretched from the Danube in the north to Yemen in the south, and from Algeria in the west to the Persian Gulf in the east. Their empire continued to be a major power in Europe, North Africa and the Middle East until the end of the First World War. Not only that, but their impact extended far beyond the areas they conquered: according to the American historian Alan Mikhail, the expansion of the Ottoman Empire disrupted trade routes with the Far East, and this compelled Spanish and Portuguese adventurers to seek out new ways to reach the Indies.[48] It isn't a coincidence that two decades after the Genovese trading colony of Kaffa fell to the Ottomans, Christopher Columbus— himself a Genovese sailor—reached North America. What is more, according to Mikhail the colonization of the Americas was a response to the realization that the Holy Land was irretrievably lost.

Although the plague-powered rise of the Ottomans had an enormous impact on Europe, the Black Death also transformed the continent from within by fundamentally changing the way in which people— particularly in the north—related to their God.

Morning Star of the Reformation

When more than half of your friends, family and neighbors die suddenly and painfully in quick succession, and the prospect of you dying imminently is very real, it is only natural to wonder about what happens after you pass away and, in a society that is overwhelmingly Christian, how best to guarantee your path into heaven. One of the most striking early manifestations of this new mood of religious introspection came from itinerant groups of flagellants who tramped across central Europe during the Black Death. When they arrived in a new town they'd head to the marketplace, strip to their waists and take out whips consisting of three or four leather thongs tipped with sharp metal spikes. After asking God to forgive their sins, they would beat their chests and backs while chanting penitential hymns. As Philip Ziegler points out, "each man tried to outdo his neighbour in pious suffering, literally whipping himself into a frenzy in which pain had no reality." One eyewitness described how the spikes sometimes got stuck so deeply in the flesh that it took several attempts to yank them out.[49]

The flagellants were mostly laypeople who believed that the Black Death was God's angry response to the depravity of medieval European society and that their dramatic acts of repentance would appease him. They claimed that their activities were authorized by God, often in the form of a letter dropped from heaven which was read out during their performances. The Church saw them as a threat to its authority because they challenged the idea that the clergy were needed to mediate between worshippers and God. The flagellants' activities undermined rituals such as confession and penance that were a key part of the Catholic faith. As the movement gained momentum, it attracted dissident clerics and became even more radical. Flagellants denounced the Church hierarchy, ridiculed its traditions, disrupted services and destroyed Church property; they were also blamed for inciting violence against Jews in the Rhineland.

By October 1349, Clement VI had seen enough. He issued a papal bull forbidding the public processions and threatening participants with excommunication. This was much more effective than the order that had attempted to put a stop to the vicious attacks on Europe's Jewish communities, and the movement quickly fizzled. The impulse that had led to the formation of these flagellants, however, wasn't so easy to stamp out. The processions were an early and shockingly masochistic manifestation of a much broader, longer-lasting change in attitudes toward religion that occurred in the wake of the Black Death. Christianity had once replaced paganism because it provided a more appealing and assuring guide to life and death during the Antonine and Cyprianic Plagues. Now, as disease ravaged the population yet again, many people began to reject the teachings of the Catholic Church.

In medieval Europe, the Jesus sect was no longer an insurgent movement of principled, self-sacrificing martyrs. The Church had grown into an extremely wealthy, powerful organization and expected Christians to pay the tithe—10 percent of their income. So many people had left property to the Church when they died that by the Middle Ages it owned about a third of all cultivated land in western Europe.[50] The papacy controlled a small state in central Italy, but the pontiff issued bulls that were supposed to be obeyed across the continent and had the power to declare war on behalf of Christendom. By the mid-fourteenth century, the Catholic Church had drifted a long way from the message of humility, compassion and faith preached by Jesus and his followers. This time round there was no upstart religion to offer an alternative to Christianity, as it had once done to paganism. Instead, the insurgency came from within the established faith.

During the Black Death and subsequent plague outbreaks, people looked to the Church for comfort. All too often, they didn't find it. Many clergy simply fled; for example, about 20 percent of parish priests in the English dioceses of York and Lincoln abandoned their posts rather than stay and tend to their flocks.[51] Those who did remain in their parishes to deliver the last rites to the dying masses were more likely to be exposed to *Yersinia pestis* and die. In many towns and villages there wasn't anyone to lead the rituals that helped people to deal with loss. An eyewitness in Avignon bemoaned the fact that "No priest came to hear the confession of the dying, or to administer the sacraments to them."[52] Boccaccio lamented that the dead were no longer "honored with tears, candles or mourners."

Even before the Black Death, the power and wealth of the Church attracted people to the priesthood who were motivated by personal advancement rather than spiritual concerns. So many clergy perished that the Church had no choice but to loosen the entry requirements in order to replace them, resulting in an influx of inexperienced and, in many cases, even more unsuitable people into the priesthood.[53] The portrayal of the clergy in the literature of the second half of the fourteenth century demonstrates how little they were respected. In Boccaccio's *Decameron*, priests, monks, mendicant friars and even nuns are on the prowl for sex wherever they can find it. Chaucer's *Canterbury Tales* satirizes English society, most of all the Church. It paints a picture of a lazy and greedy clergy, including a Monk who prefers to hunt on his fine horse rather than pray, and a Friar who has taken a vow of poverty but gleefully pockets money from destitute widows to fund his extravagant lifestyle.

While the Catholic Church failed to satisfy the spiritual needs of the population, it succeeded in making a profit off believers' existential angst. From the 1350s, on papal orders, it promoted the sale of indulgences, pieces of paper which could be purchased to reduce the time that people spent in purgatory and therefore hasten their entry to heaven.[54] If one believed Dante's portrayal of *Purgatorio*, in which for example those people guilty of envy have their eyes sewn shut with iron wire, this would probably seem like a very good deal. But clearly many people were suspicious of the Church's motivation. Chaucer's Pardoner is the most venal of all his characters, despite the theme of his sermons being *radix malorum est cupiditas*, greed is the root of all evil. He tells his audiences that, thanks to the power given to him by the Pope, his fake relics—which include a sheep's shoulder bone—will absolve them of all but the most heinous sins. After giving his spiel, the Pardoner then invites members of the congregation to come up and be absolved in exchange for cash. He reminds the crowd that if anyone doesn't take advantage of his generous offer, their neighbors will assume they are guilty of sins so terrible not even he can absolve them.

Faced with the failure of the Catholic Church to respond effectively to the trauma of the plague, people began to wonder about alternative means of salvation. There had been challenges to the authority and teachings of the Catholic Church before, but these ideas had failed to gain widespread support until the Black Death. John Wycliffe, a priest and theologian based at Oxford University, was born in the 1320s and became a leading light in the rebellion against religious orthodoxy and Church corruption in the second half of the fourteenth century. He took aim at the parish priests who had no time for preaching the gospel and comforting the needy, as well as the popes who claimed to be God's representative on earth. Wycliffe criticized the Church for veering away from the word of the Bible. He argued that there was no justification in the scriptures for many of the ideas they promoted—such as attending Mass, repenting for one's sins, praying to saints and buying indulgences. Wycliffe claimed that the clergy were not required to mediate laypeople's relationship with God; rather, the Bible was the only reliable guide to how they should conduct themselves. People should study the Holy Book—in the vernacular if they didn't speak Latin—and decide for themselves what God's message was. Wycliffe played a prominent role in the first translation of the Bible from the Latin Vulgate into Middle English in 1382.

Wycliffe's unorthodox opinions were condemned by the Church, of course, but he enjoyed the patronage of the English political elite, who saw him as a useful tool in their struggle with the Roman Church over power and money. Wycliffe's energetic and effective preaching moved followers to spread the Bible's message throughout England. His supporters became known as "Lollards."[55] Interestingly, the Parson is the only religious figure in *The Canterbury Tales* who is portrayed in a positive light, and he appears to be a Lollard. Chaucer describes him as "poor in wealth, perhaps, but rich in thought and holy works . . . who preached Christ's gospel in the most faithful fashion."

In 1415, three decades after Wycliffe's death, the Council of Constance declared him a heretic. It decreed that copies of his writings be destroyed and his remains removed from consecrated ground. The latter order wasn't carried out until 1428, when Wycliffe's body was exhumed and burned. Many of his followers weren't so lucky and were burned alive, including the Bohemian preacher Jan Hus at Constance. But the Catholic Church's heavy-handed response didn't suppress these proto-Protestant ideas. Wycliffe's ashes were cast into the nearest stream, and as a seventeenth-century writer noted: "This brook conveyed them into the Avon; Avon to the Severn; Severn to the narrow seas; they into the main Ocean. And thus the ashes of Wycliffe were the emblem of his doctrine, which now is dispersed the world over."[56]

We are taught that the Reformation began in 1517 when a young friar called Martin Luther nailed his Ninety-Five Theses to the church door in Wittenberg, central Germany, after being disgusted by Johann Tetzel's aggressive marketing of indulgences. But this familiar story ignores the fact that Luther's key arguments against the Catholic Church—not just about indulgences, but also the inadequacy and immorality of parish priests, the illegitimacy of the papacy and Church hierarchy, and the pre-eminence of the scriptures—had been raised by Wycliffe 150 years earlier in the wake of the Black Death. So why is Wycliffe only known as the "Morning Star of the Reformation," whereas Luther is portrayed as its father, mother and midwife?

One factor was the newfound accessibility of heretical ideas. When Wycliffe was alive, scribes had to copy out manuscripts by hand in a laborious and expensive process, so reading was the preserve of a small, educated elite. Then, in the middle of the fifteenth century, Johannes Gutenberg invented the printing press. The increasing use of labor-saving devices was a direct response to the challenges created by the Black Death and subsequent outbreaks of the plague, because there were now so few workers that labor-intensive processes had become unviable.[57] Printed pamphlets provided a relatively quick and cheap way of communicating with previously unimaginable numbers of people, allowing an obscure friar from a small German town to spread his anti-Church message to vast audiences across Europe. Luther's tracts were accompanied by crude, satirical woodcut images, so that in an age of low literacy his ideas reached as wide an audience as possible.[58] He was one of the bestselling authors of the sixteenth century. By 1521, 300,000 of his pamphlets and books had been printed and distributed;[59] after thirty years the figure was 3.1 million.[60] The impact of the printing press on the spread of Protestantism was so important that Luther is said to have referred to it as "God's highest and most extreme act of grace."[61]

The post–Black Death growth of universities also helped to promote a new intellectual spirit that laid the ground for the Reformation. Prior to 1348, higher education in Europe had been dominated by the great institutions in Paris and Bologna, where students from across the continent gathered to learn in Latin. The plague seems to have had a contradictory impact: at first it struck a major blow as so many experienced academics died and the pool of potential students was much reduced; but then wealthy benefactors, concerned about the plague's impact on learning and the supply of educated priests, endowed universities across the continent.[62]

The Holy Roman Emperor Charles IV, who had done so much to encourage attacks on the Jews, expressed grave concern for "precious knowledge which the mad rage of pestilential death has stifled throughout the wide realms of the world."[63] He founded the University of Prague—now known as Charles University—in 1348, and issued imperial accreditation to five other institutions over the next five years. Prior to the Black Death there were no universities in Europe located east of the Rhine and north of the Alps. Five were founded in the wake of the epidemic, not just in Prague, but in Cracow in 1364, Vienna in 1365, Fünfkirchen (modern Pécs) in 1367 and Heidelberg in 1386. These are the oldest universities in what is now Poland, Austria, Hungary and Germany, respectively. In the five years after the Black Death, three new colleges were established at Cambridge—Gonville & Caius, Trinity Hall and Corpus Christi—doubling the total number of colleges in the university.[64] The charters of these new universities and colleges cite the ravages of the Black Death. Even King's College, Cambridge, which dates to 1441, mentions the devastation of the previous century in its statutes.

New generations of theologians—as well as academics, lawyers and physicians—were educated alongside their compatriots in their home country rather than with a pan-European cohort in Paris or Bologna: Wycliffe studied at Oxford and became master of Balliol College; Hus was master of Charles University in Prague, where he had been a student; and Luther studied at the University of Erfurt (founded in 1379), then became professor of theology at the nearby University of Wittenberg (1501). These institutions provided an environment that allowed the national intelligentsia to develop an increasingly critical stance toward the Catholic Church.[65]

Many political leaders and populations, particularly in northern Europe, adopted the ideas of the Reformation and started to reject the authority of the Papacy.[66] The expansion of Protestantism was an important factor in some of the most momentous conflicts of the sixteenth and seventeenth centuries, although many wars fought in the name of Protestantism were motivated by the prospect of wresting political and economic power from Rome as much as by doctrinal issues—at times more so. Henry VIII of England's decision to break from the Catholic Church in the 1530s led to a century and a half of struggle that culminated in the Civil War (1642–51) and Glorious Revolution (1688). In German-speaking countries, the conflict between Protestant princes and the Catholic Habsburg Holy Roman emperors was responsible for the Thirty Years' War (1618–48), in which up to 40 percent of the population died from the combined impact of conflict, famine and disease in some parts of Europe.[67] The Peace of Westphalia, which determined that each prince could choose his state's religion, not only ended the conflict but also shattered the Catholic Church's supreme spiritual authority. As we will see in subsequent chapters, Protestants—specifically white Anglo-Saxon Protestants—escaping persecution in western Europe were the dominant force in the British colonies and then the United States. Protestantism now accounts for 37 percent of all Christians, and there are over 800 million Protestants in the world.[68]

The Reformation's greatest impact was on the way that people in western Europe thought. Luther's ultimate message, like Wycliffe's, was that each person should read the Bible and come to their own conclusions. This shifted the focus away from mindlessly obeying the Church's authoritative interpretation of Christianity and instead emphasized the critical faculties of the individual. Eventually, some people began to read the scriptures and reject them altogether. Instead, they tried to explain the world using reason and observation. In this sense, existential questioning triggered by the Black Death didn't just lead to the rise of Protestantism but also paved the way for the emergence of secularism.

The Black Death and the Spirit of Capitalism

To understand the key features of the feudal system that dominated western Europe in the Middle Ages, we need look no further than G.R.R. Martin's *Song of Fire and Ice* novels—or, if you prefer, HBO's adaptation, *Game of Thrones*. The occupant of the Iron Throne is only able to rule the Seven Kingdoms with the help and support of at least some of the other great houses of Westeros, each of which has its own castles and armies. The king or queen grants allied aristocratic clans control of vast chunks of land in exchange for "bending the knee"— a gesture that demonstrates loyalty and a commitment to provide military service when there is a war. The great lords then give lesser houses—the Boltons or Freys, for example—the right to control smaller parcels of land, and in return they are expected to help with raising an army. As Martin put it, when asked about the social structure of Westeros by a fan in an online forum: "it is a feudal system. The lords have vassals, the vassals have vassals, and sometimes the vassals of the vassals have vassals, down to the guy who can raise five friends."

At the very bottom of the pyramid are the serfs. They are largely invisible in *Game of Thrones*, unless they are being burned by dragons or slaughtered by zombies in the numerous battles that take place throughout the story. In a real-life feudal system, serfs account for the vast majority of the population and perform the most important function: food production. Serfs were bound in a reciprocal relationship with their feudal lord. They were granted the right to farm strips of land and graze animals on the commons, but in exchange they had to give the lords a share of their produce and spend some of their time working for nothing on the lord's demesne. Serfs weren't slaves. While not free to leave the lord's estate as and when they pleased, these peasants couldn't be sold.[69]

The standard of living for most people in Europe had barely changed since the days of the Roman Empire. The American historian Robert Brenner points out that the feudal system leads to economic stagnation because it isn't in the interests of either feudal serfs or their lords to maximize profits.[70]

The serfs' priority was to produce enough food to survive. As a result, they adopted a risk-averse subsistence strategy. Their strips of land were spread across different fields, reducing the danger that the whole harvest would be damaged by disease, bad weather or marauding animals. Similarly, they would cultivate a broad range of crops, so if one failed there would still be enough to eat. As serfs didn't have to pay rent at market rates for their land, they were shielded from the pressures of competition. This is not to say that serfs weren't involved in trade at all: if there was any surplus produce, they would sell or barter it. But they didn't organize their farming in order to produce as much as possible and sell it on the market.

Serfs were the lords' main source of income. Lords would sell surplus crops and spend the proceeds on strengthening their military capacity—for example, building castles, employing soldiers and buying weapons. This was their only rational strategy because they needed to keep the serfs in line and defend their own fief from would-be plunderers and conquerors. Lords would also spend surplus income on luxury goods that showed off their status and could be used to reward supporters and expand their following. It would have been incredibly risky to instead invest in technology that improved agricultural productivity. In a feudal society where other lords spent their money on armies and castles, a prosperous but poorly armed fief would have been a very tempting target indeed. To continue the *Games of Thrones* analogy, if the Snows had invested all their income on agricultural innovations they probably would have become wealthier in the short term, but in the medium term they wouldn't have been able to defend the North against warmongering houses that had instead spent their money on maintaining castles, equipping soldiers and keeping followers happy.

Even in the tenth and eleventh centuries, when great industrial and commercial cities sprang up in the Low Countries and northern Italy to satisfy demand for weapons and luxury goods from Europe's lords, artisan producers and merchant intermediaries were never fully exposed to market competition, the *sine qua non* of capitalism. Artisans organized themselves into guilds that limited the number of people working in a particular sector, enforced standards and restricted output, so that prices remained stable. Similarly, merchants formed companies that lobbied lords, princes and kings for charters that gave them special trading privileges and therefore restricted competition. The role of guilds and corporations, alongside the stagnant productivity of agriculture, limited the size of towns and the non-agricultural labor force. Throughout the whole medieval period, there was no increase in the number of people working in non-agricultural jobs as a proportion of the total population in most parts of western Europe, and the number of people living in towns with more than 10,000 inhabitants grew from 10 to 12 percent.[71]

How did Europe transform from a stagnant feudal system into the kind of dynamic capitalist society that Adam Smith described in *The Wealth of Nations*—one where individuals focused on maximizing profit, and the pursuit of economic self-interest led to sustained growth via the invisible hand of the market? According to the German sociologist Max Weber, the Reformation was responsible for this change in mindset. He argues that what he calls the Protestant ethic has an "elective affinity" with the spirit of capitalism. For over 1,000 years, fervent Catholics had locked themselves away in monasteries. Devout Protestants instead applied this ascetic ideal to their everyday life, working hard and investing their savings; and this change in focus was responsible for the transition from the feudal system to capitalism. Critics have pointed out that his theory doesn't really explain how self-denial leads to the unceasing pursuit of profit on an individual level and sustained economic growth on a societal one. As John Maynard Keynes noted in *A Treatise on Money* (1930): "thrift" or "mere abstinence is not enough by itself to build cities or drain fens." Rather, he argues, "it is enterprise which builds and improves the world's possessions," and the "engine which drives enterprise is not thrift, but profit." But where did the restless dynamism—the spirit of capitalism or enterprise—come from and how did it replace feudalism? To find the answer we must explore how medieval Europe responded to the demographic crash caused by the Great Pestilence and subsequent outbreaks of plague.

The death of more than half the population created a crisis for the feudal system. The lords' economic situation was considerably worse than it had been before the plague: now there were far fewer serfs to provide them with produce and labor. And if the lords had any surplus to sell, the prices they commanded were far lower than before the Black Death because, with fewer mouths to feed, demand had fallen. Consequently, the lords tried to squeeze more out of their serfs in a desperate effort to maintain their livelihoods.[72] At the same time, peasants were keen to take advantage of the shortage of workers and glut of cultivatable land to demand better conditions. The struggle played out in different ways across the continent.[73]

In eastern Europe, where lords had colonized vast areas of Steppe in the High Middle Ages, peasants were essentially free from feudal levies prior to the Black Death. Landowners were only able to persuade peasants to live on their estates by offering them extremely favorable terms. The growing scarcity of peasants after the pandemic led to a protracted struggle with the lords. Ultimately the peasants lost because, being newly arrived in the region and until then largely unoppressed, they lacked political organization. Polish and Prussian nobles managed to impose serfdom on their estates in the early sixteenth century and maintained the system until the nineteenth.

In France, lords responded to the demographic crash by building an absolutist state that provided them with income funded by universal, country-wide taxes on the peasantry rather than decentralized feudal levies. This meant that serfs couldn't play one lord against another to gain better conditions or win their freedom. But as French peasants still had access to small plots of land to meet their subsistence needs, they continued to act as feudal serfs and maintain their risk-averse approach.

It was only in England that the post–Black Death conflict between the lords and peasants resulted in the demise of feudalism and the transition to capitalism. England had a more centralized feudal state than anywhere else in Europe at the time—a legacy of the Norman conquest of 1066, when William and his followers almost completely replaced the previous feudal elite. One manifestation of England's peculiarly strong state was its national system of common law; all lords and freemen were subject to the jurisdiction of the king's court. (Unfree serfs, however, had to petition a court administered by their feudal lord.) Another was Parliament, where lords and knights would meet to discuss important topics and make laws. These institutions explain the anomalous outcome of the struggle between feudal lords and the serfs in England.

In the wake of the Black Death, feudal lords tried to use Parliament to maintain their control by limiting the social and geographical mobility of peasants. As early as 1349, the state issued an ordinance that fixed wages and prices at 1347 levels and made it illegal for serfs to live and work anywhere other than the manor they were bound to before the plague. At first, the punishment for breaking the law was a fine, but in the early 1360s penalties were increased—indicating that the previous legislation hadn't had the desired effect. Peasants who asked for higher wages or moved to another demesne that offered better terms could now be imprisoned and branded on the forehead with the letter "F" for "falsity."[74] In 1363 Parliament issued a Sumptuary Law that decreed the types of clothes people at different levels of society could wear, and even what they were allowed to eat. These rules were unenforceable—even the majority of pilgrims in *The Canterbury Tales* wore swankier clothes than were permitted—but the fact that such laws were thought necessary indicates that the lords felt threatened by the conspicuous consumption of the newly affluent commoners.

The feudal lords' efforts to impose restraints on serfs created a great deal of anger, which burst out in the Peasants' Revolt of 1381. Throughout much of the country, serfs attacked their masters and burned the manorial records that documented their obligations. Crowds marched on the capital, where they caused mayhem—burning down brothels, cutting off the Archbishop of Canterbury's head and storming the Tower of London, among other things. On paper, they were rebelling against a series of poll taxes levied to fund the Hundred Years' War. But the underlying cause was the state's concerted efforts to stop peasants from taking advantage of opportunities offered by the post–Black Death demographic collapse. Radical clerics who were influenced by Wycliffe played an important role in fomenting the rebellion and their words testify to its radical character. Most prominent of these was John Ball, who in his sermon at Blackheath in southeast London asked the gathered crowd: "When Adam delved and Eve span, who was then the gentleman?," before railing against the injustice of the feudal system: "From the beginning all men by nature were created alike, and our bondage or servitude came in by the unjust oppression of naughty men."[75]

In the end, the Peasants' Revolt was brutally suppressed by the feudal lords, but land was now so plentiful and agricultural labor so scarce that it was impossible to hold back the tides of social and economic change. Desperate, the lords eventually stopped cooperating with one another and instead began competing for peasants. Serfs streamed away from the manors they were legally bound to and settled wherever they were offered the best conditions. By the mid-fifteenth century, most English peasants were not just paying much lower feudal dues but had also won their freedom; they were even given a copy of the section of the manorial roll that set out the terms of their tenancy. The enfranchisement of England's serfs was irreversible because the peasants were now freemen who could go to the king's court to have their new terms of tenancy enforced. This created a problem for the lords: not only were there fewer peasants, who were paying less rent, but now there was no prospect of ever extracting more from them. The lords salvaged the situation by persuading the king's court that when a peasant died, the tenancy should not pass automatically to their heirs on the same terms. In time this led to a system in which lords rented plots of land to agricultural producers at market-determined rates.

In this new economic environment, only those free peasants who abandoned their risk-averse subsistence approach and adopted profit-maximizing behavior could afford to rent land. The vast majority of them didn't keep up with these changes and over the next couple of centuries became landless. Critically, for the first time since the Neolithic Revolution, most of the population could no longer grow their own crops and had no other option but to work for someone else in order to earn money to buy food and other essentials. But a handful of former peasants benefited greatly from the transition to agricultural capitalism. They used the latest technology, specialized in the most lucrative crops, kept labor costs to a minimum and sold their produce for the maximum profit. The average farming plot increased from 20 acres at the time of the Black Death to 60 acres by 1600 as inefficient producers were crowded out. Much bigger landholdings were common, however, and farms of more than 100 acres covered 70 percent of

England's cultivated surface.[76] This new, commercially minded class of yeoman farmers invested in animals to pull carts, plow and fertilize land. They grew crops that were adapted to the local soil and climate, and used crop rotation systems to improve yields. The competition between these remaining tenant farmers resulted in a new pattern of dynamic and sustained growth in output that amounted to nothing less than a Second Agricultural Revolution.

The impact of these changes can be clearly seen when we compare England to France, which remained a feudal society. In the former, agricultural productivity increased by 50 percent between 1500 and 1750. In France, productivity declined in the same period, as the rising population was forced to eke out a living on ever smaller plots of land.[77] During the sixteenth century England experienced a series of harvest failures, but there were no significant crises after 1597.[78] France suffered famines in 1693 and 1709, which together killed 2 million people, 10 percent of the population.[79] England had by this point passed through the Agricultural Revolution and was unaffected because its farmers were geared toward producing as much food as possible.

The emergence of agricultural capitalism finally allowed English society to escape the Malthusian cycle of demographic boom and bust for the first time since the Neolithic Revolution.[80] The increase in food production was so marked that the countryside was able to feed the rapidly urbanizing population. The proportion of people in England living in towns almost quadrupled to 23 percent between 1500 and 1750, while in France the figures barely changed.[81] By the late seventeenth century, the growth in England's agricultural productivity led to lower food prices and higher wages for the majority of the population. People had more money to spend on things other than the bare essentials, massively expanding the market for consumer goods. The consequences were enormous. Textile-manufacturing clusters began to develop where natural resources were available and transport links were favorable, and these grew into industrial towns and cities. But the growing disposable income of the English public also had impacts much farther afield. Rising demand for raw cotton, as well as sugar, tobacco, and other commodities contributed to European colonial expansion and the emergence of the Atlantic slave trade. For newly subjugated peoples, the effects were devastating.

Chapter 5
Colonial Plagues

European imperialists were egomaniacal about themselves, their religions, and their customs, and they had short tempers and long swords, but why were they so much more successful in the Americas and the Pacific than in Asia or Africa?

—ALFRED CROSBY

Germs, Germs, Germs

Werner Herzog's *Aguirre, the Wrath of God* (1972) tells the story of a hapless group of conquistadors as they search for El Dorado. The five-minute-long opening sequence is the epitome of Herzog's "*National Geographic* meets Theater of the Absurd" style, as one critic has referred to it.[1] A procession of soldiers clad in armor, ladies in full-length dresses, a priest, Native Americans (some in chains), chickens, pigs and llamas meander along a steep, narrow path that leads down from the mist-covered Andes to the Amazon rainforest below. The treasure hunters soon get bogged down in the dense, sodden jungle. The commander orders a smaller group to raft down the swollen river to find food and information about the location of the fabled city of gold. After the reconnaissance party encounter some early problems, their leader announces they are to return to the main party. At this point, the second in command—the eponymous Don Lope de Aguirre, played by Klaus Kinski—stages a mutiny, telling the men that untold riches lie ahead and reminding them that Hernán Cortés conquered the great Mexica (or Aztec) Empire by disobeying orders.[2] The mutineers drift down the river for the rest of the film, dying one after the next in a prolonged orgy of violence at the hands of each other and unseen assailants. By the end, only the increasingly delusional Aguirre is left alive. In the final scene he urges the dozens of monkeys that have clambered aboard to join him and his slain daughter on a mission to take over the Spanish colonies in the Americas, and in doing so to "produce history as others produce plays."[3]

Although Kinski's Aguirre is clearly delusional, his desire to conquer the colonies of New Spain with an army of monkeys and install his dead daughter as queen is only a little bit more outlandish than the conquistadors' real-life achievements. Take Aguirre's role model, for example. In 1519, Cortés set sail from the Spanish colony of Cuba on an unauthorized expedition to conquer Mesoamerica with 500 men. Shortly after arriving, he scuttled the ships to prevent anyone who was having second thoughts from leaving.* Hearing of the Spaniards' arrival, Montezuma—the ruler of the Mexica Empire—sent them lavish gifts made from gold. This gesture was probably intended to placate the invaders, but it just made them more determined to reach the great island city of Tenochtitlan, located on the site of present-day Mexico City—over 2,000 meters above sea level and a 400-kilometer trek over icy volcanoes from the coast. The imperial capital had a population of a quarter of a million—larger than any European city at the time save Constantinople and four times the size of the biggest city in Spain, Seville.[4] It was the heart of an empire that dominated a population of 5 million who lived in several hundred semi-autonomous city-states, covering an area that ranged from the Atlantic to the Pacific and stretched to the rainforest a month's march to the south. Cortés' gang were up against a huge, wealthy and heavily militarized polity that some historians have compared to ancient Sparta. And yet, in one of

---

* This was an outrageous act of bravado. Less than a century later, when Don Quixote and Sancho Panza were discussing historical figures who had achieved great fame through acts of courage, they mentioned this episode alongside Julius Caesar's crossing of the Rubicon in 49 BCE.

the most improbable feats of conquest in history, a little over two years after landing in Central America they managed to kill Montezuma, raze his capital and found the colony of New Spain.

A little over a decade later, in 1532, Francisco Pizarro achieved something even more implausible. He led a group of 106 foot soldiers and 62 horsemen on an incursion that ended in the defeat of the biggest and most advanced civilization in the Americas. At its height, just before the Spanish conquest, the Inca Empire stretched some 2,500 kilometers along the Andes and coastal plains of western South America. At Cajamarca the Spaniards faced a battle-hardened, 80,000-strong army, yet managed to capture Atahualpa, the absolute monarch, without losing a single man. Pizarro held Atahualpa captive for eight months as his subjects assembled the largest ransom in history: enough gold to fill the generously sized room in which he was imprisoned up to a height of 2.75 meters, as well as two adjacent rooms with silver. Fearing Atahualpa was conspiring against the Spanish, Pizarro killed him but kept the treasure that had been accumulated to pay the ransom: six tons of gold and 11 tons of silver. Almost all of the plunder was melted down, and each foot soldier received 20 kilograms of gold—cavalrymen twice that. Pizarro's share added up to about a quarter of a ton, plus the Incas' 15-carat gold throne weighing 83 kilograms. The conquistadors then proceeded to the capital, Cuzco, where they found more treasure, including a solid-gold llama weighing 26.5 kilograms.[5]

Cortés' and Pizarro's seemingly impossible victories, in which a few hundred and a few dozen soldiers respectively quickly conquered vast and sophisticated civilizations, were just the beginning. The Spanish went on to rule much of South and Central America for the next 300 years, brutally subjugating the population and extracting extraordinary amounts of wealth. A modern-day equivalent might be a right-wing U.S. militia or band of English football hooligans making their way to Moscow, kidnapping and killing Vladimir Putin, seizing Russia's oil and gas reserves and then declaring the territory a colony, which their descendants go on to dominate for centuries. The Spanish conquests were so remarkable that they have proved hard to explain without resorting to miracles (the pre-eminence of the Christian God) or racism (the innate superiority of Europeans). And while both of these explanations are clearly flawed, they still, consciously or subconsciously, shape the way that many people understand the creation of modern Latin America.

Jared Diamond's Pulitzer prize–winning *Guns, Germs and Steel* (1997) provides perhaps the best-known and most influential explanation for the Spanish conquest of the Americas. Put simply, he argues that Neolithic Eurasia contained more wild plants and animals that could be domesticated. This enabled Eurasians to produce more surplus food, which in turn led to the emergence of centralized, stratified, technologically innovative societies that could dominate other societies. So while Diamond sees European societies as significantly more advanced than American ones, the source of this advantage is geographical. As you will have noted from the title of his book, he also stresses the importance of pathogens: the higher numbers of domesticated animals and denser population in Eurasia increased the likelihood that infectious diseases would emerge and spread, giving Europeans the upper hand when they encountered people who hadn't developed immunity to these pathogens. *Germs* play only a cameo role in Diamond's explanation of the conquest of the Americas, however. He argues that "the Spaniards' superior weapons would have assured an ultimate Spanish victory in any case."

But the superiority of the Old World has been overstated. There weren't big disparities in living standards between late-medieval Spain and the pre-Columbus Americas. In a letter to the king, Charles V, Cortés described with amazement how Tenochtitlan's buildings, pottery, jewelry, clothes, shoes, food, markets and barber shops were either similar to or of better quality than those in Spain.[6] It has been estimated that in 1500 Spain's per-capita Gross Domestic Product (GDP) was about 1.5 times that of Central America and South America—about the same as the difference between the U.S. and UK today.[7]

In terms of military technology—or *guns* and *steel*—the Spanish did have an advantage over the Native Americans. But these were hardly the kind of disparities that could explain how tiny expeditionary forces defeated and colonized two large, complex polities that could put tens of thousands of well-trained soldiers onto the battlefield. The conquistadors' firearms had some shock value, but they were also a liability. Primitive muskets took over a minute to reload and cannon were difficult to transport across the rugged terrain. Their steel blades and armor did give them an edge in combat, but even this has been exaggerated. Some Native American weapons were very effective—slingshots that propelled baseball-size rocks at high speed, for example. The quilted armor used by the Mexica (*ichcahuipilli*) wasn't the kind of garb you'd wear to a pillow fight. It was lightweight, cool and surprisingly tough. In fact, it was adopted by many conquistadors.

Diamond argues that horses, which the Mexica and Inca would never have encountered before, played a decisive role in the outcome of the invasion as they allowed the Spanish to attack their enemies at great speed and from a considerable height.[8] Horses were, he suggests, the late-medieval equivalent of jeeps and Sherman tanks. We should not, however, exaggerate their importance. The Spanish had a very small number—initially sixteen in Cortés' invasion and sixty-eight in Pizarro's—and these would have provided little or no benefit in the most decisive of the conquistadors' campaigns, such as the three-month siege of Tenochtitlan in 1521 or against the guerrilla tactics used in the 1536 Inca rebellion.

Diamond's emphasis on *guns* and *steel* over *germs* was an argument formulated in the 1990s, before the U.S.-led invasion of Afghanistan reminded us just how ineffective military technology can be in the face of determined local resistance.* When it invaded, the U.S. was one of the richest countries in the world, and Afghanistan was one of the poorest. According to World Bank data, U.S. per-capita GDP was $38,000, over forty times higher than Afghanistan's ($877).[9] The Americans and their allies had almost unimaginable firepower at their disposal. At the peak of the conflict there were 130,000 NATO forces in Afghanistan armed with state-of-the-art weaponry. Their fighter jets and drones were the twenty-first-century equivalent of omniscient, supersonic, fire-breathing dragons, dropping tens of thousands of bombs over the course of the war.

The Taliban, on the other hand, were armed with very basic weapons that dated back to the 1980s and in some cases the Second World War. Still, the Americans found it impossible to achieve their relatively

---

* The same lesson could also have been gleaned from America's misadventures in Vietnam a couple of decades earlier.

modest political and military objectives. In 2021, after twenty years of occupation, the Western powers withdrew and the Taliban returned to power.

So if *guns* and *steel* don't explain why the conquistadors managed to conquer South and Central America so decisively, what does? The answer is simple: *germs, germs, germs.*

Five Hundred Years of Servitude

On Christmas Day 1492, one of the three ships on Christopher Columbus' first transatlantic voyage ran aground on the northern coast of what would come to be known as Hispaniola, the mountainous Caribbean island that is now divided into Haiti and the Dominican Republic. The land was incredibly fertile and inhabited by an indigenous population—the Taíno—whom Columbus described as "affectionate and without malice." As the two surviving ships were too small to carry the crew of the beached vessel, thirty-nine men were left behind to build a fortified settlement, La Navidad. While the rest of the party sailed back to Spain to announce their "discovery," those who remained were given provisions, weapons and instructions to search for gold. Just like Herzog's conquistadors, the Spaniards who discovered the Americas were driven by the desire to become fabulously wealthy.*

When Columbus returned to Hispaniola with seventeen ships less than a year later, he found La Navidad burned to the ground and the bodies of the would-be conquistadors decaying in nearby fields. The Taíno had attacked the Spaniards after growing tired of their rapacious appetite for women and gold. Their overwhelming numbers and superior knowledge of the local environment trumped any technological advantage that the invaders' guns and steel may have afforded them. But this would be a rare victory for the indigenous people of the New World.

---

* Columbus vividly explains the fascination gold held for him and his colleagues: "Anyone who has it can do whatever he likes in the world. With it he can succeed in bringing souls to Paradise."

We don't know exactly how many people lived in Hispaniola when the Spanish arrived. Columbus claimed "millions upon millions," although contemporary scholars suggest that a few hundred thousand is more realistic.[10] The indigenous population were a crucial part of the conquistadors' plans: they would mine the gold, work on the plantations, and be sold into slavery in Europe—in Columbus' own words, "as many slaves as Their Majesties order to make, from among those who are idolaters."[11] Back home, a debate raged about whether or not it was right to enslave the indigenous people of the Americas before they had learned about the Christian faith. Regardless, these plans foundered because so many of them died in the decades after 1492. In 1514 a census found just 26,000 Taíno remaining, and by the mid-sixteenth century they had all but disappeared.[12]

The decline in the native population was in part a result of the conquistadors' wanton brutality. Bartolomé de las Casas, a landowner and slaver turned Dominican friar, had spent five decades in the Americas by the time he published *A Short Account of the Destruction of the Indies* in 1552. In this book he documents how the Taíno were routinely subjected to cruelties "to which no chronicle could ever do justice." Dogs were set upon them; they were disemboweled with swords and burned alive in locked buildings. But Old World pathogens did far more damage to the indigenous population than the Spaniards' animals, weapons and matches ever could.

When Europeans started settling in the Caribbean, it was only a matter of time before the viruses and bacteria that had evolved in the Old World in the wake of the Neolithic Revolution made the jump across the Atlantic. The Taíno had never before been exposed to these pathogens and so hadn't developed resistance. They were obliterated by wave after wave of virgin soil epidemics.[13] First came illnesses like common colds and stomach bugs that had relatively mild symptoms for Europeans but were devastating for the immunologically naive indigenous inhabitants of Hispaniola. Then smallpox hit in 1518, killing between a third and a half of the population. And then, over the next few years, came a plethora of other infectious diseases. These devastating epidemics made the conquest of the New World possible. A similar tale of disease, death and conquest was repeated time and again over the next couple of centuries, first in the Caribbean, then mainland America and after that the Pacific Islands and Antipodes. As Charles Darwin succinctly put it: "Wherever the European has trod, death seems to pursue the aboriginal."

Without the help of Old World pathogens, early efforts to colonize the American mainland foundered. In 1517, Francisco Hernández de Córdoba led an expedition that landed on the Yucatan Peninsula, only to be chased away twice by a hail of arrows and stones that killed over half of the party, including Córdoba himself.[14] During one of the landings, a couple of Spaniards stole several gold items from a temple. When word of their finds reached Cuba, it piqued the interest of several would-be conquistadors. This is why Cortés was so keen to set sail for Central America; but even his early efforts ended in ignominy.

The Spanish entered Tenochtitlan in November 1519, about half a year after they first set foot on the mainland, not as conquerors but as the guests of Montezuma. Historians are not sure whether Cortés took the Mexica emperor captive or the other way round, but it wasn't until the Spanish had been in the city for seven months that open conflict broke out between the two sides. Montezuma was killed in the ensuing violence. Mexica chroniclers claim he was stabbed by the conquistadors; the Spanish describe him being stoned to death by his own people. Surrounded and vastly outnumbered, Cortés' army were forced to take flight from the island city. They set off on 30 June 1520, planning to escape along one of the causeways. But the Mexica saw them and attacked from all directions. The fighting was ferocious. All in all, two-thirds of the Spanish invaders died in what came to be known as the *La Noche Triste* (the Night of Sorrows).[15] Eyewitness accounts describe Spaniards drowning in the water, weighed down by looted treasure that they had melted into gold bars. This tale might sound a bit too much like a Herzogian allegory for the crazed greed of the conquistadors, but in 1981 a 2-kilogram ingot was dug up during building work in downtown Mexico City along the Spaniards' escape route and tests have shown that it was forged in 1519 or 1520.

It is hardly surprising that Cortés' men were so resoundingly defeated by the Mexica. They were up against a much bigger force that was fighting to defend its capital city. What really is remarkable is that just over a year later the conquistadors managed to destroy Tenochtitlan and found the colony of New Spain upon the ruins of the Mexica Empire. How can we explain such a glaring turnaround in events?

A 1,000-strong party of Spaniards arrived on the mainland from Cuba in spring 1520. Ostensibly they were sent to stop Cortés' unauthorized mission, but many of the group decided to join him. The renegades entered Tenochtitlan shortly before *La Noche Triste* and one of them appears to have been carrying smallpox. So, just after the conquistadors were vanquished, the virus ripped through the city. The victims of what the local population referred to as the *huey ahuizotl* (great rash) included the new emperor, Cuitláhuac, who had led the fight against the conquistadors after the death of his predecessor. Smallpox spread across Central America, killing between a third and a half of the population in the space of a few months.[16] A Franciscan monk accompanying Cortés describes how the locals "died in heaps, like bedbugs."[17] The Spanish, of course, were unaffected. Just as Cortés was at his lowest ebb, his expeditionary force defeated and chased out of the capital, Old World pathogens gave him a shot at redemption. The reversal in fortune was so abrupt and profound that the Spanish assumed it was divine intervention. As Francisco de Aguilar, another follower, put it: "When the Christians were exhausted from war, God saw fit to send the Indians smallpox, and there was a great pestilence in the city."[18]

It is hard to overstate the role that infectious diseases played in the creation and consolidation of New Spain.[19] Less than a year after *La Noche Triste*, the Spanish laid siege to Tenochtitlan. It took seventy-five days for the Mexica capital to fall. The besiegers destroyed large parts of the city and slaughtered tens of thousands of its inhabitants, including most of the nobility. For obvious reasons, Cortés and his colleagues' written accounts emphasize the Spanish role in the victory. In reality, the conquistadors fought alongside several rebellious tributary states, who made up about 99.5 percent of the forces arrayed against the Mexica.[20] But these allies were eventually hit by the smallpox epidemic too. The conquistadors remained healthy. While the world was falling apart for the indigenous people of Central America, the Spanish were able to watch the horrors unfold and then pick up the pieces.

Smallpox was only just the beginning. Over the next few decades, the indigenous people of Mesoamerica were afflicted by deadly epidemics again and again. Measles arrived in the early 1530s. A disease the Mexica referred to as *cocoliztli* (from the Nahuatl word for "pestilence") killed up to 80 percent of the region's inhabitants in 1545, making it the deadliest epidemic in recorded history.[21] It returned again between 1576 and 1578. The Franciscan monk Friar Juan de Torquemada described how "in the cities and large towns, big ditches were dug, and from morning to sunset the priests did nothing else but carry the dead bodies and throw them into the ditches." Half the remaining population died.[22] Recent analysis of bacteria DNA found in the teeth of twenty-nine *cocoliztli* victims buried in a cemetery in what is now southern Mexico in the middle of the sixteenth century suggests it was an infection similar to salmonella.[23] The first recorded influenza epidemic occurred in 1558, slaying another third of the population.[24] Many of the indigenous people who weren't killed by infectious diseases died from famine, as crops rotted in the fields because there was no one to harvest them. The malnourished survivors were susceptible to whatever pathogens would arrive next from Spain. The scale of the cumulative devastation is hard to imagine: the indigenous population of Mesoamerica was about 20 million when Cortés arrived but had fallen to 1.5 million a century later.[25]

Smallpox is, as Alfred Crosby puts it, "a disease with seven-league boots." When this gruesome affliction first strikes, many seemingly healthy people flee in fear. But as the disease has an incubation period of up to two weeks, the refugees all too often carry the virus with them. In this way, smallpox raced ahead of the Spanish and devastated whole communities. The first epidemic struck the Inca Empire in 1524, plunging the biggest, most sophisticated society in the Americas into disarray. The virus killed between 30 percent and 50 percent of the population, including the emperor, Huayna Capac, his designated heir and most of the court.[26] This led to a war of succession between two of Huayna Capac's other sons in which the incumbent, Huáscar, was defeated by his half-brother Atahualpa just before the arrival of the Spanish. Pizarro had made two previous attempts to invade this vast and sophisticated society, but it was only after smallpox had left it enfeebled and divided that he was able to conquer the Inca Empire with 100-odd foot soldiers and a few dozen cavalry. As in New Spain, the indigenous population were hit by successive outbreaks of infectious diseases over the next century which further weakened their capacity and resolve to resist Spanish imperialism.[27]

Across the whole of the Americas, the introduction of infectious diseases from Europe resulted in a 90 percent fall in the population, from about 60.5 million in 1500 to 6 million a century later. The global population fell by 10 percent. The decline in slash-and-burn agriculture and the reforestation of tens of millions of hectares of cultivated land resulted in a reduction in carbon dioxide in the atmosphere that is visible in the ice cores drilled by scientists in the Antarctic. The demographic collapse cooled the global surface air temperature by 0.15 degrees Celsius, contributing to the Little Ice Age in the early 1600s.[28]

But why didn't American pathogens have a similarly disastrous effect on the European invaders? After all, the Inca and Mexica lived in vast, well-connected, urbanized empires that had passed through the Neolithic Revolution over 4,000 years earlier.[29] And yet there is evidence of only one infectious disease being transmitted from Native Americans to Europeans: syphilis. Its mysterious origins are evident in the different names it acquired as it spread through the Old World in the late fifteenth and early sixteenth centuries.[30] The English called it the French pox; the French, *Morbus Germanicus*. And in Florence it was the Naples sickness. William Blake refers to syphilis as a plague: "the youthful Harlot's curse" that "blights with plagues the Marriage hearse." Syphilis certainly caused a good deal of pain, irritation and embarrassment to the people of Europe, but in terms of death and destruction its impact cannot be compared to that of Old World pathogens in the Americas.*

How do we explain the almost unilateral flow of pathogens from Europe to the Americas, despite relatively high population densities in Mexico and Peru? The infectious diseases that evolved to infect hu-

---

* Although, in a roundabout way, it might have had a lasting impact on European geopolitics. Some historians believe that Ivan the Terrible behaved as terribly as he did—murdering his son and unborn grandson in a fit of anger—because of tertiary syphilis. These murders changed the course of history: Feodor "the Bellringer," his ineffectual younger son, eventually succeeded him, leading to a period of political crisis that ended in 1613 with the accession of the Romanovs, who ruled Russia for the next three centuries.

mans in the wake of the Neolithic Revolution originated in domesticated herd animals. There were many of these animals in Eurasia,
including pigs, sheep, cows, goats and horses.[31] Guinea pigs, dogs, tur-
keys, Muscovy ducks, alpacas and llamas had all been domesticated in
different parts of the Americas. But of these, the only herd animals
were alpacas and llamas, which were found exclusively in South America. Unlike the ancestors of Eurasian farm animals, alpacas and llamas
hadn't lived in vast herds prior to domestication, limiting the opportunities for diseases to emerge and become endemic.[32] As a result, the
Neolithic Revolution in the Americas doesn't appear to have been accompanied by a devastating epidemiological revolution.

The fact that diseases caused by Old World pathogens almost exclusively killed Native Americans was interpreted on both sides as an un-
equivocal sign that God or the gods supported the Spanish invaders. It
added to the conquistadors' belief in the righteousness of their gory,
greedy mission. In contrast, the Mexica and Inca were left bewildered
and despairing. Spanish chroniclers describe indigenous people dying
by suicide, abandoning their newborn babies and murdering shamans
"to see if by this means the distemper would cease."[33] The Native
Americans were ripe for conversion to what, based on the evidence
they had available to them, appeared to be a far superior religion. They
embraced Catholicism with a fervor that is still very much apparent:
today, 40 percent of the world's Catholics live in Latin America.[34] Spanish culture wasn't adopted wholesale, however. Many of the conquistadors were young male fortune seekers who traveled alone. They settled
down with women from the Mexica and Inca nobility—those who had
survived the epidemics—and created a new hybrid, mestizo society
that drew from both indigenous and European cultures.[35]

The Spanish imposed the rotting structures of feudalism on their
colonies. The conquistadors tended to come from impoverished noble
families. Beyond finding gold, their life goals were to own an estate and
control the labor of people who worked on it. Prominent men received
land grants or *encomiendas* from the Spanish Crown that gave them
the right to tribute and labor from the indigenous people who lived on
"their" property. After much deliberation, Fernando and Isabel, the
Spanish monarchs, decided that it was not right to enslave the Native
Americans. Unlike Muslims, they had not chosen to turn away from

the one true God and had done the Spanish no harm. Nominally at least, those indigenous people who survived the waves of epidemics were not slaves; they continued to live in their own villages and couldn't be sold. Like feudal lords back home, the Spanish *encomenderos* had obligations too: they were supposed to provide their wards with religious education, protect them and pay a symbolic wage of one gold peso a year to cover the cost of their clothing. These responsibilities were often ignored, however.[36]

The Spanish never found the mythical El Dorado, but in 1545 they discovered the next-best thing: a mountain made of solid silver. The Cerro Rico at Potosí is located in the Andes in what is now southern Bolivia at an altitude of 4,000 meters, a two-and-a-half-month journey via pack animal from Lima. It contained so much high-grade silver ore that it provided about 80 percent of the silver mined across the world over the next 250 years.[37] Despite its remote location, fifty years after the deposits were discovered Potosí was a mining township with a population of 160,000 people—bigger than any city in Spain at the time. And in its shops one could buy luxury wares from all over the world, including silk and linen, Venetian glassware and Chinese porcelain.[38]

This remarkable prosperity was built on a system of forced labor called *mita*, which was adapted from—and named after—a traditional Inca institution. From the 1570s, indigenous communities living near Potosí had to provide one in seven of their adult men at any given time to work in the mines. The jobs—carrying heavy loads of ore up rickety ladders through steep, narrow shafts to the surface—were exhausting and dangerous. The *mita* was only abolished in 1812, by which time the silver in Cerro Rico was all but exhausted. The Harvard-based economist Melissa Dell has demonstrated that the negative repercussions are still evident in Bolivia: today, families living in areas where inhabitants were forced to work in Potosí are poorer, unhealthier and less educated than those in neighboring areas where there was no *mita*.[39]

Revenue from Potosí made Spain enormously rich for a while, but the newfound prosperity didn't kick-start a process of self-sustaining economic growth. Rather, feudal Spain used the almost unfathomably large proceeds of Latin American colonialism to fund a series of costly and lengthy wars. They fought a rebellion in the Netherlands that lasted for eighty years until the Protestant northern provinces seceded in 1648; a sea battle against the Ottoman Empire for dominance of the Mediterranean in 1571; and an intermittent war with the Protestant English over their interference in the Dutch Revolt and their looting of Spanish ships on their way back from the Americas. The Spanish also took part in the Thirty Years' War, fighting on the side of the Catholics against the Protestants of northern Europe, and this conflagration spilled over into a conflict against the French. Almost every country in the continent was directly or indirectly involved in a war with Spain in the 150 years after Potosí was discovered.[40]

In the end, over-reliance on Potosí silver proved disastrous. As more and more silver was carried out of the Cerro Rico the price gradually fell, and the Spanish Crown could no longer afford to finance its foreign wars. Spain wasn't able to keep up with countries like England, where stagnant feudalism had been replaced by dynamic capitalism. It lost most of its colonial possessions in the Americas in the early nineteenth century, just as Britain was building an empire. Spain would never again be a great European power, let alone a world power. Today, alongside Portugal, it has the lowest per capita income of any country in Western Europe.

The majority of silver mined in Potosí wasn't shipped to Europe, but was instead transported to the Philippines, and sold to Chinese merchants. Demand was high in China because from the sixteenth century onward, silver was the country's main form of currency. Then, in the 1570s, the Ming rulers specified that all taxes should be paid in silver.[41] This was significant because China accounted for about a quarter of the world's population at the time. Their appetite for silver drove up the price in the Far East to twice what it was in Europe. In the Philippines, European merchants exchanged South American silver for spices, silk and porcelain to be sold back home. This marked the beginning of a genuinely global economy in which the Old World was intricately connected to the New World.[42] But as the Spanish exported more and more silver, its value fell—even in China. When Potosí started producing vast quantities of silver in the last couple of decades of the sixteenth century, one ounce of gold was worth six of silver. Half a decade later, the ratio was 1.13.[43] This created a fiscal crisis because the Chinese state received all its taxes in silver, and the ensuing unrest resulted in the Ming dynasty being overthrown in a military coup in 1644. A few weeks later, the Manchus invaded from north of the Beijing Wall and founded the Qing dynasty, which ruled China until 1911.[44]

Little Britain

The conquistadors weren't the first Europeans to set foot in America: Scandinavian seafarers had sailed west across the Atlantic centuries earlier. Unlike the Spanish, they weren't searching for gold and slaves. The so-called Vikings were looking for land to graze their animals, timber for building, and resources such as walrus ivory that they could sell in Europe.[45] According to two sagas written by Icelandic scholars in the thirteenth century, the first sighting of the New World occurred around the turn of the millennium, when a ship was blown off course on its way from Iceland to Greenland—two recently settled Norse colonies in the northwest Atlantic. In subsequent years, several groups set off from Greenland to explore the coastline.

By all accounts the area they called Vinland was a favorable place to settle. Thorvald Eriksson, the leader of one of these voyages, proclaimed: "It is beautiful here . . . Here I should like to make my home." But this would-be colonialist was soon killed by an arrow fired when his party was attacked by *skrælings*, the Norse term for both Inuit and Native Americans. Not long after, Thorfinn Karlsefni led another group of 60 or 160 men—depending on which saga one reads—as well as five women and livestock. Archeological evidence suggests they were settled in L'Anse aux Meadows, on the northern tip of Newfoundland.[46] But the Norsemen faced such fierce opposition from the local population that after a couple of years they abandoned their plans and returned to the relative safety of Greenland.

The *skrælings* lived in small communities that hunted sea mammals and were far less capable of mounting an effective defense than the great Mexica or Inca Empires. So why were Cortés and Pizarro able to conquer vast swathes of Central and South America, while Karlsefni and Eriksson failed to colonize North America half a millennium earlier? The answer doesn't lie in military or state-building capabilities. In

several respects, the seafaring people of medieval Scandinavia—
variously referred to as the Normans, Norse, Rus, Varangians and
Vikings—appear to have been far better suited to building a colony in
the Americas than the sixteenth-century Spanish. Of course, they have
a reputation for being fearsome that has lasted down to the present
day. In *Asterix and the Normans*, for example, one of the latter admits
to killing twenty-four of his enemies because he wanted "to give a set
of skulls to a friend for a wedding present . . . only he wasn't too
pleased . . . everyone else had the same idea." The Norse had steel
weapons, unlike their *skræling* adversaries. They were also skillful warriors, prized as mercenaries across Europe and making up the Byzantine emperors' elite Varangian Guard.[47] And Scandinavians proved to
be remarkably successful state builders. The Normans had settled in
northwestern France, from where they went on to conquer the British
Isles and the Kingdom of Sicily—which included parts of southern
Italy and North Africa. In the ninth century, the Rus chief Rurik was
invited by warring tribes in northeastern Europe to rule them, marking
the beginning of the dynasty that lasted over 700 years and gave its
name to Russia.

The Spanish succeeded in colonizing the Americas because they
were aided by bacteria and viruses. The Norse were not and failed. In
fact, because of their own isolated existence, the European inhabitants
of Greenland and Iceland were almost as vulnerable to Old World
pathogens as the indigenous people of the New World. There is a simple epidemiological reason for this. Stuck out in the north Atlantic,
these communities were too small and remote to sustain infectious
diseases in the same way as mainland Europe. Maladies like smallpox
were endemic in late-medieval Spain. They constantly circulated
among the vast population of Eurasia and Africa, so most children
would be exposed and either die or develop immunity. But the same
diseases were epidemic in the north Atlantic island colonies; they
would periodically arrive on the ships that sailed from Denmark and
Norway, infect anyone who wasn't immune, then burn themselves out
when there wasn't anyone else to infect. Consequently, it is highly
likely that the handful of Norsemen who tried to settle in Vinland were
not carrying deadly infectious diseases.[48]

Repeated epidemics were major blows to communities that were already struggling to adapt to the Little Ice Age. Smallpox first hit Iceland in 1241, killing around a third of the population.[49] Then in the early 1400s came the plague, over fifty years after the Black Death hit mainland Europe, killing two-thirds of the population.[50] The very high death toll is a consequence of the challenges of farming in the far north. Fodder had to be collected in the short summer season to feed livestock throughout the cold, dark winter. But this couldn't happen when the Black Death struck, so disease was followed by famine. Iceland managed to survive. But the far smaller, more isolated communities in Greenland ceased to exist sometime around the middle of the fifteenth century.* Although evidence is sketchy, infectious diseases are likely to have at least contributed to the disappearance of Norse settlers. Smallpox struck Greenland around 1430.[51] And while there is no record of a plague outbreak occurring there, it is not hard to imagine infected rats hitching a ride in a shipment of grain. Alfred Crosby points out that if this was the case, "then we need inquire no further" about the cause of the colony's demise.[52] With Greenland in terminal decline and Iceland struggling to survive, the Norsemen did not make renewed attempts to colonize Vinland.

More than 500 years after the Norse had tried to settle in North America, Europeans once again began to explore. In 1539, one of Pizarro's lieutenants, Hernando de Soto, set off on a search for more treasure. He used the vast riches he had acquired in Peru to finance a private army of 600 soldiers, 200 horses and 300 pigs that landed near Tampa Bay, Florida.[53] For the next couple of years they trampled across what is now the southeastern United States, reaching as far inland as Tennessee and perhaps Arkansas. De Soto's party encountered members of the Mississippian culture, the most populous and highly organized pre-Columbian society in North America. Alfred Crosby describes these people as the "impressive country cousins" of the Mexica. The conquistadors observed that the region was heavily populated, and that there were vast cultivated fields punctuated by large settlements that featured temples on top of earthen mounds. But the locals told them there had been many more people until an epidemic struck just

---

* The Norse had managed to survive in Greenland for about four and a half centuries, longer than the Europeans have been in North America.

a year or two earlier. On their trek, de Soto's party came across several villages that had been abandoned and found houses containing the decaying corpses of people killed by the pestilence. As with the invasion of the Inca Empire, Old World pathogens had raced ahead of the Spanish. Infectious diseases might have traveled overland from Central America, arrived with previous European visitors, or been brought by the Calusa, a Native American community who lived on the southwest coast of Florida and were known to canoe to Cuba to trade in the early sixteenth century.[54]

In late spring 1542, on the banks of the Mississippi, de Soto died after suffering from a fever. Sources disagree on whether the exact location was Arkansas or Louisiana. Having failed to find great wealth, the remaining members of his party returned to New Spain. When the French explored the areas around the Mississippi River in the late 1600s, most of the large settlements and agricultural land described by de Soto had disappeared. Wild buffalo roamed what were once well-tended maize fields, and most communities had reverted to a life of part-time farming and foraging.[55] The Mississippian culture, the most advanced society in North America, which had thrived for more than 500 years, had simply vanished. By far the most plausible explanation is that the population was obliterated by successive waves of infectious diseases brought by Europeans. De Soto's would-be conquistadors might well have introduced Old World pathogens, but bearing in mind the scale of the devastation it is likely that the epidemics had multiple sources. It is possible that one of these was the English colony of Virginia, the first to be established on the North American mainland in 1607.

That same year, an English trading company—the Popham Colony—tried to set up a base in what is now southern Maine but abandoned the project after fourteen months, in large part because of opposition from numerous well-armed Native Americans. The French attempted to found a settlement near Chatham, Cape Cod around the same time, but it failed for similar reasons. Then, improbably, a small, ragtag group of English Separatists who had been exiled in Leiden landed in late 1620 and managed to start the first permanent settlement in New England. Why did the Pilgrims succeed where others failed? It wasn't because they were better prepared or more numerous. Rather, between

1616 and 1619 a savage epidemic had swept through the Massachusetts Bay area, most probably brought by European fishermen or traders who operated there. Some scholars believe it was smallpox, others viral hepatitis. Either way, it is estimated to have killed as much as 90 percent of the population.[56] If modern-day Americans want to be historically accurate, then their gratitude at Thanksgiving should be directed to the Old World pathogens that made the settlement of Plymouth Colony possible.

Whereas the previous attempts to colonize New England faced fierce resistance from the indigenous population, the Pilgrims found abandoned villages and houses containing skeletons. In fact, they built their first settlement in one of the deserted Native American villages and survived the winter by taking grain and beans from their homes and even digging up stashes buried in graves. Edward Winslow, one of the group's leaders, wrote that he was "sure it was God's good providence that we found this corn for else we know not how we should have done." This betrays his remarkable self-confidence, but also the precariousness of the Pilgrims' situation in their first few months. The epidemic that devastated the indigenous population in the years before 1620 benefited the colonists in another important way: by unsettling the power balance between rival Native American communities in the region. The Wampanoag—who had been particularly badly hit by the epidemic— were willing to ally with the English in order to strengthen their position against Native American communities who hadn't been as affected. William Bradford, another prominent Pilgrim Father, regarded Tisquantum (Squanto), the Native American who taught the settlers how to survive in their new environment, as "a special instrument sent of God." In fact, he was so willing to cooperate because his community had been completely wiped out by disease a few years earlier.[57]

The Pilgrims spearheaded a wave of Puritan immigration from Old to New England. Over the next two decades, large numbers fled Charles I's religious persecution and 21,000 of these ended up in North America.[58] The newcomers were aided by another smallpox epidemic— which they had almost certainly introduced—in 1630 that reduced the remaining indigenous population of Massachusetts by half.[59] Epidemics struck again and again over the next few decades, making the settlement of North America possible. Like the conquistadors before them, the Puritan settlers interpreted the Native Americans' destruction as a sign of Divine Providence. John Winthrop, first governor of the Massachusetts Bay Colony, noted in 1634: "For the natives, they are neere all dead of small Poxe, so as the Lord hathe cleared our title to what we possess."[60]

Alexis de Tocqueville, the French political theorist who visited the United States in the 1830s, wrote, "I think I can see the whole destiny of America contained in the first Puritan who landed on those shores." The 21,000 settlers that came in the twenty years after the foundation of Plymouth Colony were the only significant influx of people into New England until Irish Catholic immigration began in the 1840s. The colonists became the "breeding stock of America's Yankee population" and by the end of the twentieth century had multiplied to 16 million people.[61] Their influence goes well beyond numbers. In contrast to the fortune-seeking conquistadors, the Puritans traveled to the New World to build a new godly society where they could raise their families free from persecution.[62] They brought with them institutions that encouraged the emergence of capitalism, most notably a legal system that placed a strong emphasis on property rights and checks against abuse of government power. The North American colonists were better off than back home because of the absence of a powerful landed aristocracy—many of whom had controlled their vast estates since the Norman invasion of England in 1066. The political and economic system created by settlers on the northeast coast persisted after independence and helps to explain why America has developed into one of the most individualistic and wealthy societies the world has ever seen.[63]

European colonialism also had a lasting impact on Africa, but, unlike in North America, its former colonies are now some of the poorest countries in the world. Infectious diseases played a crucial role in Africa's development, as well.

The White Man's Grave

For anyone growing up in the UK in the 1980s, it was hard to escape the idea that Africa—or at least Africa south of the Sahara—was uniformly poor and helpless. It was a region "where nothing ever grows, no rain nor rivers flow," as the Band Aid 1984 Christmas song goes.[64] People in Europe didn't always think about Africa in this way, however. Medieval maps of the known world portray it as a region of great wealth. In fact, these *mappae mundi* depict a continent not just with rivers, but rivers of gold. Take, for example, the Catalan Atlas: an immense illuminated map produced in about 1375 and attributed to the Majorcan Jewish cartographer Abraham Cresques. Off the coast of West Africa a picture of a boat is accompanied by the text: "The ship of Jaume Ferrer departed for the River of Gold on the 10th of August of 1350." The atlas contains other signs that Europeans thought of Africa as a region of remarkable wealth. In the middle of the Sahel is a caricature of Mansa Musa, the fourteenth-century Malian ruler. He is seated on a throne with a gold crown on his head, and with his right hand he is offering a gold disc to a Berber on a camel. The inscription next to Musa states that "this king is the richest and most distinguished ruler of the whole region on account of the great quantity of gold that is found in his lands."

Maps like the Catalan Atlas were produced using the latest knowledge from travelers and traders who passed through Majorca. Although not necessarily geographically accurate, they tell us a great deal about how contemporary Europeans understood other parts of the world. West Africa is associated with gold because the region was the primary source of this most precious of metals in the Christian and Muslim worlds during the Middle Ages. And while the "River of Gold" is mythical, Musa existed, and his control of West Africa's gold mines made him inconceivably rich.[65] Much of what we know about Musa's wealth comes from descriptions of his spectacular pilgrimage to Mecca between 1324 and 1325. He is said to have carried 18 tons of pure gold on the Hajj and his largesse was responsible for deflating the price of gold around the Mediterranean for several years afterward.[66] Within a decade, cartographers started including him in their work. This pilgrimage literally put Mansa Musa and his vast riches on the *mappae mundi*.

Maps such as the Catalan Atlas—or, more accurately, the ideas that they represent—lured Iberian fortune seekers. In the early 1400s, Prince Henry the Navigator of Portugal gathered a team of sailors and cartographers to explore and chart the West African coast. Up until that point, all the gold that was imported into Europe was carried across the Sahara to the southern shore of the Mediterranean by camel caravans. By the middle of the century, Portuguese ships had broken the monopoly of the desert land route. Italian contemporaries referred to João II, King of Portugal in 1490s, as *il rei d'oro* due to his access to West African gold markets. The Portuguese acquired African gold through commerce rather than military victories. They established a string of trading posts (*feitorias*) along the West African coast, most notably the great fort of São Jorge da Mina on the Gold Coast in 1482. Here European goods were exchanged for gold, as well as spices and enslaved humans. The Portuguese weren't even equals in these endeavors. In most cases, the hosts dictated the terms of European fortune seekers' stays and anyone who violated the rules faced harsh punishment, including death.[67]

The motivations of the late-medieval Portuguese were very similar to those of the Spanish conquistadors. The Ottomans' expansion had closed off lucrative opportunities in the Mediterranean, so fortune seekers spilled out into the Atlantic in a frenzied search for riches, above all gold. And, just like in the Americas, powerful states stood in their way. But the experiences of Portuguese explorers contrasted starkly with those of their Spanish contemporaries. While the Mexica and Inca Empires collapsed, West African polities remained resolute. The Portuguese only ever made minor inroads in the region. They never found the mines where Musa's gold was dug up, nor did they control territory beyond a few isolated *feitorias* on the coast.

Infectious diseases are responsible for the very different outcomes. The colonization of the Americas was only possible because Old World pathogens came to the conquistadors' aid. The Portuguese had no such luck. The West African coast was linked to the rest of Europe and Asia by the trans-Saharan trade routes. Where people traveled, so did bacteria and viruses. So people living along these routes or near ports would have developed immunity to infectious diseases that were common in Europe. But Africa at this time was different from Europe in one key respect: it was relatively sparsely populated.[68] Many people in the African interior lived in isolated communities—they hadn't been exposed to Old World Pathogens and therefore hadn't developed resistance.[69] Diseases like smallpox, measles and flu might have posed a danger to this latter group, if only Europeans were able to travel throughout the continent. But mosquito-borne diseases made that all but impossible.

West Africa was and continues to be an extremely favorable environment for two mosquito-borne infectious diseases.[70] *Plasmodium falciparum* causes the most lethal form of malaria. It can only reproduce within the female mosquito if the temperature exceeds around 20 degrees Celsius for three weeks. When the weather is hotter, the cycle speeds up. *Falciparum* malaria thrives in the tropical climates. *Anopheles gambiae* mosquitoes lay their eggs in standing water, and there is plenty of this in wet and humid West Africa. Consequently, malaria was so widespread in West Africa that it would have been almost impossible to avoid being bitten by infected *Anopheles* mosquitoes.[71] Innate immunity provides nowhere near full protection.[72] Even today, malaria kills hundreds of thousands of people in sub-Saharan Africa every year, most of them young children exposed to the disease for the first time. Those who don't die in childhood can be reinfected and harbor the plasmodium, but as one's body develops resistance it is rare to show anything more than mild symptoms. Malaria, then, is a relatively harmless condition among adults who have lived in West Africa all their lives. In contrast, *Plasmodium falciparum* is deadly to adults who haven't grown up in a region where it is endemic, and a significant proportion of European would-be settlers were killed by malaria soon after they arrived.

Yellow fever is also common in West Africa, but the epidemiological dynamics are different. The virus tends not to be deadly in childhood, and after one infection you have lifelong immunity and can never again serve as a host to the pathogen. But yellow fever is a very serious disease for adults. Victims suffer massive internal bleeding. The blood collects in their stomach and coagulates into black slime, which is then vomited up. It is referred to as yellow fever because one of the symptoms is jaundice, which, of course, turns the skin yellow. About one-third of those who develop symptoms die.[73] Unlike malaria, yellow fever virus can burn out in a particular area when there are no longer enough non-immune bodies to infect. But it returns again when there are sufficient new children or immigrants to sustain another epidemic. Despite the differences between malaria and yellow fever, the outcome was the same from the perspective of Europeans: they were killed in horrifying numbers, while the adult population of West Africa appeared unaffected.

The fact that European attempts to settle in the Americas foundered without the help of infectious diseases suggests that the Portuguese would have struggled to colonize West Africa even if malaria and yellow fever hadn't intervened to help the indigenous population. But these mosquito-borne diseases created a defensive force field that made military conquest all but impossible. Writing in the sixteenth century, João de Barros, the historian who is referred to as the "Portuguese Livy," lucidly captured the frustrations of the would-be colonists:

> But it seems that for our sins, or for some inscrutable judgment of God, in all the entrances of this great Ethiopia that we navigate along, He has placed a striking angel with a flaming sword of deadly fevers, who prevents us from penetrating into the interior to the springs of this garden, whence proceed these rivers of gold that flow to the sea in so many parts of our conquest.[74]

In the late eighteenth and early nineteenth centuries, when Britain was on its way to becoming the dominant colonial force in the world, malaria and yellow fever—the flaming sword of deadly fevers—still made tropical Africa all but unconquerable. The American historian Philip Curtin estimates that around this time between 30 and 70 percent of Europeans died in their first year on the West African coast; little wonder that the region was known to the British as "the white man's grave."[75] Malaria and yellow fever accounted for 80 percent of these deaths.[76] Earlier statistics didn't distinguish between the two diseases, but later figures suggest that malaria was responsible for five to ten times more deaths than yellow fever.[77] For those Europeans who managed to survive in the colony for a year, mortality fell as they became infected, survived and acquired immunity—although there was still about a one-in-ten risk of dying each year.

The interior of the African continent was even more deadly. Colonial explorers tended to travel inland via navigable rivers. The "rivers of gold" that appeared on medieval maps were in reality "rivers of death."[78] In the late fifteenth century, João II sent a party of eight men to travel up the Gambia River to find Mansa Musa's descendants.[79] All but one died. If Cortés, Pizarro or Aguirre had attempted to search for El Dorado in Africa rather than the Americas, they would have almost certainly been killed by infectious diseases too. In the first half of the nineteenth century, Europeans who dared to venture inland still perished in astonishingly high numbers. Curtin's data suggests that the average European would have survived for just four months in Mali—an annual mortality of 300 percent!

In 1805, Mungo Park, the Scottish physician and explorer, led a Colonial Office–sponsored expedition that aimed to chart interior West Africa. It took the party of forty Europeans eleven weeks to complete the first leg of the trip, an overland trek from the Gambia to the Niger in the rainy season. By the time they arrived at Bamako, all but ten of the party were dead and the survivors were weakened by illness. Park and four other survivors traveled by canoe along the Niger, but they drowned in the rapids near Bussa, 1,600 kilometers downstream.[80] In 1827 Mungo Park's son Thomas set out to discover what had happened to his father, but he died from fever before reaching the interior. The British Navy then sent three iron-hulled steamers up the Niger in 1841–42. These were equipped with state-of-the-art chemical filters designed to protect the sailors from the "miasma" that was assumed to be the source of deadly tropical fevers. Unfortunately, they did not filter out mosquitoes—it was almost another half-century before scientists understood how malaria and yellow fever were transmitted—and the expedition fared only slightly better than Park's: fifty-five of the 152 Europeans died.[81]

The threat posed by infectious diseases made it impossible for Europeans to colonize most of sub-Saharan Africa. In 1870, only one-tenth of the African land mass was under European control. Compare this to the Americas, where the conquest of the Mexica and Inca had occurred three and a half centuries before, and the whole continent either was or had been under European occupation. The major European colonies that were established in Africa before the late nineteenth century were located in the more temperate, less disease-ridden regions. Algeria in the far north was held by France, and the Cape Colony and Natal in the far south by Britain; in both cases, large numbers of Europeans emigrated there. But in the tropical regions it wasn't possible for would-be settlers to take and hold territory. Instead, Europeans were restricted to a few settlements along the coast, and focused their efforts on monopolizing trade in humans, gold, ivory and other valuable commodities—as is apparent in the names they gave to West Africa, such as the Gold Coast and Côte d'Ivoire.[82]

The Heart of Darkness

If you compare the Catalan Atlas with maps produced almost 500 years later, you would be forgiven for thinking that medieval Majorcan cartographers knew more than the Victorian imperialists about sub-Saharan Africa. Whereas the former included impressionistic scenes of the interior that contained at least a hint of reality, the latter left almost everywhere but the coast blank. This all changed in the final third of the nineteenth century: by the early 1890s, when Joseph Conrad captained a steamboat that traveled the Congo River, there were few, if any, holes remaining in Europeans' knowledge of Africa. According to Marlow, Conrad's narrator and alter ego in *Heart of Darkness*, the gap in cartographic knowledge that had existed just a few decades previously "had got filled since my boyhood with rivers and lakes and names. It had ceased to be a blank space of delightful mystery—a white patch for a boy to dream gloriously over." By the turn of the twentieth century, more than nine-tenths of the African land mass was occupied by European countries, with only Abyssinia (Ethiopia) and Liberia—which had belonged to the American Colonization Society—spared. The continent "had become a place of darkness," Marlow remarks, by which he seems to mean that European exploitation and oppression had turned it into an almost unimaginably unpleasant place.[83]

Historians usually explain the "Scramble for Africa" as a consequence of European industrialists' desire to get their grubby hands on new sources of raw materials and prize open markets where they could sell their goods. It is certainly true that the Industrial Revolution led to a surge in manufacturing activity, so the factory owners would have been keen to identify sources of cheap natural resources, as well as people to buy their wares. But these ambitions were remarkably similar to those of Europeans going all the way back to the late-medieval Portuguese. The main difference is that, from the 1880s onward, colonialists *were* finally able to establish and maintain colonies in Africa. What had changed?

Technical developments, such as the steamship and the Maxim gun—the first automatic firearm—were important.[84] But that's only part of the story. Europeans had to survive long enough to navigate their steam-powered boats into the interior of the continent, and then fire ten bullets a second into the flesh of the local population. Innovations in transport and weaponry only abetted the Scramble for Africa in conjunction with improvements in the prevention and treatment of malaria. Quinine was crucial in this respect.

In the natural world, quinine is found in the bark of cinchona trees that grow in the eastern foothills of the Andes. In the late 1500s, Spanish Jesuits observed indigenous people treating fever with a kind of proto-tonic water that consisted of ground bark mixed with sweetened water. By the middle of the seventeenth century, "Jesuit powder" was used across Europe as a treatment for malaria, which was endemic to much of the region at the time—albeit mostly the milder *vivax* strain that was able to reproduce in colder temperatures. Oliver Cromwell, who headed an austere Protestant dictatorship after the execution of Charles I in 1649, came down with malaria but stubbornly refused to take a medicine that was so closely associated with papists.[85] He died shortly afterward. Charles II, who replaced Cromwell, had no such qualms and survived a bout of what was then referred to as the ague.

In 1677, ground cinchona bark was included as a treatment for fevers in the latest edition of *Pharmacopeia Londinensis*, the Royal College of Physicians' list of medicines. But quinine fell out of fashion in the eighteenth century, in part because physicians in the tropics observed that it didn't prevent or cure the periodic devastating yellow fever epidemics, which early modern medicine didn't distinguish from malaria. In its place, doctors used cutting-edge treatments like bloodletting, which involved making an incision in a vein so that the patient lost enormous quantities of blood—sometimes up to 3 liters, more than half of the total volume in the body. This certainly wasn't an effective treatment—in fact, as malaria often leads to anemia, it was worse than doing nothing.[86]

The rehabilitation of cinchona bark began with the disastrous 1841–42 Niger Expedition. Thomas Thomson, one of the British Navy doctors on the mission, used it in small amounts to treat some of the party and noticed a positive effect. Over the next couple of years he experimented with larger doses. In 1846, he published his findings in *The Lancet*, the prestigious London-based medical journal. Soon afterward, the head of the British Army's Medical Department sent a circular to West African colonial governors advising them to use cinchona bark, and word spread quickly among Europeans in the region. In 1854, an iron-hulled steamboat—the *Pleiad*—traveled up the Niger on another Navy-sponsored expedition. The only significant difference between this mission and the one that took place in 1841–42 was that everyone on board took regular doses of quinine. It turned out to be an unprecedented success, penetrating further into Africa than any Europeans had done before and then returning to the coast without losing a single member of the crew.[87] It marked the beginning of the beginning of the Scramble for Africa.

David Livingstone, the Scottish missionary and explorer, occupies a prominent—although highly problematic—place in the pantheon of Great British Men. He made it his life's mission to bring "Christianity, Commerce and Civilization" to the people of the African continent, declaring: "I Will Open a Path into the Interior, or Perish." In the 1850s he became the first European to traverse Central Africa from coast to coast, filling in many of the blanks on the map and demonstrating that it was now possible to travel into the heart of the continent. Livingstone's account of his journey made him famous and led to an upsurge in interest in Africa. He inspired other missionaries, explorers, traders and then ultimately colonial powers to follow in his footsteps.

Thanks to quinine, Livingstone managed to succeed where the likes of Mungo Park and his son had failed. He was also a medical doctor and had been convinced by the growing evidence that it prevented deadly tropical diseases. Before setting off for Africa, Livingstone bought huge quantities of quinine from the Apothecaries' Hall in London. After experimenting with different amounts, he reasoned that it was necessary to take a dose large enough to make his ears ring. His concoction of quinine with jalap, rhubarb and calomel was later marketed by Burroughs Wellcome & Co. as "Livingstone's rousers."[88] This didn't prevent him from getting very sick—his journals suggest he had dozens of bouts of malaria. But he didn't perish. His travels into the African interior also provide a sad reminder of what happened to Europeans when quinine wasn't available. In 1862, Livingstone's wife, Mary, was unable to keep quinine down due to sickness. She quickly died. And when the chest carrying David's supplies of quinine went missing in 1870, he wrote in his journal: "I felt as if I had received the sentence of death." Livingstone became very unwell, but he didn't die—most probably because he had built up some immunity from his many previous infections. Eventually he was found by Henry Morton Stanley, another explorer whose travels were made possible by quinine, and was able to replenish his supplies.[89]

Philip Curtin estimates that with the increased use of quinine in the second half of the nineteenth century, coupled with the decline of dangerous treatments like bloodletting, European mortality in tropical Africa fell by "at least half and perhaps more."[90] The region remained a very dangerous place for Europeans: quinine didn't totally eliminate the risk of malaria and there was still no prevention or treatment for the other dreaded mosquito-borne killer, yellow fever. Jesuit powder didn't slay the "angel with a flaming sword of deadly fevers" that guarded the continent. But it did weaken her. Five hundred years after Portuguese explorers had first coveted Africa's vast natural resources, settler mortality fell to a level that made colonialism possible.[91] Explorers, including Livingstone and Stanley, could now chart the key geographical features of the region, filling in Conrad's "blank spaces." When European countries claimed territories in the Scramble for Africa, they were now habitable for colonial administrators and soldiers in a way they had never been before.

The continued threat posed by infectious diseases in tropical Africa had an enormous impact on the specific form that colonialism took. The region attracted ambitious and unscrupulous Europeans motivated by making as much money in as little time and with as small a capital expenditure as possible—and then cutting and running before they were struck down by disease. They weren't colonial settlers. So, unlike in New England, they didn't bring their families with them, settle down and build institutions in the image of their home country. Rather, the Europeans who colonized Africa in the last decades of the nineteenth century created "extractive institutions" that used violence and the threat of violence to coerce the population into mining natural resources and transporting them to the coast, where they were shipped to Europe. The ultimate aim of this brutal endeavor was not to build a new and better society, but to enrich a small group of Europeans by draining wealth from the region.[92]

Arguably the most appalling example of such a colony was created by Leopold II of Belgium.[93] Frustrated with being the king of a minor European power with no overseas possessions, he hired none other than Henry Morton Stanley to help him build an empire in Africa. In the late 1870s and early 1880s, the quinine-fueled explorer staked out a vast territory between the Atlantic and the African Great Lakes for his patron. It was seventy-six times the size of Belgium and amounted to one-thirteenth of Africa's total area. Founded in 1885, the Free State of Congo was Leopold's private property—although he never traveled there because he feared the impact that infectious diseases would have on his health. The Belgian king presented his venture to other European heads of state as a philanthropic project that would stop Arab slavers, promote free trade and spread peace. The colony's flag reflected these lofty aims. The yellow star on a dark-blue background was supposed to symbolize the shining light that Belgians were bringing to the darkest corner of Africa. In reality it was an enterprise that aimed to enrich Leopold, with no concern for the harm that it would do to the local population.

The Belgians' first major infrastructure project was a 400-kilometer-long railway from the coast to Stanley Pool, where the Congo River became navigable. Conrad arrived in the Congo in 1890, when it was being constructed, and witnessed the harrowing conditions under which African workers labored. He described chain gangs with iron collars around their necks and others who, exhausted from their exertions, sat under trees, waiting to die. From Stanley Pool, steamships traveled hundreds of kilometers into the interior. Perhaps the most disturbing scene in *Heart of Darkness* occurs at one of the most distant river stations. Through binoculars, Marlow observes that Kurtz, the delinquent company agent whom he has been sent to find, has impaled the severed heads of Africans on fence posts surrounding his garden. This incident isn't a figment of the author's imagination. A very similar story was reported in Europe several years after Conrad left the Congo and appears to have spurred him to write his fictionalized firsthand account of European colonization. Conrad described what he witnessed as "the vilest scramble for loot that ever disfigured the history of human conscience." But the worst was yet to come.[94]

When Conrad worked as a steamboat captain on the Congo River, the main loot was ivory. Toward the end of the 1890s there was a boom in demand for rubber, which was used to insulate electrical wires and make bicycle, and later car, tires. Congo's equatorial rainforest was, along with Brazil, the world's main source of natural rubber. Other European colonial powers responded to this economic opportunity by planting vast rubber plantations in tropical Asia, but it takes at least ten years before the trees produce a decent crop. Leopold set out to make as much money as possible in the intervening period. By the turn of the twentieth century, half of the colony's budget was spent on the *Force Publique*. This army of occupation-cum-corporate police would move from village to village. They kidnapped the women and children and sent the men deep into the rainforest to collect rubber. If they failed to bring back their quota, the soldiers would respond with wanton brutality—killing, raping and maiming their captives. One particularly notorious photo from the period shows a father staring forlornly at a tiny dismembered hand and foot that once belonged to his daughter but now lie on the floor in front of him. Alas, this was not an isolated incident. The Belgians cut off so many limbs that there was a rumor among the Congolese that dismembered body parts were used to make the canned corned beef that formed an important part of the European diet in the tropics.[95]

According to the American writer Adam Hochschild, when the Congo Free State was created in 1885 it had about 25 million inhabitants; by 1923, when the rubber boom was over, there were 7.7 million. For every 10 kilograms of rubber exported, the population fell by one. Congolese didn't only die as a direct result of the *Force Publique*'s violence: Belgian rule caused massive disruption to the lives of people living in Central Africa, leading to famines and plummeting birth rates. As soldiers, caravans of porters, steamboat crews and displaced people moved across the colony they spread diseases from the coast to the interior, where many communities had lived relatively isolated existences prior to the Belgians' arrival. Half a million people died from sleeping sickness in 1901 alone. Smallpox was another major killer. One observer reported visiting a smallpox-ravaged village in which the vultures had become so fat on their diet of human flesh that they were unable to fly.[96]

While colonization was disastrous for the people of the Congo, it made Leopold fabulously rich. He spent most of his money on construction—so much so that he became known as the "Builder King." In his home country he paid for monuments and museums in Brussels, a railway station in Antwerp and a golf course, hippodrome, promenade and parks at the seaside resort of Ostend. In the south of France he built a dock for his 15,000-ton yacht and bought an estate on Cap Ferrat, Villa Les Cèdres, which in 2017 was on the market for over $410 million, making it the most expensive home in the world at the time. Another major outlay was Caroline Lacroix, who was sixteen and earning a living from prostitution when she met sixty-five-year-old Leopold. He lavished enormous sums of money on her over the next ten years until his death, including 3 million francs on dresses at Callot Soeurs in Paris.[97]

Even after the Congo became independent in 1960, half a century after Leopold's death, the impact of colonialism lingered. In contrast to North America, where the colonial legacy was democracy and rule of law, in the Congo it was authoritarianism and plunder. The Belgian state connived with the former colony's military and the CIA to murder Patrice Lumumba, just a few months after he became the first democratically elected prime minister. In 1965, after various mutinies, rebellions and secessions, Mobutu Sese Seko—who had been a sergeant in the colonial *Force Publique* and was then head of the Congolese National Army—seized power. He would be the country's dictator for the next thirty-two years. Mobutu ruled with a brutality and venality that was not dissimilar to Leopold's, and amassed a fortune of several billion dollars—bigger than the king's. His tastes were similar too. Mobutu was infamous for chartering a Concorde to take him on shopping trips to Paris, and he bought a yacht and several palatial homes in Europe, including one in Roquebrune-Cap-Martin, only 20 kilometers from the Belgian king's former home in Cap Ferrat.[98]

Mobutu was removed from power in 1997. Still, despite being rich in natural resources including diamonds, gold, timber, copper, cobalt and coltan, Democratic Republic of Congo (D.R.C.) is one of the poorest countries in the world today. According to World Bank data, three-quarters of the population live in extreme poverty—that is, on less than $1.90 a day—and the annual GDP per capita is just over $1,200, the third-lowest in the world. The D.R.C.'s is a typical story—albeit an extreme version—for the nations that were created in the Scramble for Africa at the end of the nineteenth century and won their independence in the second half of the twentieth. The ten poorest countries in the world are all former colonies in sub-Saharan Africa. It is not unreasonable to conclude that these societies would have been better off if Europeans had never discovered a moderately effective treatment for malaria and the region had remained a white man's grave.

Chapter 6
Revolutionary Plagues

When we revolt it's not for a particular culture. We revolt simply because, for many reasons we can no longer breathe.

—FRANTZ FANON

I Can't Breathe

On 25 May 2020, a cashier at a Minneapolis convenience store called the police after a customer paid for a packet of cigarettes with a counterfeit $20 bill. Mobile phone footage of what happened next shows one of the responding officers restraining the suspect in the street outside. The policeman, who is white, kneels on the neck of an African American man, crushing his head against the pavement and restricting his airway. The suspect pleads for his life. "I can't breathe," he says repeatedly. "Please. Please. Please. I can't breathe. Please man." Members of the public implore the officer to stop. His three colleagues watch, doing nothing. After nine and a half minutes, the man accused of paying for smokes with a fake banknote is dead.

The murder of George Floyd sparked an unprecedented outpouring of sadness and anger about police brutality toward African Americans. Up to 26 million people participated in demonstrations in support of Black Lives Matter (BLM) that summer, making them the largest protests in United States history.[1] Dying at the hands of law enforcement is, however, only the most shocking and violent manifestation of the discrimination that Black people face. The median household wealth of African Americans is $17,600 compared to $171,000 for whites,[2] and they are almost six times more likely to be incarcerated.[3] The demonstrations that rocked the U.S. in the summer of 2020 were motivated by concerns that were much more fundamental and went beyond one brutal killing: although the United States abolished slavery at the end of the Civil War, it never rid itself of white supremacy and Black subjugation. As a result, statues that literally put Confederate politicians and generals on pedestals in Southern state capitals were rallying points for protesters.

But New World slavery and its legacy are not exclusively a North American problem. Only about 3 percent of the 12.5 million humans trafficked across the Atlantic ended up in what would become the United States.[4] The slave ships' most common destination was the European colonies in the Caribbean, where African slave labor was first used over a century before they were first shipped to Britain's North American territories in 1619. Many descendants of Afro-Caribbean slave laborers migrated to Europe, where the sentiments expressed by BLM found a receptive audience. Shortly after the murder of George Floyd, residents of Bristol in southwest England pulled down a statue of Edward Colston—a seventeenth-century merchant and slave trader—that had stood in the city center for over a century, as if to celebrate the role that he and his hometown played in trafficking Africans across the Atlantic.[5] In fact, a plaque on the plinth described him as one of Bristol's "most virtuous and wise sons." For years locals had petitioned the city council to remove it, but they got nowhere. Finally, in June 2020, protesters dragged the statue of Colston through the streets and threw it into the murky River Avon.*

In order to comprehend the contemporary world, we must understand how an institution as horrific and iniquitous as American slavery came into being. For most people alive today, the primary objection to slavery is that it is fundamentally dehumanizing to treat one person as the property of another. There are less principled grounds for objection

---

* The protests that occurred in summer 2020 also provided an opportunity for people to express their anger at the legacy of colonialism more generally. For example, in the Belgian city of Antwerp red paint was thrown over a statue of Leopold II.

too. The founder of economics, Adam Smith, agreed that New World slavery was morally repugnant, but he also pointed out that it was economically inefficient. In *The Wealth of Nations* Smith argued that "the work done by free men comes cheaper in the end than the work performed by slaves." This is because enslaved workers who had no prospect of being freed could only be encouraged to be productive through violence and threats. At the same time, there were enormous incentives for slaves to try to sabotage their workplaces, attack their supervisors and escape from a living hell. According to Smith, the cost of violent supervision required to keep an enslaved labor force in line made it prohibitively expensive. If European settlers were economically rational, they would have employed free laborers from their home countries because they were a less threatening, more manageable and ultimately cheaper option.

Adam Smith saw slavery as a manifestation of humanity's will to dominate other people. But is this the whole story? It's clear that the proprietors of slave plantations in the New World were capable of treating laborers with great cruelty in order to maximize their profits. But it seems improbable that the planters were so sadistic that they would choose to engage in this hideous practice when it was essentially costing them money. Was there a hidden logic to their cruelty? As we'll see, the emergence of American slavery and the ideology of racism used to justify it had a great deal to do with infectious diseases—and who could, or could not, survive them.

Slavery and Epidemiology

The history of slavery goes back far beyond the European colonization of the Caribbean. It emerged soon after the adoption of settled agriculture and should be conceptualized as the extension of the logic of domestication of animals to unfortunate members of our own species.[6] When men and women became slaves they were no longer treated as fellow humans but as beasts of burden. They could be held in captivity, worked to the point of exhaustion, beaten into submission, and exchanged for something else. But there was something new and peculiar about American slavery. For thousands of years, skin color had no bearing on who was seen as a suitable candidate for enslavement. It was in the Americas that people of African origin became associated with servitude for the first time.

In fifth-century-BCE Athens, as many as 80,000 people—a quarter of the population—were slaves who played no role in the city-state's democratic processes.[7] They comprised both Greeks and non-Greeks who were captured during wartime and through piracy. Ancient Rome also had a large number of slaves, most seized in the wars of expansion that the Roman army fought across the Mediterranean and its hinterlands. After the conquest of Epirus in 167 BCE, 150,000 Greeks were enslaved despite the high esteem in which Romans held Hellenic culture.[8] Some slaves in the Greco-Roman world may have been Black Africans, but they were in a small minority and skin color wasn't a characteristic that was associated with servitude. Indeed, Roman emperors and other high-ranking officials came from across the empire—including the provinces of Africa and Arabia—and although it isn't clear how dark their skin was, we can be fairly sure they weren't light-skinned Europeans.

There was a booming trade in humans in the medieval Mediterranean. The basic principle of slavery was that it was acceptable to enslave anyone who didn't follow your own religion. Catholic Italian slave traders sometimes stretched this to include Orthodox Christians.[9] In the western Mediterranean the main source of slave labor was Muslims captured during the Christian campaign to retake the Iberian Peninsula—known as the Reconquista—which culminated in the defeat of the Nasrid Kingdom of Granada in 1492. Genovese and Venetian merchants bought young men, and more often young women, in the Black Sea slave markets—and sold them throughout the eastern region. These included Georgians, Armenians, Circassians and other Caucasian people.[10] At this time, most slaves would work as domestic servants. There were exceptions, however. In the Arab world, young men from the Black Sea region were bought to serve as an elite caste of soldiers or Mamluks. Slaves became masters when the Mamluks seized power in 1250, ruling much of the Middle East from Cairo until 1517.

In the thirteenth century, Norman crusaders established sugarcane plantations on Cyprus and began exporting their produce to western Europe.[11] The work was initially done by feudal serfs, but as demand for sugar grew and sugar cultivation expanded, the plantations increasingly used slave laborers bought in the slave markets of the Black Sea or captured in wars against the Greeks, Bulgarians and Turks.[12] This model spread to Crete, Sicily and then westward to the Balearic Islands.[13] The sugarcane plantations established in the thirteenth and fourteenth centuries shared many of the key characteristics with the slave societies that emerged in the sixteenth and seventeenth centuries in the Americas: slave labor was used to cultivate and process a cash crop on estates owned by western Europeans and transported by ship to be sold back in Europe.

The association between Black Africans and slavery only began in the fifteenth century. The post–Black Death expansion of the Ottomans disrupted the economic life of the Mediterranean, leading European explorers, soldiers and entrepreneurs to spill out into the Atlantic Ocean. Spain conquered the Canary Islands, and the Portuguese settled previously uninhabited archipelagos such as Madeira, the Azores, Cape Verde and São Tomé and Príncipe.[14] The warm, humid climate, volcanic soil and plentiful water were ideal for cultivating sugarcane, and entrepreneurial aristocrats established plantations to satisfy the ever-growing demand in Europe. The major challenge they faced was finding workers to clear the forest, cut terraces into the sides of mountains and build irrigation systems, and, once this was done, cultivate, harvest and process the crop. With the Reconquista coming to an end, access to the Black Sea slave markets blocked by the Ottomans, and all the islands except the Canaries uninhabited, they found a variety of alternative sources of forced labor.[15] This included Berbers from northwest Africa and *conversos*—Iberian Jews and Muslims who had converted to Christianity yet were treated with deep suspicion. But as Spanish and Portuguese merchants developed closer links with West Africa, it became the most reliable source of slaves. In fact, Black Africans were increasingly being transported back to Europe too: by the mid-sixteenth century they constituted over 7 percent of Seville's population and 10 percent of Lisbon's.[16]

When Columbus set foot on Hispaniola he inadvertently found some of the most fertile land on the planet and a warm, humid climate that was perfect for growing sugarcane. His second voyage in 1493 brought sugarcane plants to the Caribbean. At first the conquistadors tried to use Native Americans to work the land, but, as we know from the previous chapter, the indigenous population was devastated by Old World pathogens.[17] On Columbus' third voyage to the Caribbean in 1498 he advocated importing Africans who were already working on sugar plantations in Atlantic outposts like Madeira and the Canary Islands. Soon afterward the transatlantic slave trade began. Within twenty-five years there were more enslaved Africans than Taíno in Hispaniola. By the middle of the sixteenth century the indigenous population had totally disappeared.[18] As West Africa was connected to Europe and Asia by overland and now sea routes, the local population had been exposed to Old World pathogens and fared much better. Between 1550 and 1650, 650,000 Africans were trafficked to Spain and Portugal's American colonies—more than twice the number of Europeans who crossed the Atlantic in that period.[19]

The early conquistadors' decision to use enslaved Africans on their sugar plantations had unexpected but momentous consequences: it inadvertently set the whole of the American tropics on an inescapable path toward racialized slavery because the nascent transatlantic slave trade carried not only people but also some of the mosquitoes and microbes that made West Africa a deadly place for Europeans.[20]

The *Anopheles gambiae* mosquito, which transmits the most lethal falciparum strain of malaria in West Africa, didn't make it across the Atlantic. Instead, the malaria plasmodium was carried to the Americas in the blood of trafficked West Africans—many of whom would have been recently infected by falciparum and therefore carrying the plasmodium. The Caribbean is home to a number of other species of the *Anopheles* mosquito that were capable of transmitting *Plasmodium falciparum*. But they are not as effective as their African cousins because they are less drawn to human blood. As a result, malaria—which was the major killer in West Africa—was not as deadly in places like Hispaniola.[21]

Yellow fever was a different story. The species of mosquito that transmits this virus from human to human, *Aedes aegypti*, prefers to lay its eggs in water vessels rather than in swamps or puddles; as a result, it was well suited to crossing the Atlantic in slave ships. Once it had made it to the Caribbean, *Aedes aegypti* found sugarcane cultivation an ideal ecosystem in which to reproduce: the plantations were full of clay pots that were used to crystallize sugar but would fill with water in the wet summers, effectively doubling up as mosquito breeding sites.[22]

The arrival of West African pathogens turned the Caribbean into a new white man's grave. Yellow fever epidemics rather than malaria were the major killer of Europeans, but the basic outcome was the same: almost everyone who had grown up in West Africa would have been exposed to yellow fever and acquired lifelong immunity, whereas new settlers from Europe hadn't developed any tolerance and so died in droves.[23] As a result, African labor became the economically "rational" option for plantation owners.

Thanks to research commissioned by the British Army, we have a good idea of the differences in death rates between newly arrived Africans and Europeans in the Caribbean in the first half of the nineteenth century.[24] During peacetime, 1.5 percent of soldiers based in Britain died every year. Being stationed in other temperate regions such as the Mediterranean, North America or southern Africa did not have much of an impact on mortality rates. But when they were sent to tropical areas, the risk of death rose markedly. In the American tropics more than one in eight soldiers died every year, about ten times the death rate of soldiers in temperate zones.[25] Early-nineteenth-century medical science wasn't able to distinguish between yellow fever and malaria, but the data demonstrates that Europeans in the Caribbean died mainly from "fevers" which were responsible for 84 percent of British troops' deaths in Jamaica and just under half in the Lesser Antilles, which includes Barbados.[26]

Given that people working on plantations would have been more exposed to mosquitoes than soldiers stationed in ports and towns (and that for every death two more people got seriously ill), it's clear that agricultural laborers imported from Britain would have fared very badly in the Caribbean. Mortality was much lower among trafficked West Africans who had already acquired immunity to yellow fever and malaria. This can be seen in the disparity in death rates between African soldiers in the British Army—who had been rescued from ships crossing the Atlantic by the Royal Navy as part of its efforts to enforce the 1807 ban on the slave trade—and their white counterparts. When stationed in Sierra Leone, about 3 percent of African soldiers died every year. In the Caribbean the risk of dying increased slightly to 4 percent, but was still three times lower than for white British soldiers.[27]

A very clear illustration of what happened to European settlers who tried to establish colonies in the Americas without African slave labor is the disastrous Scottish attempt to build a trading settlement in what is now Panama at the end of the seventeenth century. The Scottish Darien Company's expedition was funded by public subscription and thousands of people had invested their life savings in the enterprise. In total, this amounted to between a quarter and half of Scotland's wealth.[28] In 1698, 1,200 people set sail to "New Edinburgh" with a year's food supply and the "the nation's finest woollen hose, tartan blankets, ornamental wigs, and leather shoes—25,000 pairs" to trade with the natives.[29] Within eight months of arriving, over three-quarters of them were dead and the survivors returned to Scotland. Tragically, just before this party arrived back in Scotland to tell their compatriots about the disaster, the Darien Company sent another group of 1,300 people to New Edinburgh. Within nine months, all but 100 of the second group were dead. Infectious diseases weren't the only problem encountered by the Scottish colonialists—as you can imagine, there wasn't much demand for itchy socks or warm blankets—but they were the most significant cause of failure.[30]

Incredibly, the impact of Scotland's Central American misadventure is still felt today. At the end of the seventeenth century, although England and Scotland were separate nations, they had shared the same monarch since 1603. England was keen for the two countries to unite, but many Scots wanted to retain their independence because they feared being overwhelmed by their much bigger neighbor. The failure of New Edinburgh didn't just kill 2,000 people; it also wiped out all the money that had been invested in—or gambled on—this doomed project. Cannily, the English promised to compensate the investors if they agreed to closer ties between the two countries. Even committed Scottish nationalists supported the 1707 Act of Union when faced with the possibility of financial ruin. "Thus," wrote the historian John McNeill, "Great Britain was born, with the assistance of fevers from Panama." Over 300 years later, the union is a major political issue and pro-independence parties currently hold a majority in the Scottish parliament. New Edinburgh was a particularly spectacular example of the damage that infectious diseases wrought among white colonial would-be settlers in the American tropics. But the colonies that lasted did so because plantation owners quickly learned that trafficked West Africans provided a much more reliable source of labor than Europeans.

After the notable success of Spanish plantations in the Caribbean, other nations began to establish colonies to cash in on growing demand for sugar.[31] The English settled in Barbados in 1627 and set about developing cane plantations. As with Hispaniola and other islands, the original inhabitants were quickly wiped out by infectious diseases. But the plantation owners didn't immediately turn to enslaved Africans to solve the perennial problem of who would work for them. Unlike in southern Europe, there wasn't a recent tradition of slave labor in the British Isles. At the time the English wouldn't have associated slavery with Black Africans; rather, it would have brought to mind their countrymen who had been kidnapped from coastal settlements or ships by Barbary pirates and taken to North Africa.[32] Plantation owners adapted the traditional English system of apprenticeship, in which a novice worked for a master tradesperson for nothing for a fixed amount of time so they could learn their trade.[33] In the Americas, indentured servitude involved a laborer signing up to work on a plantation without pay for a set period of time, usually between three and seven years. In return, the employer would cover the cost of the transatlantic journey, as well as food and board for the period of employment. When the contract finished, the former servants were provided with land, goods or money to build a new life in the New World.[34]

On the face of it, it made perfect sense for Barbadian landowners to use indentured laborers from home. This was not just because, as Adam Smith noted, free workers were easier to control and were therefore cheaper in the end. It also helped that back home the Agricultural Revolution had created plenty of underemployed landless laborers who were looking for new opportunities, and it wouldn't be until the nineteenth century that the Industrial Revolution provided vast numbers of new jobs for them. In the aftermath of the English Civil War, plantation owners didn't even have to look that far afield to find workers. Oliver Cromwell shipped several thousand political opponents, many of whom were Irish, to the Caribbean.[35] The term "barbadoesed"—to be exiled to Barbados—was in common use in the middle of the seventeenth century. With no way of making a living in this strange land, many exiles had little choice but to enter indentured servitude.

Ten years after the colony of Barbados was first settled, there were about 2,000 white indentured laborers compared to 200 enslaved Africans.[36] The former were disparagingly referred to as "buckra" by the latter—supposedly because they had to sit in the "back row" of the church.[37] These impoverished white settlers struggled to survive in tropical America. Yellow fever would have had a far more devastating impact on plantation laborers than on those who worked in other roles, because toiling in the fields brought them into frequent contact with disease-bearing mosquitoes—hence the lyrics of a song sung by enslaved Africans on Caribbean plantations: "New-come buckra, He get sik, He tak fever, He be die, He be die."[38] Yellow fever killed about 6,000 people, half of the white population of the island, in the mid-seventeenth century.[39] Faced with the loss of so many workers, English plantation owners started to copy the model pioneered by the Spanish and use slave labor from Africa. By the 1680s, enslaved Africans had all but displaced European indentured laborers in the Caribbean.[40]

The climate and soil were so advantageous to sugar producers in the American tropics that by the end of the seventeenth century the Caribbean supplied the vast majority of sugar to the European market. Regardless of whether a colony was Spanish, Portuguese, English, French or Dutch, the setup on the cane plantations was similar. Slave labor from tropical West Africa toiled on European-owned plantations to produce sugar for export. As production boomed, prices fell. What was once a rare luxury became an everyday household item used to sweeten tea, coffee, chocolate and rum punch, among other things. Between the beginning and the end of the eighteenth century, per capita annual consumption of sugar in Britain rose from 4 pounds to 18 pounds.[41] This massive expansion in Caribbean sugar production was only possible because of the huge numbers of enslaved African laborers who cultivated and processed cane on yellow-fever-infested plantations.

The transatlantic slave trade created suffering on an almost unimaginable scale. Between the start of the sixteenth and the middle of the nineteenth century, 12.5 million Africans were transported to the Americas—the largest involuntary migration in human history.[42] Almost 2 million perished, crammed below deck, shackled, as they crossed the Atlantic. Those who survived the journey were sold to the highest bidder and became their property. Parents were separated from their children and husbands from their wives. Once on the plantation, they were forced to carry out back-breaking labor harvesting and processing sugar and other crops, in constant fear of violence at the hands of their masters. Women were subject to widespread rape and sexual coercion. Perhaps the most notorious sexual predator was Thomas Thistlewood, a British plantation owner in Jamaica whose diary describes 3,852 acts of sexual intercourse with 138 enslaved women over thirty-seven years in the mid-1700s.[43] A recent study based on the DNA provided to the biotech company 23andme by 50,000 people demonstrates that he was far from the exception.[44] Almost twice as many males were transported across the Atlantic as females, and yet African women provided twice as much DNA to the modern-day population of former British colonies in the Caribbean.

There was nothing new about degrading stereotypes of slaves, but in the New World people of African heritage were for the first time exclusively associated with servitude.[45] It is the specifically racial nature of modern American slavery that distinguishes it from pre-modern forms of forced labor. But once Black Africans had become inextricably linked with slavery in the European imagination, modern ideas about race were developed in order to justify this iniquitous situation.

The massive expansion in the transatlantic slave trade and American slavery in the seventeenth and eighteenth centuries coincided with a period of great intellectual energy in Europe, the Age of Enlightenment. One of its major preoccupations was ordering the natural world into various categories. This included humans, who were classified into different races, each with their own supposed physical, intellectual and moral characteristics. The pseudoscientific, racist taxonomy of humans had a clear hierarchy, with the white Europeans who came up with the schema placed at the top. Immanuel Kant, for example, wrote that the "race of the whites contains all talents and motives in itself." Black Africans, in contrast, "can be educated, but only to the education of servants" or, in other words, "they can be trained." Native

Americans were, according to Kant, "uneducable" and "lazy," which might have served to soften European guilt for colonizing their continent and literally decimating them. Curtin points out that immunity to infectious diseases was a major factor in these stereotypes. The idea that Black people are well suited to a life of hard labor was influenced by African immigrants' apparently unique ability to survive on the plantations in tropical regions of the Americas. In contrast, Native Americans were seen as a "weak race" because they often died after their first encounters with "white people."[46]

Freedom and Revolution

In August 2019 the *New York Times* launched its *1619 Project,* with the aim of "placing the consequences of slavery and the contributions of Black Americans at the very center of the United States' national narrative." The inaugural magazine issue, which has been turned into a bestselling book, contained an array of articles that emphasized the profound influence that racialized slavery has had on almost every aspect of contemporary American society, from traffic jams to health care. The project's title and the date of the publication referred to the arrival of the first trafficked Africans in Britain's North American colonies exactly 400 years earlier; the twenty-odd men and women had been transported across the Atlantic by Portuguese slave traders, but were then seized off the coast of Mexico by English pirates and brought to Point Comfort in Virginia. The fact that Africans have been present on the continent since 1619 is remarkable: even the Pilgrim Fathers—whose story plays such a central role in American mythology—didn't get there until the following year.

The year 1619 did not mark the moment when North America became a slave society, however. As in Barbados, indentured servants were the preferred source of laborer in England's North American colonies at first. These workers comprised two-thirds of the 250,000 Europeans who arrived in the New World in the 1600s.[47] The number of Black people arriving was tiny in comparison: there were fewer than 7,000 across all the colonies in 1680, accounting for less than 5 percent of the population.[48] And they were treated like indentured servants rather than slaves; "set to work alongside a melange of English and Irish servants, little but skin color distinguished them."[49] Many gained their freedom after working for their masters for a period of time; some of them even managed to amass large landholdings and purchased their own trafficked Africans to work on them.

The first record of what can be recognized as racialized slavery doesn't appear until 1640, when three indentured laborers from Virginia—two white and one Black—ran away from their place of work. After they were captured, the colony's highest court sentenced the two Europeans to four additional years of servitude. In contrast, the unfortunate African American—whose name was John Punch— was condemned to "serve his said master or his assigns for the time of his natural Life here or elsewhere." Still, at the time, John Punch was very much an exception to the rule.[50]

It wasn't until the end of the seventeenth century that the number of African Americans in North America took off—in both absolute and relative terms. From under 7,000 in 1680 (5 percent of the population), their number increased to almost 17,000 in 1690 (8 percent), 28,000 in 1700 (13 percent), and then kept on growing.[51] By 1750, there were al- most a quarter of a million Black people living in the North American colonies, roughly 20 percent of the population. When we look at colony-level statistics, it is clear that the proportion of African Ameri- cans barely changed in the northern colonies; the increase in numbers is almost totally accounted for by the southern colonies. By 1700, Afri- can Americans represented 43 percent of the population in South Car- olina and 28 percent in Virginia, for example. Fifty years later, the numbers were 61 percent and 44 percent respectively.

As their numbers increased, the status of African Americans began to change for the worse. Beginning in the last decade of the seven- teenth century, new legislation transformed African Americans from servants into slaves.[52] In 1696, South Carolina was the first colony to pass a so-called slave code, a set of laws that governed slavery and de- fined enslaved African Americans as the personal property of their owners. This legislation borrowed heavily from Barbados' 1688 legisla- tion. Other states followed, and by the time the Revolutionary War began slavery was legal throughout the Thirteen Colonies. Then, in the late eighteenth century, the northern states began to repeal their slave codes. In 1780, Pennsylvania passed a gradual emancipation law and Massachusetts ended slavery three years later.[53] By the early 1800s, all the northern states had passed legislation that abolished slavery. The southern states, of course, remained strong defenders of slavery until they lost the Civil War, at which point they reluctantly and halfheartedly freed their African American slave laborers.

How can we explain the emergence of slavery in the south from the end of the seventeenth century but not in the northern colonies? The most common answer to this question is that it was incredibly labor-intensive to cultivate the type of crops grown on plantations that were suited to the climate and soil. According to this argument, tobacco, sugarcane, rice, and later cotton cultivation generated so much demand for labor in southern colonies that the only way to satisfy it was with trafficked Africans. But this argument doesn't really fit the evidence. Farmers and entrepreneurs in the northern colonies were also in need of workers, but they continued to use free and indentured labor from Europe—just as Adam Smith would have expected.[54]

In fact, the single biggest factor behind the sudden and marked increase in enslaved African Americans between 1680 and 1750 in the southern colonies—but not the northern ones—was infectious diseases. Unlike the Caribbean, where yellow fever was the major hazard, in the North American colonies it was malaria that played a decisive role. There was no malaria in the region before the European colonists arrived. The deadliest strain—*Plasmodium falciparum*—came from West Africa, possibly via the Caribbean. We know that falciparum malaria traveled in the bodies of infected people because its vector, the *Anopheles gambiae* mosquito, didn't make it across the Atlantic.[55] On the American mainland falciparum was transmitted by *Anopheles quadrimaculatus*, a species of mosquito common in low-lying parts of the east coast. It is not as effective at spreading the plasmodium as its West African "cousins," but it is better than Caribbean species because of its preference for human blood.[56] So malaria wasn't as devastating as in West Africa, but it was far more consequential than in the Caribbean.

Falciparum malaria first appeared in Virginia and South Carolina in the mid-1680s—that is, just before African American slavery began to catch on in the North American colonies.[57] The timing is not an accident. As with so many other disease outbreaks we've encountered in this book, it coincided with a period of climate disruption. In this case, El Niño events were much more frequent in the 1680s than in the preceding two decades, which may have aided the spread of malaria by creating the stagnant pools of water in which *Anopheles* mosquitoes need to breed.[58] The climate influenced the distribution of malaria in North America in another important way: as *Plasmodium falciparum* requires long stretches of relatively warm temperature in order to reproduce, it could survive in the southern colonies but not in the northern ones. In fact, the geographical boundary between areas where the parasite could and couldn't reproduce falls more or less exactly on the Mason-Dixon Line that divided Maryland from Pennsylvania and Delaware.[59]

In the south, agricultural workers who hadn't developed immunity to falciparum malaria were likely to get very sick. As a result, European indentured laborers were no longer wanted, and nor did they want to settle there.[60] From an amoral economic perspective, West African labor suddenly became a much more appealing proposition for plantation owners. The Italian economist Elena Esposito estimates that the arrival of falciparum malaria in the 1680s explains the rapid rise in numbers of African Americans in the southern colonies from that time—a conclusion that holds even when other possible explanations for the expansion of slavery are taken into account, such as the suitability of a county's soil for crops like tobacco and cotton.[61] In fact, malaria had the biggest impact on the expansion of slavery in counties where labor-intensive crops were grown, presumably because the economic benefit of healthy workers was greatest there.

Not only were plantation owners aware that people who were trafficked from West Africa were far less susceptible to malaria than those who came of their own volition from western Europe. According to Esposito they also had an understanding that people who grew up in certain parts of Africa were less susceptible to malaria than others. Posters advertising slaves for sale were surprisingly specific about where in Africa the people came from: they mention places such as Sierra Leone, or the Windward and Rice Coast. Esposito's analysis of a database of 3,000 Africans sold in the slave markets of Louisiana between 1719 and 1820 shows that those who came from the most malaria-ridden regions of West Africa—who therefore had the highest level of immunity—commanded significantly higher prices than those who did not.[62]

The situation in Georgia was peculiar, but it underscores the crucial role that malaria played in the spread of slavery. When the colony was established in the 1730s, its trustees decided to build a society of small-scale farmers from Britain. African American slaves were initially banned from the province—a decision that was driven by military concerns. The leaders were worried about the threat posed by the Spanish in neighboring Florida; they reasoned that the best way to defend Georgia was with an army of British settler colonialists who would fight tooth and nail to defend their land, rather than a few plantation owners and lots of enslaved Africans who had no incentive to maintain the status quo. This might have made sense from a military perspective, but within a handful of years the strategy proved economically unviable because of the impact malaria had on the new arrivals.

In 1740, James Habersham, who arrived in Georgia as a missionary but became a merchant and politician, complained about the scarcity of workers: "I don't know where I could purchase, or hire, at any reasonable rate, one servant." Contemporary Georgians were acutely aware that the labor shortage was a result of the Europeans' susceptibility to malaria. One noted that Europeans "succumb to Distempers which render them useless for almost one half of the Year," while another complained that because of their great susceptibility to malaria, "a white servant cost three times what he could produce." With the exclusion of African Americans posing an existential threat to the nascent colony, Georgia overturned its ban on racialized slavery in 1751 and four years later adopted a slave code that was very similar to neighboring South Carolina's. By 1760, African Americans accounted for 37 percent of the population.[63]

Although the number of enslaved African Americans in the southern colonies was rapidly increasing, white European settlers were still a significant proportion of the population. They put up with the initial, debilitating bouts of fever in order to take advantage of all sorts of relatively lucrative, high-status positions in the slave economy. Those Europeans who didn't die developed immunity to falciparum malaria, as did their surviving children. At this point the descendants of settler colonies were capable of working on the land without getting gravely ill, but the die was already cast: there was an entire ideology in place to justify a racialized class system in which it was seen as natural that African Americans toiled on plantations while the white population raked in the profits.

The fact that the white southern population eventually acquired resistance to malaria proved important in the founding of the new nation. When the Continental Congress voted to adopt the Declaration of Independence in the summer of 1776, it was by no means a certainty that the rebels would be able win the war. The British sent a large naval fleet and 34,000 soldiers to North America in order to crush the uprising. But after three years of fighting, the Revolutionary War had reached a stalemate. The British planned to break the deadlock with their so-called Southern Strategy. Up to this point, the conflict had been fought mainly in the north—particularly in New England, where support for the rebels was strongest. The British sent 9,000 troops to the south, where they believed the population was loyal to the king and would rally to support the imperial army. Although mass support didn't materialize, General Charles Cornwallis's army was a superior fighting force and won the majority of its battles against the colonies. But the Southern Strategy fell apart during malaria season.

Although many of the British soldiers had been in North America for a year or two, they were stationed in New York and New England and had not developed resistance to falciparum malaria. During the late summer and autumn of 1780, a large number of Cornwallis' troops fell sick with malaria. They recovered in the winter and then headed for the uplands of Virginia in the spring of 1781; the general hoped this move would "preserve the troops from the fatal sickness, which so nearly ruined the Army last autumn." But then Cornwallis was ordered by his superiors in New York to march to what he described as a "sickly defensive post" in the Tidewater, a low-lying coastal plain. Having endured one malaria season at most since their arrival in North America, the British soldiers' immune systems were ill prepared for what lay ahead compared to members of the Continental Army and militiamen, many of whom had spent their whole lives in the south.

In early August, the British Army set up camp in Yorktown. In late

September they were surrounded by the enemy, which included not just American forces but also newly arrived French soldiers who had come to help their fellow revolutionaries. Cornwallis surrendered twenty-one days after the siege began. He had no choice: over half of the soldiers under his command were unable to fight due to falciparum malaria. The newly arrived French soldiers were also susceptible to malaria, but because it takes about a month from being bitten by an infected mosquito to the onset of symptoms, they didn't fall ill until after the British had given up.[64] Seven thousand British troops were captured at Yorktown, a quarter of their forces in North America. This changed the trajectory of the war.

In 1781 the revolutionaries were really struggling. The Congress was bankrupt and the Continental Army had mutinied twice earlier in the year. But with war raging back in Europe and across much of the empire, defeat at Yorktown demonstrated to the British that there was little chance of regaining its American colonies. It marked the end of major combat operations in the Revolutionary War and the beginning of negotiations between the United States and Great Britain, culminating in the British agreeing to recognize U.S. independence at the Treaty of Paris in 1783. Although John McNeill is careful not to completely ignore the role of Great Men like George Washington, he drolly suggests that the female *Anopheles quadrimaculatus* mosquitoes should be considered one of the "founding mothers of the United States." As he points out, malaria killed eight times more British troops than American guns.

A couple of decades later in the Caribbean, mosquitoes—in this case *Aedes aegypti*—once again came to the assistance of a colony that was fighting to win independence from another European Great Power.

Black Jacobins and Yellow Fever

François Makandal was born into a well-to-do Muslim family in West Africa in the first half of the eighteenth century.[65] At the age of twelve he was captured and transported across the Atlantic to Saint-Domingue, the French colony that covered the western third of Hispaniola. Contemporaneous accounts of Makandal's life are scant and contradictory, but we know for sure that he worked on a sugar plantation and lost his right arm in an industrial accident while grinding cane at night.[66] After this he fled to the mountainous interior, where he became the charismatic leader of the island's fugitive former slaves—the so-called Maroons. Some sources suggest that he was an oungan, or Vodou priest. According to C.L.R. James, the Trinidadian historian and author of *The Black Jacobins* (1938), Makandal claimed to be able to predict the future and persuaded his fiercely loyal followers that he was immortal. For many years he led a campaign to destroy the colony's French community by poisoning their water supplies. In 1758, the French apprehended him and then burned him at the stake in front of a large crowd in Cap-Français, the capital. His followers were convinced that he escaped death by metamorphosing into a mosquito and flying away.[67] If Makandal did indeed transform into this insect it was a prescient choice, because a generation later the humble *Aedes aegypti* would play a critical role in the Haitian Revolution, the only time in history when enslaved Africans succeeded in overthrowing their European oppressors.

Today, Haiti, as it is now known, is the poorest country in the western hemisphere. But in 1789 Saint-Domingue was one of the most productive and profitable territories anywhere in the world. Despite being about the same size as Massachusetts, it produced two-fifths of the world's sugar and over half its coffee.[68] Exports had doubled between 1780 and 1789 as a result of booming demand in Europe, generating enormous wealth for French plantation owners, merchants and the state.[69] But Saint-Domingue's productivity depended on the forced labor of almost half a million enslaved people of African descent. Together with the 50,000 Maroons, who—like Makandal—had fled slavery and eked out a living in the mountains, Black Africans constituted almost 90 percent of the population, with the rest rich and poor whites, along with a smaller population of free mulattoes. Saint-Domingue had the largest enslaved population in the Caribbean, almost twice that of Jamaica, the next biggest. While there were 700,000 enslaved African Americans in the United States at the time, they only accounted for about a quarter of the total population.[70]

C.L.R. James describes how plantation owners and their agents "hated the life and sought only to make enough money to retire to France or at least spend a few months in Paris."[71] One of the main reasons why the French were so keen to get out of the colony was infectious diseases, and in particular yellow fever. The threat of dying was not high enough to discourage impoverished aristocrats from making a quick *livre*, but it wasn't low enough for them to bring their families over and settle down forever. As a result, plantations were run to maximize short-term profit. Nowhere was this more apparent than in the treatment of enslaved Africans. More than half of all enslaved Africans died within five years of arriving in Saint-Domingue—not from yellow fever but from overwork, malnutrition and crowded, unsanitary conditions which made them susceptible to dysentery, typhoid and tetanus.[72] In an effort to stem the tide of deaths—and presumably increase slaves' productivity—the Colonial Ministry in Paris issued a series of decrees in the mid-1780s calling upon plantation owners and their agents to give enslaved laborers a day off per week, provide enough food so they wouldn't starve, and refrain from murdering them. The French population in Saint-Domingue vehemently opposed these decrees and the court in Cap-Français refused to recognize them.

There was a simple economic reason for the brutal treatment of enslaved Africans: they were cheap to replace—so cheap, in fact, that it was more cost-effective to buy new laborers every few years than to provide them with decent living standards and encourage them to have children. The numbers of enslaved Africans being imported into Saint-Domingue increased markedly in the second half of the eighteenth century, from 10,000 a year in the mid-1760s to 15,000 by the early 1770s, and 40,000 on the eve of the French Revolution.[73] The short-term economic calculations of plantation owners overlooked the fact that this approach destabilized Saint-Domingue society because it meant the majority of enslaved workers had been born in Africa: they remembered life before servitude, longed to be free again, and recognized that if they didn't rise up they would most likely be dead within a few years.[74]

In the 1780s, perceptive French visitors realized how dangerous the situation had become, with one likening Saint-Domingue to Mount Vesuvius. The French Revolution further unsettled Saint-Domingue. The political turmoil set the so-called *grands blancs*—the royalist plantation owners and their allies—against the *petits blancs*—the poor French who supported the revolution. And it sowed resentment among the mulatto and Black population when it became clear that, as in the United States, the revolutionary ideals of *liberté*, *égalité* and *fraternité* did not apply to them. While the revolution quickly swept away the remnants of feudalism in France, the white supremacist slave society remained unchanged in the Caribbean colonies. That is, until the Black population of Saint-Domingue took matters into their own hands.

In 1791, enslaved laborers attacked their French masters with machetes, burned the plantations and smashed sugar-processing machinery. Massively outnumbered, the colonialists fled. They begged the National Assembly in Paris to send troops to crush the rebels and restore slavery. But the revolutionary government, increasingly influenced by the radical factions, declined to intervene. Instead they ratified what had already been achieved in practice: slavery was abolished in Saint-Domingue in 1793. The rebel army joined their former enemy, the French state, and their leader, François-Dominique Toussaint Louverture, became the colony's lieutenant-governor and commander-in-chief.

The British aimed to take advantage of the situation and invaded Saint-Domingue in 1793. They were welcomed by the French plantation owners, who hoped that they would help restore the old order. For five years, the British occupied the southern and western parts of Saint-Domingue. In that time, 25,000 British soldiers fought in the colony. But with 60 percent of these forces dying within a few months of arriving, most from yellow fever, they failed to make much progress against the rebels.[75] In 1798 the British Army cut its not insignificant losses and returned to Europe.

Toward the end of 1799, Napoleon seized power in a coup. He had built his reputation over the previous decade as a brilliant military commander who successfully defended the revolution from internal and external threats. The First Consul longed to reassert French control over Saint-Domingue, which although still technically part of France had taken an increasingly independent path under Toussaint Louverture. Napoleon hoped to reimpose slavery and revive the slave plantations, which would then be distributed to his loyal supporters.

The reconquest of Saint-Domingue was also part of a grand strategy: to use the colony as a base from which to expand the French Empire into North America. France nominally owned the vast but sparsely popu-lated territory of Louisiana, which extended from the Gulf of Mexico to the Canadian border, and from the Mississippi to the Rockies. But in reality French control didn't go far beyond Nouvelle Orleans, which at the time had a population of about 8,000. Napoleon wanted to de-velop the region to grow grain to feed the population of Saint-Domingue, but also to get one over on his archenemy, Britain, which had lost most of its colonies in North America two decades earlier.

When it became known that France was planning to invade Saint-Domingue, the Ministry of War in Paris was inundated with men want-ing to take part. Like Napoleon, they assumed that victory would be a foregone conclusion, providing opportunities to accumulate great wealth. In December 1801, an expeditionary force of 30,000 soldiers set sail for the Caribbean under the command of Charles Leclerc, Napo-leon's brother-in-law.[76] Napoleon and Leclerc were aware that their soldiers would suffer greatly from yellow fever in Saint-Domingue—even though they thought it was "miasma" rather than a mosquito-borne virus that posed the threat. The expedition left in winter so that the French army would have several months to reconquer the colony and restore slavery before the rainy season arrived and the *Aedes ae-gypti* population exploded. The French commanders were so confident that they could achieve a swift victory that they didn't plan for a pro-longed campaign that stretched into the summer. This hubris would prove very costly.

The French had an early success in May 1802, when they captured Toussaint Louverture during what was meant to be a parley between him and a French general. The rebel leader was transported to France and imprisoned in a castle in the Jura Mountains, where he died the following year. But apart from this one ignominious episode, French efforts to reconquer Saint-Domingue were a disaster. After a decade of conflict, the rebel army was a disciplined, well-armed fighting force led by brilliant military commanders—especially Jean-Jacques Dessalines, who assumed leadership after Toussaint Louverture was captured. *Aedes aegypti* was a crucial weapon in their arsenal. The rebels knew from experience that newly arrived Europeans died in droves every summer during the rainy season, when mosquitoes thrived, and they planned to fully utilize the advantage that their immunity to yellow fever offered them. As Dessalines prepared to attack the French for the first time in March 1802, he reminded his troops: "The whites from France cannot hold out against us here in Saint-Domingue. They will fight well at first, but soon they will fall sick and die like flies."[77]

The insurgents did everything they could to avoid the kind of conventional pitched battle that the French were expecting. They used the rugged terrain to their advantage, launching surprise attacks and then disappearing into the mountainous interior. This not only negated any tactical or technological superiority the colonial army had; it also bought the rebels time until the yellow fever season arrived.[78] It proved to be a wildly effective strategy. When the rains came, the French fell sick in terrifying numbers. In a letter to Napoleon written in summer 1802, Leclerc lamented: "The colony is lost . . . What general could calculate on a mortality of four-fifths of his army and the uselessness of the remainder?"[79] Leclerc himself died from yellow fever in November. Twelve thousand reinforcements arrived from France early the following year, but they suffered the same fate. According to John McNeill, a total of 65,000 French troops were sent to reconquer Saint-Domingue. Over 50,000 died, the vast majority from yellow fever. The rebels were, of course, barely affected by the disease. It was as if Makandal really did live on as a mosquito and had returned to finally fulfill his plan to poison the French.

In the summer of 1803, war broke out again in Europe between Napoleon and his client states on the one hand, and the Third Coalition, which included the British, Habsburg and Romanov Empires, on the other. The Royal Navy renewed its blockade of French ports, making it impossible for Napoleon to send more reinforcements to the Caribbean. Bearing in mind the struggles that French troops had experienced in the past couple of years, this probably would have been futile anyway. Nevertheless, it marked the point at which Napoleon realized victory was unachievable. He is supposed to have muttered, "Damn sugar! Damn coffee! Damn colonies!"[80] If he had better understood the ultimate cause of his army's downfall, he would have perhaps cursed *Aedes aegypti* and RNA viruses too.

On New Year's Day 1804, the rebels proclaimed the birth of the new state of Haiti, a name derived from the Taíno term for the island of Hispaniola. The French defeat at the hands of the Haitian rebels—and the island's mosquitoes—helped to shape the modern world. Without a base in Saint-Domingue, Napoleon had little choice but to abandon his grand plan of building an empire in the western hemisphere. In December 1803, France sold its North American colonial possessions to the United States for $15 million. The Louisiana Purchase was a crucial milestone in the growth of the new country, doubling its size and expanding its boundaries from the Mississippi River all the way to the Rockies. Fifteen new states were eventually carved out of the land acquired from the French. The U.S.'s westward expansion was disastrous for Native Americans, but it went a long way to shaping the vast country that became a global superpower in the twentieth century.

Disunion

The Haitian Revolution sent shockwaves throughout the Atlantic world. The former slaves of Saint-Domingue had risen up and vanquished a European power with a population forty times its own. This demonstrated just how vulnerable white plantation owners in the Caribbean were: they were not just massively outnumbered by an angry enslaved population but also faced an invisible enemy that struck down forces sent from Europe to save them.

It isn't a coincidence that Britain banned the Atlantic slave trade in 1807, three years after Haiti declared independence. At the time, this move wasn't seen as a first step toward the abolition of slavery; rather it was an attempt to preserve the institution.[81] The British hoped that banning the trade in human beings would cut off the cheap supply of African labor and force plantation owners to take better care of "their property," therefore reducing the risk of rebellions spreading from Haiti to other colonies in the region. This strategy failed. There were uprisings in Barbados in 1816, Demerara (today's Guyana) in 1823, and then Jamaica in 1831–32. Even though the Caribbean slave plantations remained hugely profitable, and an increasingly important part of the British Empire's economy, the government in London decided to abolish slavery altogether in 1833.[82] The story of Haiti serves as a vital corrective to the self-congratulatory narrative that I was taught at school, which emphasized the role of William Wilberforce, the enlightened white savior. Enslaved Africans played a crucial role in winning their own freedom by making the risk of another Haiti too much for the British government to bear.[83]

In the U.S., Congress also abolished the importation of slaves in 1807—although it didn't take effect until the following year and smuggling continued. The Haitian Revolution increased North American plantation owners' fears that slavery could be abolished there too—as the French revolutionary government had done in 1793.[84] This anxiety influenced their excessive response to the threat posed by the anti-slavery movement in the north, which in turn contributed to the polarization that was already cleaving the country apart. The arrival of falciparum malaria in the late seventeenth century had set the colonies in the south and north on diverging trajectories, and by the beginning of the eighteenth century the differences between the two regions had become stark. Enslaved African labor was a crucial part of the southern plantation economy, whereas the north's growing manufacturing sector relied on free labor from Europe; this led to very different understandings of liberty.[85] In the northern states, freedom implied resistance to the southern slave states that had dominated national politics since the revolution. To white southerners, it meant the absence of federal interference in states' affairs, particularly when it came to slavery.

The fragile alliance between North and South was thrown into crisis in 1860 with the election of Abraham Lincoln, the standard-bearer of a newly formed Republican Party that strongly opposed the westward expansion of slavery. He became president without receiving a single Southern Electoral College vote. Elena Esposito's statistical analysis demonstrates how malaria played an important role in the polarization of American politics during this time. Support for what was then the pro-slavery Democratic Party in the 1860 presidential election was strongest in counties that had the highest rates of malaria—presumably because African American slave labor and the racist ideology that justified it were most strongly entrenched in these disease-riddled areas. Feeling that their way of life was under threat and with no way to address their concerns through the democratic process, the Southern states seceded.

For the North to win the Civil War, it had not just to defeat the Confederate armies in battle but force the South to remain part of the United States. This would likely involve controlling large areas of enemy territory and enforcing what we now refer to as "regime change" upon the slave states.[86] As a result, much of the war was fought in the part of the country where falciparum malaria was endemic. The Union Army was bigger and better supplied, but it struggled to win battles. The reasons for this include incompetent leadership, brave adversaries and logistical problems. Another important factor was that most of the Northern soldiers had not developed immunity to malaria, whereas most of the Southern soldiers had. According to one estimate, 40 percent of Union soldiers fell ill each year with the disease. The debilitating fevers were massively disruptive to the war effort and, if they didn't kill sufferers outright, made them susceptible to other infectious diseases such as dysentery and measles. Throughout the Civil War, twice as many Northern troops died from disease as were killed in battle by Confederate guns.[87]

Malaria didn't change the outcome of the Civil War: the North won despite the disproportionate toll that *Plasmodium falciparum* had on the Union Army. But it probably delayed victory by months or even years, which in turn had a momentous effect on the postwar settlement.[88] At the outset of the conflict in spring 1861, Lincoln was trying to maintain a fragile war coalition that included not only his fellow Republicans but also Northern Democrats and Unionists in border slave states that hadn't seceded. His objectives were therefore relatively modest: to keep the South in the union and restrict the expansion of slavery. He realized that promising to abolish slavery would have ripped this alliance apart. But by the summer of 1862, as the North's war effort continued to struggle, Lincoln was willing to consider more radical measures. He came round to the idea that abolishing slavery could break the deadlock. African American slave laborers were, after all, a crucial part of the Southern economy and also played a big role in providing logistical support to the Confederate Army. They were, according to Lincoln, "undeniably an element of strength to those who had their service, and we must decide whether that element should be with us or against us."[89] On 22 September he concluded that abolishing slavery had become "a military necessity, absolutely essential to the preservation of the Union." Then, 100 days later on New Year's Day 1863, the Emancipation Proclamation declared "that all persons held as slaves . . . are, and henceforward shall be free."

In 1865, soon after the North won the Civil War, the Thirteenth Amendment to the United States Constitution was ratified—and with that, almost nine decades after the Declaration of Independence proclaimed all men to be free and equal, slavery was outlawed. But the Northern victory in the Civil War didn't suddenly end white supremacy and Black subjugation. Many African Americans continued to work on their former plantations as indebted sharecroppers in slave-like conditions. Jim Crow laws maintained segregation and restricted Black voters. Almost fifty years ago, James Baldwin argued that little had changed in the preceding century: "for Black people in this country there is no legal code at all. We're still governed, if that is the word I want, by the slave code." The murder of George Floyd and the massive Black Lives Matter protests that broke out across the country in the summer of 2020 indicate that, more than a century and a half after the abolition of slavery, there remains a long way to go until African Americans have the same rights to life, liberty and the pursuit of happiness as their white compatriots.

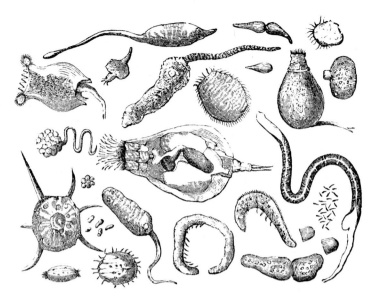

It wasn't until the late nineteenth century that scientists began to understand how "animalcules" cause disease. Over the past century, scientists have discovered that bacteria and viruses perform a wide range of roles that are vital to the functioning of our planet, our bodies, and even our minds.

Although Neanderthals were bigger and stronger than *Homo sapiens*, they weren't ape-like cavemen. In fact, the latest research suggests that Neanderthals were just as intelligent as our paleolithic ancestors. So why did they disappear about 40,000 years ago, while our own species survived?

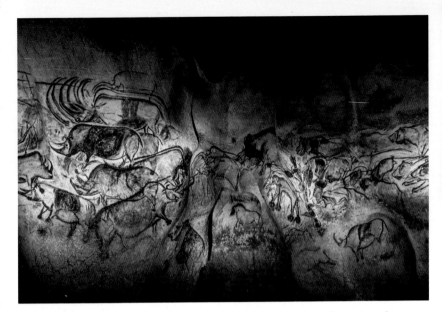

Scholars who argue that it was *Homo sapiens'* superior ingenuity and creativity that allowed them to vanquish Neanderthals often cite evidence such as the 30,000-year-old Chauvet cave paintings. But an increasing body of evidence points to the pathogens that our ancestors carried as they migrated out of Africa. These would have had little impact on *Homo sapiens* but were deadly to Neanderthals, as they hadn't developed immunity.

Nine-thousand-year-old "Cheddar Man" was one of the first permanent inhabitants of the British Isles. His hunter-gathering ancestors were almost completely wiped out about six thousand years ago by farmers who migrated from the Eastern Mediterranean region. This population replacement was most probably aided by infectious diseases that jumped from domesticated animals to humans after the adoption of agriculture.

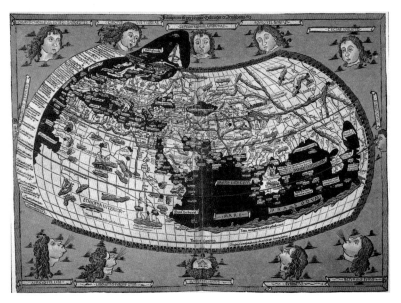

The Romans forged trade links from sub-Saharan Africa to the Far East, which made the empire vulnerable to infectious diseases from beyond their borders. From the second century CE onward, a series of devastating pandemics transformed the Mediterranean, resulting in the disappearance of paganism and the emergence of Christianity and then Islam as the dominant religions.

The Black Death killed over half of Europe's population. It had a more limited impact on the nomadic Ottomans who, over the next century, expanded from their base in western Anatolia, conquering the Balkans and threatening to push further westward. In 1498, when Albrecht Dürer created a print of the Four Horsemen of the Apocalypse, he styled War and Plague as Ottoman janissaries.

Within a few decades of discovering the New World, the Spanish managed to conquer the vast, wealthy, and technologically advanced Mexica and Inca Empires—including Tenochtitlan, the mighty Aztec capital shown here—with just a few hundred soldiers. These seemingly miraculous victories would have been unthinkable without the helping hand of Old World pathogens.

The fourteenth-century Catalan Atlas shows a river of gold in Africa. Beneath it, Mansa Musa sits on a gold throne with a gold crown on his head, offering a gold disc to a Berber on a camel. For five hundred years, Europeans coveted West Africa's riches, but malaria made the region an unconquerable "white man's grave."

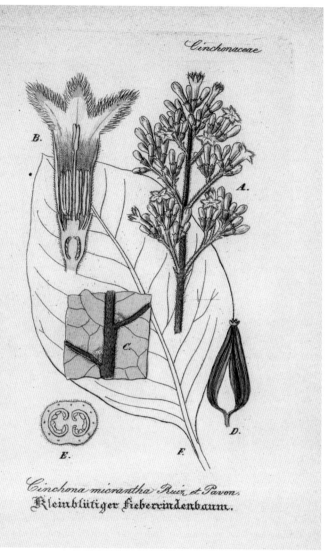

Cinchonaceae

Cinchona micrantha Ruiz. et Pavon.
Kleinblütiger Fieberrindenbaum.

In the late 1500s, Spanish Jesuits observed that indigenous people in the Andean foothills treated fever with ground bark from the cinchona tree. When European explorers realized that quinine—the active ingredient— prevented malaria in the middle of the nineteenth century, their risk of death fell by half and the Scramble for Africa became possible.

On New Year's Day, 1804, Haiti declared independence from Napoleon's France, the greatest military power of the time. In a decade-long insurgency, the former slaves led by Toussaint Louverture perfected guerrilla tactics that took advantage of their immunity to yellow fever, a mosquito-borne virus that killed a large proportion of European troops.

The Industrial Revolution—as depicted in this L. S. Lowry painting from 1928, *Coming Home from the Mill*—brought unprecedented economic growth to the UK, but for the masses who worked in factories, it was a disaster. In the first half of the nineteenth century, life expectancy was lower than at any time since the Black Death.

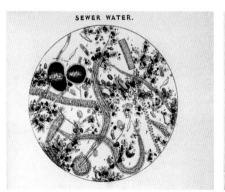
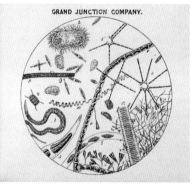

In the middle of the nineteenth century London had no way to deal with the tons of excrement its three million inhabitants produced each day. As Charles Dickens pointed out in *Little Dorrit*: "Through the heart of the town a deadly sewer ebbed and flowed, in the place of a fine fresh river."

Gustav Klimt's Faculty Paintings were commissioned in 1894 to celebrate the scientific achievements of the University of Vienna. His depiction of *Medicine* instead captures the failure of medicine to rid the world of disease and death. Hygeia, the Greek goddess of health, stands in the foreground, oblivious to the tangle of suffering bodies behind her. Klimt would go on to die of the Spanish flu at the age of fifty-five.

In 1958, in an effort to tackle rampant infectious diseases, the Chinese Communist Party urged citizens to "exterminate the four pests": rats, flies, mosquitoes, and sparrows. The campaign was a disaster, contributing to a famine that killed tens of millions of people. Despite this setback, life expectancy more than doubled in the thirty years after the end of the Chinese Civil War, due in large part to a precipitous decline in deaths from infectious diseases.

Chapter 7
Industrial Plagues

*A greater revolution for humanity than the theories of
Copernicus, Darwin, and Freud put together came with
the invention of the toilet.*

—GOCE SMILEVSKI

We Have Lift-off

The United Kingdom underwent a remarkable transformation during
what the British historian Eric Hobsbawm refers to as the long nineteenth century, which ran from the French Revolution in 1789 to the
beginning of the First World War 125 years later. At the start of this
period, the vast majority of the population lived in something approxi-
mating a John Constable landscape or a Thomas Hardy novel. Society
was predominantly rural, and most people worked in agriculture. Although wind and water power were used to mill grain, the main source
of power was humans and draft animals, just as it had been since the
adoption of farming. A significant proportion of the rural population
were employed in the textile industry, though this tended to be on an
ad hoc basis using handlooms in their own homes. Then, in the space
of a few decades, everything changed.

The invention and gradual improvement of the steam engine in the
eighteenth century allowed humans to utilize the power of fossil fuels
on an industrial scale for the first time in history. The changes began in
the textile sector, where steam-driven machinery enabled Britain to

produce enormous amounts of cloth. The quantity of raw cotton imported—mainly from the American South—increased from 11 million pounds in 1785 to 588 million pounds in 1850, and the output of textile mills rose from 40 million yards of cloth to over 2 billion in the same period.[1] The intensification and expansion of manufacturing permanently altered society. The new machinery needed to be housed in purpose-built factories located close to coal deposits and ports. As the handloom was rendered obsolete, millions of families were forced to move from the countryside to booming industrial towns to seek employment in the "dark satanic mills" of William Blake's poem "Jerusalem." By the early twentieth century, most people in the country inhabited a world that looked much more like a L. S. Lowry painting or Charles Dickens novel than Constable or Hardy's bucolic depiction of England. The new urban working classes lived in large, crowded cities and worked in vast factories where coal-fired machinery churned out acrid smoke and goods to be transported across the world by steam-powered trains and ships.

For many Britons, the fact that the Industrial Revolution occurred first in their country is a source of national pride; they see industrialization as the natural consequence of their innate superiority, specifically their pre-eminence in science and engineering. Yet this jingoistic explanation doesn't make sense, because the technical knowledge that made innovations in the British textile sector possible existed throughout Europe, and had done so for several generations.[2] Why, then, was the United Kingdom the first country in the world to go through the process of industrialization? It certainly helped that Britain had large and easily accessible coal deposits that were already being used for domestic fuel, as Britons had cut down most of their woods and forests over the previous centuries to make way for agricultural land and to use in shipbuilding. It was also critical that wages in Britain were markedly higher than in the rest of Europe—as a result of the post–Black Death transition from feudalism to agricultural capitalism. Consequently, investment in steam-driven machinery to reduce reliance on the workforce made much more economic sense in Britain than in parts of the continent where coal was scarce and expensive, and labor plentiful and cheap.

The legacy of previous infectious disease outbreaks catalyzed the

Industrial Revolution in a number of other ways too. Most of the raw cotton used to produce textiles in the factories of northern England was cultivated in the American South by malaria-resistant enslaved Africans. And sugar, which provided the growing urban working classes in the UK with a cheap source of calories in the form of jams, cakes and biscuits, was produced by enslaved Africans in the Caribbean.[3] Furthermore, a large proportion of the vast profits from colonialism and slavery were reinvested in Britain. In this way, the suffering of enslaved Africans and colonized peoples paid for the construction of vital infrastructure such as the roads, canals, docks and railways that made the Industrial Revolution possible.[4]

The repatriation of colonial loot did not automatically lead to economic growth and social transformation, however. You will recall that when Spain was inundated with American gold and silver in the sixteenth and seventeenth centuries, it did not kick-start a process of self-sustaining economic growth. Rather, it led to untrammelled inflation and a series of ill-advised wars, because Spain's feudal economy was not capable of using the newfound wealth productively. It was only because Britain was going through the transition from feudalism to capitalism that it was able to invest the proceeds of colonialism in profit-generating enterprises that were responsible for the economic and social transformation of the long nineteenth century. The British economic miracle didn't occur simply because of its industrialists' entrepreneurial spirit. The state intervened to make sure that the odds were stacked in the favor of the domestic economy: for example, British companies could export cotton cloth with almost no tariffs, but their producers were charged duties of up to 85 percent to import textiles into the UK.[5]

As we saw earlier, capitalism didn't appear suddenly in the industrializing towns and cities of northern England in the eighteenth and nineteenth centuries. It emerged gradually in the rural shires over several hundred years as a result of the struggle between lords and peasants following the Black Death. The feudal system tended toward economic and social stagnation; in contrast, the system that replaced it was dynamic because a new class of commercially minded tenant farmers applied the latest technology in order to maximize profits on their increasingly large holdings.

Agrarian capitalism aided the Industrial Revolution in several ways. The vast majority of the population became landless as entrepreneurial peasants crowded out their inefficient cousins, and the increasing use of new technology reduced demand for labor in the countryside. Agricultural productivity rose sharply. The growing surplus contributed to feeding families who had been forced to migrate to towns and cities in search of work. In the 1830s, British producers grew 98 percent of grain consumed in the UK, even though the population had tripled in size since the mid-eighteenth century.[6] So, although the sugar used to produce cakes and biscuits was imported from the Caribbean, the flour came from closer to home.

This new emphasis on continuous innovation, improving productivity, and profit maximization transformed agriculture. But when those principles were applied to manufacturing, the economy really took off. The self-interested greed of individual businessmen and the invisible hand of the market created a turbo-charged economic boom that changed the world beyond recognition. As John Maynard Keynes puts it:

> From the earliest times of which we have record—back say to two thousand years before Christ—down to the beginning of the eighteenth century, there was no very great change in the standard of life of the average man living in the civilized centers of the earth. Ups and downs certainly. Visitations of plague, famine, and war. Golden intervals. But no progressive, violent change.[7]

Then, everything changed. For most of the 1700s, the British economy grew by a little less than 1 percent per year.[8] This figure is low by modern standards, but even at this rate the economy doubled in size in less than seventy years. As industrialization kicked in over the last two decades of the eighteenth century, growth picked up. It reached 2.5 percent a year in the middle of the nineteenth century, before falling back to 2 percent. These figures are modest compared to the growth rates experienced by China over the past few decades. But in a world where economic growth had been close to zero since the adoption of agriculture, this was unprecedented. The British economic historian Simon Szreter suggests that the modern-day equivalent would be growth rates of between 15 percent and 20 percent a year over several decades—rates that even China hasn't come close to. As Hobsbawm points out, "for the first time in human history, the shackles were taken off the productive power of human societies, which henceforth became capable of the constant, rapid and up to the present limitless multiplication of men, goods and services." Writing in the middle of the nineteenth century, Karl Marx and Friedrich Engels were awestruck by the productive capacities of the Industrial Revolution that "had accomplished wonders far surpassing Egyptian pyramids, Roman aqueducts, and Gothic cathedrals."[9]

The population of England and Wales had been pretty constant at between 5 and 6 million between 1650 and 1750. Then it smashed through the Malthusian ceiling because of the dual impact of the Agricultural and Industrial Revolutions. The growth rate picked up in the second half of the eighteenth century. It doubled from about 9 million in 1801 to 18 million by mid-century, and had reached over 35 million by the outset of the First World War.[10] The landless, impoverished masses flooded from the countryside to the towns, attracted by wages that were consistently higher and in real terms tended to rise, albeit sporadically.[11] At the start of the nineteenth century, London—with a population of about a million—was the only city in the UK with more than 100,000 inhabitants, and two-thirds of the population lived in the countryside.[12] By 1871 the situation was vastly different: seventeen provincial cities had more than 100,000 people, Glasgow and Liverpool were home to half a million, and London had swollen to a metropolis of 3 million. Despite the growth in population, two-thirds of Britons now lived in urban areas.[13]

The Industrial Revolution led to vast increases in productivity, wealth creation, population growth and urbanization. It was critical in creating the world we live in today. Many assume that industrialization was also a boon to human health, and a quick glance at the data seems to support this notion. In 1700, average life expectancy at birth in England and Wales was about thirty-six years; it reached forty in the early nineteenth century, and by the start of the First World War was about fifty-five years.[14] Because the marked increases in wealth and health occurred at roughly the same time, it is widely believed that economic growth led automatically to improved human welfare. This is the crux of the theory that as countries get richer they pass through an "epide-miological transition" in which life expectancy improves as fewer people die young from infectious diseases, and more people are killed at an older age from chronic diseases such as cardiovascular disease and cancer.[15]

In fact, the reality is much more complex and troubling. Between the 1820s and the end of the 1860s—a time of unprecedented techno-logical development and wealth creation—average life expectancy in Britain remained stagnant at around forty-one years.[16] It was only in the last three decades of the nineteenth century that health began to improve. These national-level figures obscure a more complicated pic-ture at the local level, however. Life expectancy in rural areas tended to be higher than the national average. In rural Surrey, south of Lon-don, life expectancy was forty-five years in the middle of the nine-teenth century. And health improved slowly but steadily throughout the period. Remarkably, this was despite the great economic hardship that most people in the countryside were experiencing as technology reduced the demand for labor.[17] In London, life expectancy was thirty-seven. This figure was four years below the national average and it hid stark inequalities between the wealthy parts of the city in the west and the poor districts in the east.

The new provincial towns and cities really dragged down the na-tional life-expectancy figures. They were not only considerably lower than the figure for England and Wales, they also fell markedly in the second quarter of the nineteenth century.[18] The numbers are skewed by very high infant mortality rates, with one in five babies dying before their first birthday.[19] In the central areas of Manchester and Liverpool, you could expect to live for around twenty-five years—a shorter life-span than at any time since the Black Death.[20] The figures are even worse when we focus just on the poor. Life expectancy for factory la-borers was seventeen in Manchester and fifteen in Liverpool.[21] Death rates were so high among the urban working classes that the popula-tion was only able to sustain itself because of the continual inflow of people from the surrounding countryside, and increasingly from Ire-land. As northern towns and cities were the epicenter of the Industrial Revolution, this is clear evidence that economic growth and increasing real wages did not automatically lead to improvements in health via the

invisible hand of the market. Instead, the rapidly growing urban population in the late nineteenth century was experiencing what Simon
Szreter terms the "4 Ds": disruption, deprivation, disease and death.

Hell Upon Earth

In a comedy sketch performed by *Monty Python*,[22] four men dressed in
white dinner jackets sit around a table smoking cigars, drinking wine
and discussing their humble beginnings in broad Northern accents.
The scene begins with Ezekiel—played by John Cleese—exclaiming:
"Who'd have thought thirty years ago that we'd be sitting here drinking
Château de Chasselas." The characters then proceed to outdo each
other with increasingly absurd accounts of how miserable their child-
hoods were:

> HEZEKIAH: "Aye. In them days, we'd have been glad to have
> the price of a cup of tea."
> OBADIAH: "A cup of cold tea."
> EZEKIEL: "Without milk or sugar."
> JOSIAH: "Or tea!"
> HEZEKIAH: "In a filthy, cracked cup."
> EZEKIEL: "We never used to have a cup. We used to have to
> drink out of a rolled-up newspaper."

And so they continue with ever more outlandish claims about their
housing, working conditions and family life until Ezekiel delivers the
coup de grâce: "I had to get up in the morning at ten o'clock at night,
half an hour before I went to bed, drink a cup of sulphuric acid, work
twenty-nine hours a day down t'mill, and pay t'mill owner for permission to come to work, and when we got home, our Dad and our mother
would kill us, and dance about on our graves singing 'Hallelujah.'" To
this, Hezekiah replies: "But you try and tell the young people today
that and they won't believe you."

Unbelievable as it might seem, the conditions that the urban poor
had to endure during the Industrial Revolution weren't so far from the

experiences of Ezekiel and his buddies. The millions of destitute families that migrated from the countryside to the towns and cities in search of work found employment in the factories, but the days were long, tedious and dangerous. Even minors weren't spared. The content of the Factory Act of 1833 gives you a taste of the working conditions at the time. Most strikingly, it limited children between the ages of nine and twelve to forty-eight hours of work a week. Even these restrictions were contested by economic liberals, who viewed child labor laws as unjustified state intervention in the functioning of the free market.[23] To provide some relief from the misery of their situation people drank, and among the urban poor alcoholism was widespread. The quickest way to get out of Manchester was by the bottle, as a popular saying went. One consequence of what Hobsbawm calls "a pestilence of hard liquor" was widespread domestic abuse.[24]

In the *Monty Python* sketch, Obadiah, played by Graham Chapman, scoffs at Cleese when he says he "used to live in this tiny old house, with great big holes in the roof." "We used to live in one room, twenty-six of us, no furniture. Half the floor was missing; we were all huddled together in one corner for fear of falling!" Again, this was only a slight exaggeration. It was not uncommon for whole families to live in one small room of a poorly built tenement building without furniture because they'd been forced to pawn or sell their possessions in order to buy food. Perhaps the most shocking feature of urban workers' living conditions was the absence of sanitation. Britain's towns and cities had grown rapidly and haphazardly, and lacked basic infrastructure such as sewerage and safe drinking water. Human waste was thrown on to the unpaved streets, stored in cellars and piled up in overflowing cesspits. From there, it fed into the streams and rivers that were the main source of water. Engels, Marx's collaborator and patron, who lived in Manchester in the mid-nineteenth century, described the "filth, ruin, and uninhabitableness" as "Hell Upon Earth." Anyone who could afford it would live outside the slums, often to the west—and therefore upwind—of the industrial center. This pattern of urban segregation is still apparent in many European cities today, including London and Paris.

The crowded and unsanitary conditions in working-class urban districts created new habitats in which previously uncommon pathogens thrived. Infectious diseases weren't receding here. In fact, in the middle of the nineteenth century they accounted for about 40 percent of deaths in England and Wales, with the figures much higher in urban areas.[25] In London they were responsible for 55 percent of deaths, and in parts of Liverpool and Manchester the figure was about 60 percent. In *The Condition of the Working Class in England* (1845) Engels calculates that the risk of dying from infectious disease was four times higher in large industrial cities such as Manchester and Liverpool than in the surrounding countryside. One of the primary culprits was airborne tuberculosis, which is spread when a person coughs or sneezes and someone else inhales droplets that contain TB bacteria. Another was waterborne diarrheal diseases. Crowded and unsanitary living conditions aided the transmission of these maladies.

But according to British historian Richard Evans, cholera was the "classic epidemic disease of Europe in the age of industrialization."[26] Even though cholera didn't kill as many people in the 1800s as endemic ailments such as tuberculosis and waterborne diarrheal diseases, the speed and violence with which it struck made it as feared as plague had been in previous centuries.[27] *Vibrio cholerae* spreads via water contaminated by the feces of an infected person. When it reaches the gut, the immune system attacks it. But there's a twist: as the pathogens die, they release an incredibly powerful toxin that causes the plasma—the transparent liquid component of our blood—to drain into the intestines. From there, it is expelled from the body through explosive diarrhea and projectile vomiting. In severe cases, victims can lose a quarter of the body's fluid within a few hours. Severe dehydration makes sufferers appear shriveled. Ruptured capillaries turn the skin black and blue. Within a few days of the onset of symptoms, a little more than half of victims would have been dead. Cholera continued to terrify even after it had killed: in some cases, due to post-mortem muscle contractions, the limbs of corpses twitched violently after death, giving the impression that the carts carrying victims' bodies for burial were teeming with life.[28]

Cholera had been endemic in the Ganges Delta for many centuries. It first broke out of its original home in 1817, carried by East India Company troops as they tramped across the subcontinent; the Marquis of Hastings lost a third of his 10,000 men to cholera while fighting the Marathas.[29] As more people began to travel between India and the rest of the world on increasingly fast ships, cholera was transmitted beyond South Asia. *Vibrio cholerae* hitched a lift in the guts of travelers, and their soiled clothes and bed linen, where it could stay alive for weeks. Cholera first arrived in the UK in 1831, just as the Industrial Revolution was transforming Britain's economy and society. With their poor hygiene and unsanitary water supplies, the working-class districts of towns and cities provided a perfect environment for the bacteria to spread. As Evans points out, "these conditions might almost have been designed for it."[30] The middle and upper classes, who lived in more expansive, cleaner areas and often had the option to flee to their country residences when outbreaks occurred, were far less affected. The differential impact of cholera is apparent in statistics from London during the 1848–49 and 1854 outbreaks, when the inhabitants of working-class districts in the east died at up to twelve times the rate of residents in leafy Kensington or St. James's and Westminster.[31]

When cholera first appeared in Europe in the early 1830s, doctors had no idea what it was or how to treat it. They came up with all sorts of bizarre "cures," including pouring scalding water on the bellies of the sick and injecting turpentine and mutton stew into the intestines via the anus. The authorities responded with the same public health measures that had been developed to stop the spread of the plague: the military enforced quarantines and cordons sanitaires to limit the movement of travelers, and doctors compelled the sick to isolate in hospital. These measures would have had limited impact on outbreaks because infected feces could still flow into the waterways. They did, however, raise the suspicions of the local population. Wherever outbreaks occurred, doctors, soldiers and officials turned up in urban slums to restrict the movement of people and take away the sick, but these outsiders appeared to be unaffected by the gruesome disease. We now know that this is because cholera is transmitted by infected water, which the visitors would have tended not to drink. At a time when the fetid stink that lingered around crowded urban slums was widely believed to be responsible for infectious diseases, the fact that visitors who were also exposed to this miasma were largely unaffected was difficult to explain.

Many people looked at all these facts—the symptoms, the sudden appearance of outsiders, the disproportionate burden on the lower classes—and surmised that cholera wasn't a previously unknown disease at all, but a plot by the authorities to poison the urban poor.[32] This time Jews avoided the blame—even in eastern and central Europe where the feudal system persisted. Instead, popular suspicion focused on the authorities who led the public health response to the outbreak, as the power of the state had expanded enormously since the Black Death but had done little or nothing to improve most people's lives.

Throughout Europe, the spread of cholera was accompanied by civil unrest and riots. The army officers who enforced lockdowns were assaulted and sometimes killed in Germany and Russia. In Hungary, crowds attacked castles and massacred the nobility, whom they blamed for poisoning the population. In Britain, popular anger was directed at doctors as they took patients to the hospital for isolation and treatment. This was not only because physicians played a more prominent role in the public health response than in eastern and central Europe. By the time of the first cholera outbreak, distrust of doctors had reached fever pitch. In 1829, William Burke was convicted and hanged for murdering sixteen people and selling their bodies to the University of Edinburgh Medical School for dissection. His co-defendant, William Hare, turned state informant in return for immunity.

The case attracted substantial public interest, with 25,000 people turning out to watch Burke's execution. A small riot occurred at the public dissection of Burke's body at Edinburgh Medical School when the crowds of medical students massed outside realized there wasn't room for them. The murders raised public awareness that bodies were needed for medical research. As Evans points out, this "rekindled long-held popular resentments against the anatomists, and the cholera epidemic was widely held to be another example of the same business." So when the crowds attacked doctors as they tried to transport suspected cholera victims to hospitals for isolation, it was because they genuinely feared that patients were going to be killed and their bodies used for medical research.[33]

Governments across Europe responded to this violent opposition by abandoning public health interventions aimed at halting the spread of cholera.[34] Britain's laissez-faire approach to public health mirrored the economic policy of the time, and meant that the country was ill prepared when cholera struck again.

Shopkeepers of the World Unite

The sketch of the four nouveau riche Northerners reminiscing about their humble roots while sipping on their Château de Chasselas illustrates an important consequence of the Industrial Revolution: it provided opportunities for men such as Obadiah and his friends to rise from abject poverty to comfortable wealth within a generation. This disrupted long-established power structures. At the beginning of the nineteenth century, most of the population were excluded from taking part in political decisions at both the national and the local level. Britain was dominated by a few thousand families who owned most of the land and monopolized the important political offices. In many cases, these people were descended from the Normans who came over from France with William the Conqueror in 1066. Although Members of Parliament were elected, the system was full of idiosyncrasies. For example, Old Sarum was a tiny hamlet in the south of England with only three houses but it sent two MPs to Westminster, whereas London had just four and many of the northern industrial cities—including Manchester—had no representation at all.

While pre–Industrial Revolution British society was undemocratic, it wasn't stingy. In urban areas, the ruling oligopolies of wealthy landlords, merchants and professionals took proprietorial pride in what they saw as "their" towns and cities. They organized and funded a variety of initiatives that improved the urban environment—particularly the streets—including paving, lighting and regular cleaning. In the countryside, the paternalistic landowning class presided over a generous welfare system.[35] According to the Old Poor Law, anyone in need was entitled to receive relief from the parish where they were born—of which there were about 10,000 in England and Wales. It usually took the form of food or money handouts and was paid for by a progressive tax on the value of landholdings known as the "poor rate." This system had been formalized at the start of the seventeenth century and was a response to the breakdown in the feudal system and dissolution of the monasteries, which provided a safety net in the Middle Ages. It was not only popular among the recipients, who believed it was their birthright to receive help from more fortunate members of the community when times were hard. It was also supported by the landowning elite, who bore most of the cost and who saw it as a way of conserving the status quo amid growing calls for equality and the revolutionary chaos then engulfing France.[36] But as the commercialization and mechanization of agriculture reduced employment opportunities in the countryside, the Old Poor Law became increasingly expensive. Between the middle of the eighteenth century and the start of the nineteenth, national expenditure on poor relief rose tenfold.[37] As the population flooded from the countryside to the towns and cities, the welfare system—which was administered by rural parishes—struggled to cope.

The Industrial Revolution created enormous pressure for political reform. This didn't just come from businessmen such as Obadiah and his friends; they joined forces with the increasingly politicized urban working classes. By the early 1830s, the government could no longer resist demands to broaden participation in politics.[38] Some historians have argued that this was the only point in modern British history when revolution was a distinct possibility. The government responded by passing a series of reforms that broke the alliance between employers and their workers, enfranchising the former but keeping the latter out in the cold. First, the Great Reform Act of 1832 established new constituencies in growing industrial towns and gave the vote to any adult male who occupied premises on which the rent was more than £10 a year. This increased the electorate in national elections to about one in seven adult males.[39] Then, in 1835, the Municipal Corporation Act established representative local government voted for by a town's taxpayers.

This legislation ended the relatively homogenous, predominantly Anglican landowning elite's stranglehold on British politics. A share of power was handed over to the country's businessmen, many of whom were Nonconformists—that is, Protestants who rejected the authority of the Church of England, including Methodists, Unitarians and Quakers, who were noted for their commitment to temperance, hard work and frugality. The Old Testament names of Obadiah, Ezekiel, Josiah and Hezekiah in the *Monty Python* sketch are an allusion to the fact that many of the successful businessmen to emerge from the Industrial Revolution were from Nonconformist sects. Some of the new electorate were wealthy factory owners who employed large numbers of workers, but the majority were small-scale entrepreneurs who, although in a much better position than the urban working classes, were in a constant struggle to remain solvent and avoid falling back into the deprivation they had so recently escaped.[40] What Simon Szreter calls the newly enfranchised "shopocracy" was staunchly opposed to national taxes and local rates, particularly when the funds were used to support what they saw as the feckless poor. As the old political elite and the new heterogeneous electorate had very little in common, they found it difficult to agree on anything apart from the fact that they shouldn't spend each other's money. Consequently, for a generation or two after the reforms of the 1830s, the only electable governments were those that were committed to the laissez-faire ideology of minimal taxation and limited state intervention.

The New Poor Law, passed in 1834, rejected the generous, paternalistic approach to welfare taken by the landed elite, replacing it with a system that represented the values of the new voters. The legislation was drafted by Edwin Chadwick, a barrister, and the economist Nassau William Senior, neither of whom was sympathetic to the plight of the poor.* They believed that the old system of welfare handouts encouraged dependence and indolence, which in turn created more poverty. The stipulation that poor relief could only be accessed in one's native parish was seen as an unnecessary restriction on the free movement of labor. The New Poor Law aimed to distinguish the "deserving" poor—the sick and elderly—from what its authors saw as scroungers, by making welfare support so disagreeable for able-bodied people that they would ask for help only in the most desperate circumstances.

Chadwick and Senior certainly succeeded in designing a system that was very unpleasant for anyone who wanted to claim poor relief. To access support, families had to enter the workhouse. The fundamental principle of this dreaded institution was that life within it must be even worse than the worst existence one could have outside. This was an almost impossible feat in the first half of the nineteenth century, but its architects rose to the challenge. Parents were separated from each other and their children. Work was designed to be difficult and tedious, including breaking large stones into smaller pieces and

* During the Great Irish Famine of 1845, Senior remarked that it "would not kill more than one million people, and that would scarcely be enough to do any good."

crushing bones to make fertilizer. Food was in such short supply that in 1845 a government inquiry found occupants of the Andover workhouse fighting over the bones they should have been crushing in order to suck out the marrow. Charles Dickens, in *Oliver Twist*, suggested that the poor now had the option of starving slowly in the workhouse or quickly at home.

The problem with the New Poor Law wasn't simply that it was cruel. The emphasis on punishing the so-called undeserving poor overlooked the reality that people were often destitute because of factors beyond their control. In the mid-nineteenth century, the cyclical nature of the capitalist system resulted in regular economic downturns and massive, albeit temporary, layoffs that left enormous numbers of people without a means of earning money. For example, when demand for cloth slumped in 1842, two-thirds of textile workers in the town of Preston near Manchester were left without jobs.[41] The workhouses were, nevertheless, popular with taxpayers as expenditure on welfare payments to the sick, old and poor fell from 2 percent of national product—probably the highest figure in Europe—to 1 percent.[42] This was early-Victorian austerity or structural adjustment, albeit starting from a very low base.

While working on reforming the welfare system, Chadwick was shocked by the unsanitary environment in which the working classes lived and the impact that this had on their health. To be clear, his politics hadn't suddenly changed. He doesn't appear to have been concerned about the suffering of the urban proletariat, and he still supported the laissez-faire approach to regulating factories. He remained, for example, against controls on child labor and limiting the working day. Rather, Chadwick realized that the poor health of the working population undermined factories' productivity and created a drag on the economy.[43] After 1834, he became a leading light in what became known as the sanitary movement, arguing that the health of the urban poor could only be improved by cleaning up towns and cities and constructing sewerage and water infrastructure. This idea united people from across the political spectrum. Dickens, for example, who was a vehement critic of Chadwick's New Poor Law, was a prominent supporter of sanitary reform because he realized how important it was for ameliorating the wretched living conditions of the urban poor which he described so vividly in his novels. William Farr, who oversaw Britain's censuses and vital registration system at the General Register Office, was another influential advocate. From 1840 onward, he published regular lists of the districts in England and Wales with the highest death rates to shame and shock local governments into sanitary reform.

The sanitary movement was influenced by the "filth theory of disease," which was based on the idea that the foul stench of sewage and other waste was responsible for illness. Given that the poor areas of towns and cities were both the smelliest and most disease-ridden, it is not hard to understand why so many people found the filth theory believable.[44] In order to improve health, the sanitary movement argued that it was necessary to build an integrated water and sewerage system that would pipe clean water into homes and remove dirty water far beyond the city limits. Chadwick referred to creating an "arterial-venous" city.

The petit bourgeois electorate was at the height of its power in the mid-nineteenth century, and Chadwick failed to persuade politicians that such vast infrastructural projects were viable. In London, in the early 1840s, the authorities took a more piecemeal approach that involved getting rid of the cesspits and diverting human waste into the drains that had been built to carry rainwater to the Thames. This removed the stench of excrement from the local neighborhoods, but pumping several hundred tons of raw sewage directly into the river every day transformed it into what Benjamin Disraeli, the Tory leader in the Commons and Chancellor of the Exchequer, described as "a Stygian pool reeking with ineffable and unbearable horror." Dickens described the impact in *Little Dorrit* (1855–57): "Through the heart of the town a deadly sewer ebbed and flowed, in the place of a fine fresh river." To make matters much worse, the issue of water supply wasn't addressed. A patchwork of unregulated private companies continued to draw water from the polluted Thames. When cholera inevitably returned to London in 1848, it killed over 14,000 people—twice as many as in the first outbreak.[45]

The government eventually passed the UK's first Public Health Act in 1848. It was no coincidence that this happened just as the second great outbreak of cholera was devastating British cities. The panic shocked the state into action. As an article in *The Times* pointed out, cholera was "the best of all sanitary reformers."[46] Chadwick became one of three commissioners of the General Board of Health, which was charged with supervising local governments' construction of water and sewerage systems. The Act allowed municipal authorities to borrow from the central state at subsidized rates to fund the construction of water and sanitation infrastructure; this money would then be paid back over a long period of time by the local taxpayers.[47] But the petit bourgeois voters, whose main concern was to keep taxes low, were so appalled that the central government was pressuring municipal authorities to increase local rates that Chadwick was forced into retirement in 1854.

Many town and city councils did take advantage of the cheap loans to improve the water supply, but their efforts were not motivated by a desire to improve the health of the urban poor. Rather, because water was a useful input in manufacturing processes, such projects provided immediate benefits to business owners. In many cases, factories used half of the increased volume of water that was piped into towns.[48] The municipal authorities were much less willing to borrow money to construct sewerage systems. In fact, two decades after the passage of the 1848 Public Health Act not one provincial town or city had built the kind of integrated water and sewerage networks that Chadwick advocated.[49]

The early Victorians had the technology and engineering expertise to build integrated water and sewage systems. During the first half of the nineteenth century, there was a boom in the number of private companies that supplied water to the factories and houses that could afford the cost, and the wealthy installed flush toilets in their homes in large numbers. But without city- or town-wide solutions, these disjointed private initiatives tended to have a negative impact on public health, as the waste often emptied into streams and rivers that were also sources of drinking water.[50]

While the construction of water and sewerage infrastructure would have been expensive, the cost was not beyond the means of mid-nineteenth century Britain. The middle and upper classes found enormous sums of money to invest—or gamble—on the shares of companies that built the country's steam train network during the "railway manias" of the 1830s and 1840s. Local government also played a role. As steam trains were considered crucial for towns' prosperity and prestige, municipal politicians fell over themselves to help railway companies. Entire city centers were rebuilt to accommodate tracks, stations and yards.

It was not lack of technology or money that stopped society from dealing with the deadly unsanitary conditions in working-class neighborhoods of provincial towns and cities; rather, it was the absence of political will. Providing sanitation and clean water to the masses is an enormously expensive undertaking, but one that delivers huge long-term economic and non-economic benefits. Such projects are not viable for private companies motivated by short-term returns on investment, so the problem of sanitation can't be solved by the invisible hand of the market. Instead, it is imperative that the state steps in, at the very least to coordinate. Unfortunately, local and national governments in the mid-nineteenth century were beholden to the parochial interests of small business owners who voted for politicians promising to keep taxes low, and in spite of recurrent cholera outbreaks local leaders refused to invest in preventative health infrastructure. In the second half of the nineteenth century the political context changed once again, moving in a direction that made sanitary reform not only possible but desirable for municipal authorities to undertake.

From Free-Market Economics to "Gas and Water Socialism"

During the third cholera epidemic that struck the UK in 1854, a physician named John Snow conducted what is now one of the most famous epidemiological studies ever undertaken. He didn't believe the dominant filth theory and instead had a hunch that cholera was a waterborne disease. Snow got a chance to test his hypothesis when there was an outbreak in central London that killed 500 people in a week. He interviewed people who lived in the area and discovered that all those who had come down with cholera had one thing in common: they had drunk water from a pump on Broad Street, Soho.[51] He found that workers at a brewery close to the epicenter of the outbreak were unaffected because the brewing process involves boiling the water, and the employees only drank beer when at work. But the most incontrovertible piece of evidence came when he persuaded the local authorities to remove the pump's handle, making it unusable. The outbreak subsided almost immediately.

It took a long time for germ theory—the idea that specific diseases are caused by particular microbes that invade the body—to become mainstream. Van Leeuwenhoek, the curious Dutch haberdasher and lens grinder, first discovered the microscopic world in the middle of the seventeenth century. At the end of the eighteenth century, the physician Edward Jenner noticed that milkmaids seldom caught smallpox. He deduced that their work brought them into contact with cowpox, which had much milder symptoms but conferred crossover immunity against smallpox. Jenner used this insight to develop a "vaccine"—*vacca* being the Latin for cow. This was a remarkable achievement that has earned Jenner a place in the public health pantheon, but it was the consequence of a serendipitous observation rather than an insight into the way infectious diseases are transmitted. It wasn't until the mid-nineteenth century that physicians including John Snow began to gather evidence to show that the "animalcules" that had so enchanted van Leeuwenhoek might be responsible for transmitting diseases.

Snow is now regarded as one of the great heroes of British public health, and you might assume that his meticulous research would have led to an immediate clamor for reform. At the time, however, his discovery had little impact. A committee appointed by Parliament to investigate the causes of the 1854 outbreak—whose authors included William Farr of the General Register Office—endorsed the filth theory of disease and explicitly dismissed Snow's research, stating: "After careful inquiry we see no reason to adopt this belief."[52] And when Snow died in 1858, his thirty-three-word obituary in *The Lancet* did not even mention his research on cholera.[53]

In the end, it was the Great Stink of London, not John Snow, that prompted the government to commission an extensive underground system of sewers in the city. In the summer of 1858 the hot weather cooked the Thames into a foul-smelling sludge, making life almost unbearable for the capital's inhabitants. This was not just a problem in the working-class East End, but also in the newly completed Houses of Parliament at Westminster in the heart of London. Many politicians retired to their rural constituencies to avoid the smell; the few stalwarts struggled on, holding handkerchiefs over their noses. In order to make sure that this would never happen again, Parliament passed legislation that forced London's municipal authorities to build a sewerage system that transported human waste far to the east of the city. This vast project used 318 million bricks to build 82 miles of underground tunnels.[54] It was the first large-scale sewer network in the country and it put London at the forefront of sanitation engineering in Europe. Remarkably, with improvements and additions, these Victorian sewers still form the backbone of the city's sanitation system, even though the population has increased threefold since the mid-nineteenth century. And in 1866, when Britain was once again hit by a cholera epidemic, London was largely spared—with one notable exception. An outbreak occurred in the East End, one of the few parts of the city that hadn't yet been connected to the sewers. Four thousand East Enders died.[55] This finally convinced William Farr of the General Register Office—who had dismissed John Snow's ideas ten years before—that cholera was, in fact, a waterborne disease.

Even then, the UK's provincial towns and cities were resistant to making improvements to their sanitation and water infrastructure.[56] The impetus for change was the Second Reform Act in 1867, which quadrupled the number of men who could vote in urban local elections. Suddenly, more than 60 percent of working-class men were enfranchised and their support was critical to anyone who wanted to get elected.[57] This transformed the nature of municipal politics. Local governments were no longer in thrall to the shopocracy, the small-business owners who had dominated electoral politics since the 1830s and were primarily concerned with keeping taxes as low as possible. The new voters were far more receptive to the ambitious plans of city leaders to build vast and expensive water and sewerage infrastructure precisely because they didn't pay local taxes and therefore wouldn't have to fund the projects directly.

Joseph Chamberlain, who was elected mayor of Birmingham for three consecutive terms in the mid-1870s, embodied this political ethos. He was a wealthy industrialist and, like many of the new economic elite, came from a Nonconformist background. Chamberlain was influenced by the philosophy of municipal activism first preached by Nonconformist ministers in Birmingham. Proponents of the "civic gospel" argued that the deprivation, disease and death that blighted industrial towns and cities was a moral abomination and that their wealthy congregations had a duty to improve the lives of the urban working classes.[58] Under Chamberlain's leadership, the city of Birmingham pioneered a politically and economically viable strategy for putting the civic gospel into practice. It took out low-interest, long-term loans from the central state and commercial banks and spent this money on building sanitation and water infrastructure, as well as other projects that improved the well-being of the population. At the same time, the city created municipally owned monopolies over water, gas, electricity and public transport. These enterprises were run at a profit, with the money used to pay off the loans.

Chamberlain's strategy proved very popular among the newly enfranchised working classes, who had the most to gain but didn't have to pay taxes. As a successful businessman, Chamberlain's views on the matter were respected by many influential people who would otherwise have been skeptical. While Chamberlain and his colleagues were in large part driven by altruism—which set them apart from Chadwick and his ilk—the economic benefits of their strategy weren't lost on them either. They understood that ignoring health was counterproductive. A sickly working class was not just bad for the urban poor, who got ill and died; it was also bad for wealthy business owners, who relied on them to labor in their factories. Detractors referred disparagingly to the reforms as "gas and water socialism." But the urban poor and the city's economic elite formed a new cross-class alliance that undermined the petty-bourgeois shopocracy and their laissez-faire ideology which had scuppered efforts to improve sanitation and public health.[59]

As the civic gospel spread, the new breed of municipal politicians didn't just want their towns and cities to be wealthy. Taking inspiration from their idealized vision of the great city-states of classical Greece and Renaissance Italy, they aimed to use the prosperity to encourage their inhabitants to flourish.[60] From the mid-1870s onward, all the efforts of the sanitary movement over the previous four decades began to coalesce.[61] The General Register Officer continued to publish regular data on local death rates. Just as Farr had hoped, these figures became a source of pride and shame for municipalities, and factory owners began to seek out the towns and cities with the lowest death rates to invest in.[62]

By the beginning of the twentieth century, the majority of local governments in the country had followed the lead of Chamberlain and Birmingham and taken control of their town's utilities. In 1905, the total sum of money spent by local governments was greater than that of the national government for the first and only time in modern history as they poured money into improving public health.[63] Accordingly, over the last quarter of the nineteenth century urban death rates tumbled—primarily due to a steep decline in waterborne infectious diseases rather than airborne maladies such as tuberculosis.[64] There were no major cholera outbreaks in the UK after 1866 and deaths from the more common but less terrifying diarrheal diseases decreased precipitously. In the 1870s, life expectancy in Britain's towns and cities finally rose above 1820s levels. From there, it kept on increasing. And unsurprisingly, as the UK was predominantly an urban society by this point, national life expectancy followed the upward trajectory, having stalled for half a century.

Death in Hamburg

In the last decades of the nineteenth century, almost all of Europe's major cities saw a massive improvement in sanitation—with one notable exception. Hamburg, an autonomous German city-state located on the River Elbe near where it flows into the North Sea, was one of the biggest ports in the world. By 1892, the population had reached 800,000 as people moved from the countryside to the city in search of work on the docks and in factories. At the end of the nineteenth century Hamburg was still governed by a senate composed of eighteen members of the city's most powerful merchants who were appointed for life. The oligopoly was bound by familial and social ties, and it was concerned with one thing: promoting and protecting the trade on which its fortunes depended.

Hamburg's political structure was uniquely ill suited to cope with the social problems that industrialization and urbanization created. As its economy boomed, the authorities spent vast sums of money on port facilities and a new town hall. There wasn't even a professional civil service to run the city-state on a day-to-day basis. Sanitation and the water supply were overlooked, even though raw sewage poured into the Elbe, from which the population drew its drinking water. One doctor, writing in the 1860s, lamented the city leaders "scarcely believable ignorance and indifference . . . with regard to what one might call public health care."[65] This is about as far as you could get from the gas and water socialism that emerged from voting reforms in the United Kingdom in the 1860s and 1870s.

As one of the biggest ports in northern Europe, Hamburg was also a main point of departure for people migrating to America. In the last decades of the nineteenth century and first decades of the twentieth, hundreds of thousands of Russian Jews passed through the city as they migrated westward to escape persecution and poverty. In 1891 and 1892 the numbers were particularly high because the Romanov authorities had ejected Jews from the empire's cities. In Hamburg, the refugees were housed in very basic barracks by the docks and the waste from the latrines poured straight into the Elbe. In August 1892 there was a cholera outbreak, the last one to hit the continent. Because an epidemic raged in Russia at the time, it is widely assumed that Jewish communities carried the bacteria with them as they traveled across Europe. The working-class areas of the city were particularly badly affected by cholera because, unlike in some of the more salubrious suburbs, the water wasn't filtered; 10,000 people died in six weeks.[66]

The authorities' initial response to the outbreak was incompetence and dithering: not wanting to interfere with the flow of trade, they sat on the news that people were dying of cholera for six days before making it public. Obviously this made the situation much worse than it needed to be, as people weren't informed and couldn't take precautions. When it became clear that Hamburg had a fully blown outbreak on its hands, it called in Germany's top scientist, Robert Koch, who in

1884 had been the first person to identify the bacterium that causes cholera. Walking through the working-class areas of the city, he was shocked by the overcrowded and unsanitary conditions. Turning to his companions, Koch remarked: "Gentlemen, I forget that I am in Europe." This remark suggests a lack of respect for other cultures, but it also reveals how far Hamburg deviated from other great cities in the region. Koch was eventually able to arrest the spread of cholera by constructing a clean water supply and instructing the public to use only that source. The indignity of the 1892 outbreak altered Hamburg for good, encouraging a variety of reforms that improved public health, but it also made politics more inclusive and eventually created a professional civil service.[67]

The same year as the Hamburg outbreak, the first effective cholera vaccine was created—although it took several more years of testing in Calcutta for it to become accepted. While cholera vaccines are still used today, their development was far too late to explain the decline of the disease in Europe. Cholera didn't disappear because of innovations in medical technology but because of improvements in hygiene and sanitation driven by political reform.

The examples of Hamburg—as well as the provincial towns and cities of the UK fifty years earlier—demonstrate that economic growth alone does not guarantee the health and well-being of the population. Clearly, the combined actions of self-interested individuals are not capable of delivering broad-based development. John Maynard Keynes is supposed to have said that such an idea assumes that "the nastiest of men for the nastiest of motives will somehow work for the benefit of all." In the absence of strong state intervention, economic growth enriched a small elite but resulted in disruption, destitution, disease and death for the masses. In almost every country that industrialized in the nineteenth century, including most of Europe, the U.S. and Japan, the urban working classes experienced a generation-long decline in health and life expectancy.[68] Eventually, the state intervened to mitigate the deprivation and ensure that growth was converted into improved well-being and health. The one notable exception to this is Sweden, where the government passed comprehensive public health legislation in the 1870s in anticipation of the disruption that was to come. As a result, when Sweden went through its Industrial Revolution in the last decades of the nineteenth century, it largely managed to avoid the death and disease part of the four Ds.[69]

In the UK, the national government did play a role in these developments, through providing loans and sharing best practice. But it was not directly involved in efforts to improve the lives of the urban working classes in the last three decades of the nineteenth century.[70] This changed when the New Liberal government that included Winston Churchill and David Lloyd George won a landslide victory in the 1906 general election. They ushered in a new era of centrally organized and funded state activism. Within the space of a few years, the government had established initiatives including old age pensions, labor exchanges, free school meals and workers' national insurance against sickness and unemployment.[71] Similar developments occurred across the industrialized world. For example, Otto von Bismarck had introduced a welfare program in the 1880s—referred to as *Staatssozialismus* by his liberal and conservative critics—in a vain attempt to undermine support for the Social Democratic Party.* In the U.S., the New Deal was created by Franklin D. Roosevelt in the 1930s in response to the devastation of the Great Depression.

By the middle of the twentieth century, the modern welfare state had started to take shape in many industrialized liberal democratic societies. Its activities expanded to perform a range of tax-funded functions including road-building, health care, social security, housing and education. Governments began to concern themselves with such a broad range of social issues that their activities became the target of comedians as well as free-market economists. In another famous *Monty Python* sketch, John Cleese plays Mr. Teabag, a bowler-hatted civil servant who works at the Ministry of Silly Walks, a department with a budget of £348 million—worth £5.7 billion in today's money. Of course, part of what makes the scene funny is Cleese's bizarre gait and the way it jars with our perceptions of staid Whitehall bureaucrats. But the idea of a lavishly funded Ministry of Silly Walks also satirizes how big—critics would say bloated—the state had become in the third quarter of the twentieth century. When the skit first aired on TV in 1970, it must have seemed inconceivable that a rebooted version of the

---

* Although not in Hamburg, which was an autonomous city-state.

free-market economic liberalism of the previous century would soon return to prominence. But by the start of the next decade, it was very much back on the domestic and international policy agenda. And once again it would have devastating and often deadly consequences on health—both in high-income countries like the U.S. and the UK and in the world's poorest nations.

Chapter 8
Plagues of Poverty

The existing gross inequality in the health status of the people, particularly between developed and developing countries as well as within countries, is politically, socially, and economically unacceptable and is, therefore, of common concern to all countries.

—ALMA-ATA DECLARATION

Gustav Klimt versus Steven Pinker

In 1894, Gustav Klimt was asked to produce a series of paintings for the ceiling of the University of Vienna's newly built Great Hall. Given the theme of "Light conquering darkness," the academe must have hoped that this commission would celebrate their scientific achievements.[1] The faculty paintings were destroyed by the Nazis at the end of the Second World War, so all we have to go on are a few black-and-white photographs. Still, it is not difficult to see why many of the university's staff were horrified by Klimt's work. Take the depiction of *Medicine*—it combines aesthetic beauty with acerbic satire and razor-sharp social criticism. Hygeia, Apollo's granddaughter, and the goddess of good health and cleanliness, stands imperious in the foreground, staring over the heads of any mortals that might deign to look at her. She is either oblivious or indifferent to the suffering going on in the background, where a tangle of naked bodies—some of them emaciated, others grimacing with pain—represents the river of life. In the center of this mass of humans is a skeleton.

Klimt's message is clear: life is painful, death is certain, and modern medicine hasn't altered this fundamental reality.* The rather depressing stance reflects his personal experience. Born in 1862, he lived through the revolutionary period in which doctors finally discarded ideas that had first emerged in Ancient Greece and adopted explanations such as germ theory that now form the basis of modern medicine. Despite this progress, disease and death played a prominent role in Klimt's life. His younger sister passed away as a child. He lost his brother and father within a few months of each other in 1892. His mother and another sister suffered from mental illness. Klimt died at the age of fifty-five in 1918, one of at least 50 million people to succumb to the Spanish flu pandemic.[2]

The acrimonious disagreement between the *fin-de-siècle* Viennese professors and Klimt remains relevant today. The Austrian faculty weren't unique in having faith in the ability of academic endeavor to improve the human condition. As the British philosopher Anthony Kenny notes, the Enlightenment is characterized by the belief that humans were traveling on the "perpetual path of progress . . . moving forward to a happier future, to be made possible by the development of the natural and social sciences."[3] Steven Pinker is undoubtedly the most prominent contemporary advocate of this swaggering, triumphant narrative of history. His bestselling book *Enlightenment Now: The Case for Reason, Science, Humanism, and Progress* (2018) argues that, over the past few centuries, the application of science and reason has allowed us to escape the ignorance, superstition and misery of the past and create a world that is not just healthier, but also wealthier, more peaceful and increasingly respectful of human rights. Inherent in Pinker's argument is the idea that our current economic and political system is fundamentally responsible for this progress and, at most, is only in need of a minor tune-up to optimize the way it functions.

---

* Although perhaps not all academics disapproved: Sigmund Freud worked at the University of Vienna around that time, and it isn't too big a leap to imagine that he might have approved of Klimt's sentiment.

Such booming confidence can seem tone-deaf in a world that is facing impending climate disaster; has been devastated by brutal wars in Ukraine, Syria, Yemen and elsewhere, fought with little or no concern for civilian life or international law; is scarred by obscene inequalities between rich and poor; and is only just starting to overcome a pandemic that has killed an estimated 15 million people.[4] But in the most reductive way, liberal optimists like Pinker are right when they claim that the world is getting healthier. If one looks at data from the World Bank, it's clear that global average life expectancy has improved markedly, from about fifty years in the middle of the twentieth century to almost seventy-three today.[5]

And yet the aggregate figures cited by Pinker to show that the world is getting healthier obscure stark inequalities in life expectancy and hide a huge amount of misery. If we are really taking in the big picture, millions of people still die every year from infectious diseases that are preventable and treatable, mostly poor people living in poor countries. So, although there have been enormous improvements in medicine in the century that has passed since Klimt painted his masterpiece, its key message remains pertinent. Despite the remarkable advances in public health, human existence is still plagued by disease and death.

Plagues and Poverty

If you are reading this book in Japan or Norway, you can expect to live until your mid-eighties. In the UK and U.S., the figures are slightly lower, at eighty-one and seventy-seven, respectively. But if you happened to be born in any one of a dozen countries in sub-Saharan Africa, the odds are that you won't survive past your fifties. In Nigeria, Chad, Sierra Leone, Central African Republic and Lesotho, the average person can expect to live a full three decades less than in the healthiest countries. These disparities are, to a large extent, caused by infectious diseases that have little or no impact on high-income countries but kill millions of people every year in low-income ones.

As we saw in the previous chapter, waterborne maladies were rife in Britain and other industrial and industrializing societies in the mid-nineteenth century. Beginning in the 1870s, improvements in sanitation and water infrastructure led to a steep decline in common diarrheal diseases and the disappearance of cholera. Yet 3.6 billion people—almost half the world's inhabitants—still don't have access to toilets that get rid of their waste in a safe manner and 2 billion people have to drink from sources that are contaminated with human excrement.[6] As a result of these unsanitary conditions, 1.5 million people—mainly young children in low-income countries—die every year from water-borne diarrheal diseases such as rotavirus.[7] Cholera outbreaks still occur periodically and tend to strike particularly hard when normal life has been disrupted. For example, the biggest recent epidemics took hold after Haiti was hit by an earthquake in 2010 and during the recent Yemeni Civil War in 2017. Tuberculosis was another major killer in the slums of industrializing Europe, but it declined in high-income countries as living and working conditions improved, antibiotics were developed and national immunization programs were introduced in the mid-twentieth century. And yet, despite the fact that there is a cheap and reasonably effective vaccine available—it costs a couple of dollars per dose—and TB can be treated with a course of antibiotics, it is still the most deadly infectious disease in the world. It kills about 1.2 million people a year, almost all of whom live in lower- and middle-income countries.

While malaria has always been most deadly in tropical regions of Africa, it was endemic in the American South and parts of Europe until relatively recently. Malaria declined sharply in these regions in the first half of the twentieth century as a result of determined efforts to reduce mosquito breeding grounds by draining wetlands and spraying standing water with chemicals. By the 1950s malaria was no longer a serious public health problem in the U.S., and Europe was declared malaria-free in 1975. (In 2011, however, Greece recorded its first cases of locally transmitted malaria in half a century. The country was in a deep economic crisis, when steep budget cuts impacted public health measures to control the mosquito population.) Once again, progress has been much slower in sub-Saharan Africa. While the global number of malaria cases and deaths has fallen steadily over the last couple of decades, it still kills more than 600,000 people every year. Most of the victims are young children and almost all are in Africa.

New infectious diseases emerged in the twentieth century too. In the early 1980s, doctors in New York noticed that homosexual men and intravenous drug users were developing rare infections that normally only occurred in people with severely compromised immune systems. What came to be known as HIV-AIDS cut swathes through the gay community and heroin users in North America until the development of effective antiretroviral (ARV) drugs in the mid-1990s. ARVs not only prevent HIV patients from developing symptoms and full-blown AIDS, they also reduce the viral load to such an extent that it cannot be transmitted to others. Today, anyone diagnosed in a timely manner can live a long and healthy life by taking just one pill a day—if you could afford it.

For almost a decade after the development of ARVs, the pharmaceutical companies that held the patents refused to lower the price, even for patients in low-income countries. They charged about $10,000 to treat an HIV-AIDS patient for a year, an astronomical sum when compared to the average annual income in sub-Saharan Africa at the time, which was less than $600 dollars. Meanwhile, HIV-AIDS was spreading far beyond marginalized communities. Even today in South Africa, almost one in five people between the ages of fifteen and forty-nine have the disease.[8] Tragically, in the ten years it took pharmaceutical companies to cave in to pressure and allow the production of generic versions that cost just $350 a year, at least 10 million people died and more than double that number contracted the virus.[9] The price of ARVs is only part of the problem, however. Under-resourced health systems in sub-Saharan Africa still struggle to reach patients. Despite the fact that HIV-AIDS has been preventable and treatable for two decades and affordable generics are increasingly available, 1.5 million people are infected with the disease and almost 650,000 die from HIV-related causes each year.[10]

The continued high incidence of infectious diseases in sub-Saharan Africa constitutes a major barrier to economic growth. Sick people cannot go to school or work, often need a family member to take time off to care for them, and require medical attention that can force a family into catastrophic debt. Research from Burundi demonstrates that each time a child gets sick with diarrhea, the average cost to a family, in terms of health care and lost earnings, is $109—almost twice the average monthly salary.[11] In Uganda, treatment of TB is free but associated non-medical costs such as travel to and from the health center still account for more than one-fifth of annual household expenditure for most patients.[12] When thousands or even millions of people are affected by infectious disease in this way, it hinders the whole economy. The same study on Burundi calculates that diarrheal diseases cost the country more than half a billion dollars every year—that is, 6.4 percent of the Gross National Income. It has been estimated that TB cost the world about two-thirds of a trillion dollars in lost economic growth between 2000 and 2015, mainly in low- and middle-income countries. Without drastic action the losses will be even greater over the next fifteen years, as cases of TB have not fallen markedly but the economies are bigger.[13] The American economist Jeffrey Sachs and his colleagues have demonstrated that malaria has a deleterious impact on economic growth, with countries that are not afflicted by malaria enjoying five times the GDP per capita of those that are.[14] Another group of economists estimate that HIV-AIDS reduced economic growth by between 2 and 4 percent a year across Africa in the 1990s.[15]

Sachs and his collaborators argue that infectious diseases create a "poverty trap" that is almost impossible to escape.[16] Poor people are more likely to get ill, making them even poorer and even more prone to infectious disease. Low-income countries tend to be afflicted by more infectious diseases, which in turn undermines economic growth and makes it very difficult for them to prosper. The prevalence of infectious diseases in sub-Saharan Africa helps to explain why it is not only the poorest region in the world but has become even poorer in relative terms over the last few decades, as economic growth has failed to keep pace with the rest of the planet.[17] Is it possible for countries to break the negative feedback loop and escape the poverty trap?

Springing the Trap

China is the most notable example of a country that managed to massively reduce the burden of infectious disease in the second half of the twentieth century. It offers policy lessons for the rest of the world—

especially low-income countries, but even rich ones like the UK and U.S. The concept of public health has long played an important role in traditional Chinese medicine. According to the two-millennia-old *Canon of the Yellow Emperor*, a court physician is said to have advised the mythical ruler: "To administer medicines to diseases which have already developed . . . is comparable to the behavior of those persons who begin to dig a well after they have become thirsty."[18] In the West we celebrate Edward Jenner as the pioneer of vaccines, but the Chinese have been inoculating their population against smallpox for over 1,000 years.[19]

In the nineteenth century China fell on hard times—so much so that it is common to refer to the period between the First Opium War (1839–42) and the foundation of the People's Republic in 1949 as the "Century of Humiliation." Interference from Europeans, the fall of the Qing dynasty, a two-decade-long civil war and Japanese occupation all contributed to reducing China to an anarchic and desperately poor society. One particularly deadly symptom of economic and political disruption was the devastation wrought by infectious diseases, which were responsible for more than half of all deaths in China in the mid-twentieth century.[20] This included diseases that had afflicted Britain before and during the Industrial Revolution—waterborne pathogens such as cholera and other forms of diarrheal disease and airborne maladies like tuberculosis, measles, smallpox and plague. But the Chinese population was also cut down by ailments more associated with tropical regions such as malaria and schistosomiasis, which is caused by a parasitic worm that lives in fresh water.[21] In some regions of China, as many as a third of all babies died before they reached the age of one—although across the whole country the figure was about half that.[22]

At the end of the civil war in 1949, average life expectancy in China was just thirty-two—almost a decade lower than the national average in Britain during the unhealthiest years of the Industrial Revolution.[23] Over the first three decades of communist rule, health improved rapidly. By 1960 the figure had risen to 43.7 years, which was not dissimilar to sub-Saharan Africa (40.4) or India (41.4). And then, in 1980, it rocketed to 66.8 years, shooting past sub-Saharan Africa (48.4) and India (53.8).

The health transformation in the first thirty years of the People's

Republic of China occurred even though China was very poor and only achieved moderate economic growth rates. According to World Bank figures, GDP per capita in China was just $89.50 a year in 1960, compared to $137.20 in sub-Saharan Africa and $82.20 in India. By 1980, the Chinese figure had doubled, while sub-Saharan Africa and India's more than tripled.

What is more, this was a tumultuous period in China's history. In the late 1940s and early 1950s, hundreds of thousands, possibly millions of landlords and richer peasants were killed as the rural poor asserted their newfound power over their former exploiters.[24] Then Mao attempted to transform the Chinese economy by reorganizing the countryside into communes and forcing peasants to concentrate their energy on producing steel. At least 45 million people died from starvation during the so-called Great Leap Forward between 1958 and 1962.[25] When Mao attempted to purge bourgeois elements from society in the Cultural Revolution (1966–76), another 1.5 million people died in the upheaval and 20 million were banished from the cities to the countryside.[26]

The improvements in Chinese longevity between 1949 and 1980 were almost entirely the result of a reduction in infectious diseases.[27] In fact, infectious disease control was so effective that it caused a population boom as more children survived infancy: while there were about 540 million Chinese at the end of the civil war, the figure rose to almost a billion over the next three decades. This had important implications. The one-child policy introduced in the late 1970s was a response to concerns about rapid demographic growth. But before population control started to have an impact, the hundreds of millions of babies born in Maoist China grew into adults, many of whom migrated to cities to work in the factories responsible for the economic miracle that occurred from the 1980s onward.

So how did China achieve this remarkable health transformation? It began in the early 1950s with top-down, campaign-style efforts to prevent infectious diseases, one of the most effective of which was mass immunization.[28] China vaccinated almost all its 600 million inhabitants against smallpox; its last outbreak was in 1960, two decades before it was eradicated globally. Vaccinations against the plague resulted in an 80 percent drop in cases in the first year alone. TB cases fell by 80 percent in a decade due to increased use of the BCG vaccine. The Chinese state also organized "patriotic health campaigns," in which people were exhorted to take part in activities that interrupted the transmission of infectious diseases—projects to provide safe drinking water and improve sanitation, for example, and efforts to get rid of the vectors that carried disease. One particularly impactful campaign formed part of the Great Leap Forward. In 1958, the state urged the population to "exterminate the four pests," which were rats, flies, mosquitoes and sparrows—the latter because they were accused by the Chinese Communist Party of being capitalist birds due to their penchant for "stealing" large amounts of grain and fruit from hard-working peasants.

The population responded enthusiastically to the call to arms. Mao's slogan "Man Must Conquer Nature" became a rallying cry. According to official figures, patriotic Chinese killed more than 1 billion sparrows, 1.5 billion rats, 11 million kilograms of mosquitoes and 100 million kilograms of flies.[29] But it was the massacre of birds, in particular, that disrupted the ecological balance and had disastrous consequences. Across China, people hunted for sparrows with sticks and slingshots. Where they found nests, they killed the chicks and smashed the eggs. Groups of people banged drums, gongs and pots until the exhausted birds fell off their branches and out of the sky. On its own terms, this campaign was a massive success: it appears to have driven the country's sparrow population to the brink of extinction. But sparrows don't eat just grain and fruit; they also consume insects. With the threat from natural predators vastly reduced, the locust population boomed and then feasted on the harvest in a manner far more destructive than anything that sparrows could have achieved. In this way, the campaign to "exterminate the four pests" contributed to the famine that killed 45 million people during the Great Leap Forward. By 1960, the government realized their mistake and replaced sparrows with bedbugs on the most-wanted pests list.

In the mid-1960s, the Chinese state introduced a bottom-up approach to public health led by "barefoot doctors" (so called because in the southern provinces they balanced their medical duties with work in the waterlogged rice paddies). These were local people who looked after the health care needs of their community. Barefoot doctors continued to work part-time in agriculture but were also part-physicians, part-nurses and part-sanitation engineers who received between three months and a year of basic training in medicine and public health.[30] Their role included raising awareness about sanitation, providing advice on family planning, organizing vaccination programs and treating common illnesses using insights from both Western and traditional medicine. By the mid-1970s there were 1.8 million barefoot doctors across the country, assisted by twice that number of health aides.[31] Prior to the introduction of these medical cooperative schemes, the majority of the population had almost no access to health care and people were only sporadically engaged in public health activities. Barefoot doctors filled this enormous gap and in doing so made a significant contribution to the steep decline in infectious diseases.

Mao died in 1976 and was eventually replaced by Deng Xiaoping. Under Deng's leadership, China began to implement reforms that prioritized economic growth over everything else. As China became integrated into the global economy, hundreds of millions of people moved from the rural interior to coastal cities to work in factories that manufactured goods for export. Within a couple of decades, China went from being one of the poorest countries on the planet to a global economic and political superpower. But the Chinese industrial revolution was accompanied by a health crisis. Unlike in nineteenth-century England, this didn't occur in the booming urban areas: Chinese city authorities were generally proactive in building water and sanitation systems. It was the rural interior that suffered the most, in large part because the economic reforms abolished agricultural communes and with them the free, decentralized, barefoot-doctor-led health care and public health system.

People were now required to purchase health insurance, but 90 percent of the rural population couldn't afford to pay; for the uninsured, one visit to the doctor could easily cost a poor family a third of their annual income.[32] Barefoot doctors' work was abandoned because individuals weren't willing to pay for preventative public health programs. Patients even had to pay doctors for vaccinations and, as a result, immunization rates fell to under 50 percent.[33] Infectious diseases surged, including measles, polio, TB and schistosomiasis.[34] On the national level, life expectancy continued to improve—it rose from 66.8 in 1980 to 71.4 in 2000—but the rate of increase was five times slower than in the preceding two decades due to the growing burden of infectious diseases among the rural poor of the Chinese interior.

Over the last twenty years, the Chinese Communist Party has changed its approach, once again taking a leading role in addressing the challenges posed by disease and poverty. Between 2005 and 2011, China managed to extend health care from 50 percent to 95 percent of the population.[35] This was a remarkable achievement in a country of 1.3 billion, and was only possible with the full political and financial support of the state. As a result, infectious diseases have fallen sharply in the last decade and it is now rare for them to kill children and adolescents.[36] At the same time, the government has made a concerted effort to improve the well-being of the poorest people in rural areas. The booming economy allowed the state to spend $244 billion on reducing extreme poverty and, in a reversion to the pre-reform Maoist approach, over 3 million party cadres went to the countryside to bolster these efforts.[37] In 2021, President Xi announced that China had eradicated extreme poverty. Although he was referring to the national measure of extreme poverty, which is comparable to the shockingly low World Bank threshold of $1.90 a day, this is still quite an achievement given that as recently as 2000 almost half the population lived below the poverty line.[38]

My intention here isn't to advocate communism. Rather it's to demonstrate that, just as the state was crucial in defeating infectious diseases in late-nineteenth-century Britain, it was also vitally important in China's escape from the poverty trap in the late twentieth century. Yet we must not overlook the massive downsides to the Chinese model of development. The improvements in health and wealth have been achieved despite an Orwellian disregard for individual freedom and human rights—from the Great Leap Forward to the present-day treatment of the Uighurs, and of course the response to Covid-19. Notwithstanding, it was the iron fist of the totalitarian state that pulled China out of the poverty trap rather than the invisible hand of the market.

Kicking Away the Ladder

Millions of people still die every year from preventable and treatable diseases in sub-Saharan Africa because of lack of political will. If politicians—both domestically and on the international stage—prioritized prevention and treatment, then the impact of infectious diseases would quickly become negligible, just as it has in China. The paralysis in much of sub-Saharan Africa is, in part at least, a legacy of colonialism. The Turkish-American economist Daron Acemoglu demonstrates how the settlement patterns of European colonialists between the seventeenth and nineteenth centuries were determined by infectious diseases.[39] Where death rates were low—in New England, for example—men brought their families, settled down and built new societies in the image of the ones they'd just left; in this endeavor they were aided by infectious diseases that decimated the indigenous population. These colonies grew into wealthy democracies that although imperfect were relatively responsive to the needs of the electorate.

Where mortality from infectious diseases was high, the outcome was very different: entrepreneurial colonialists built extractive institutions that were designed to make as much money as possible, as quickly as possible, before they returned home to their families. This happened most clearly in sub-Saharan Africa, where malaria and yellow fever made the region almost uninhabitable for Europeans. Acemoglu argues that the character of the colonial state survived independence and continues to influence the development trajectory of former colonies. Accordingly, many sub-Saharan states lack the ability or willingness to plan and implement the kind of public health measures necessary to prevent the spread of infectious diseases—such as investing in basic water, sanitation and health systems. Nor are they in a position to use the money flowing into the region—from the sale of natural resources, lent by commercial banks, and given by foreign states in exchange for political allegiance—to kick-start a process of self-sustaining economic development.

There is certainly something in Acemoglu's thesis. We don't have to look far for examples of how the legacy of colonialism impacted post-colonial governments' ability to deal with infectious diseases. For example, when the Congo became independent in 1960, there were just

a few dozen Congolese university graduates and no doctors or engineers, and only three out of 5,000 management-level positions in the
civil service were held by Africans.[40] A large part of the money that
flowed into postcolonial states in the decades after independence was
appropriated by corrupt politicians and technocrats—just as European
colonialists had done. If the resources weren't stolen, they were
frequently wasted on poorly conceived infrastructure projects that
were often constructed at the suggestion of Western consultants. We
shouldn't, however, be too fatalistic about the destiny of postcolonial
Africa. Many African politicians worked hard to improve the health
and well-being of their countries, despite having the cards stacked
against them. In fact, in the 1970s they very nearly succeeded.

When the WHO was founded in 1948 it consisted of fifty-five member states, most of them relatively wealthy countries in Europe and the
Americas. Three decades later it had expanded to 146 members as recently independent former colonies joined up.[41] In Africa alone, nearly
fifty countries were created between the formation of the WHO and
the end of the 1970s. Another significant event occurred in 1973 when
the People's Republic of China joined. These developments radical-
ized the WHO, which is a membership-based organization that makes
decisions on the principle of one nation, one vote through the World
Health Assembly. Idealism at the WHO reached a pinnacle in 1978 in
the Soviet city of Alma-Ata, now Almaty in Kazakhstan. The health
ministers of 134 countries launched the "Health for All" movement,
which aimed to deliver basic health care to even the world's poorest
inhabitants by the end of the millennium.

The conference agreed that investment in health facilities and drugs
would not be enough to improve health in poor countries. Rather, the
Alma-Ata Declaration argued that fundamental political and economic
reform—in terms of tackling iniquitous power relations between former colonies and their colonizers, and mobilizing communities to take
an interest in health care—was essential to achieving its goal. One of
the main sources of inspiration was the remarkable improvements in
health that China had achieved over the previous thirty years, and in
particular the role of barefoot doctors.[42] If the Alma-Ata Declaration
had been implemented, it would have provided low-income countries
with the equipment they needed to clamber out of the poverty trap.

Unfortunately, the optimism of Alma-Ata was quickly undermined by high-income countries—most notably the U.S. and the UK, where the arrival of Ronald Reagan and Margaret Thatcher on the scene in the late 1970s and early 1980s marked a fundamental shift in political consensus. Their new economic orthodoxy harked back to the laissez-faire approach of the previous century. In this new environment, "Health for All" was deemed too radical and too political. The focus shifted to taking out infectious diseases one by one using medicines and technology, without tackling the poverty and powerlessness that are the underlying causes of ill health. The U.S. and its allies reduced their funding to the WHO. Instead they funneled money for global health projects into organizations like the World Bank, which gave them more control because member states' voting power is proportional to their financial contribution.[43]

The U.S. and UK also used international financial institutions to undermine low-income countries' efforts to tackle infectious diseases through structural adjustment programs. In the late 1970s, interest rates increased, the dollar strengthened, and the prices that African countries received for the natural resources they exported fell. Poor countries' debts spiraled out of control and it became clear that it wouldn't be possible to pay them back. From the early 1980s, the World Bank and International Monetary Fund (IMF) began to bail out indebted countries. International financial institutions lent money, but the loans came with certain conditions designed to make sure the recipients were able to pay them back. The story of the economic failure of so-called Structural Adjustment Programs has been told elsewhere.[44] States were forced to lower tariffs on imports, privatize state-controlled industries and concentrate their efforts on producing goods for export. These reforms failed to transform heavily indebted economies so that they would be able to repay the World Bank and IMF loans. GDP per capita in sub-Saharan Africa was about 10 percent lower in 2000 than it had been twenty years earlier.[45] In China and other parts of East Asia, by contrast, where governments avoided following the World Bank and IMF's free-market diktats and the state played a central role in development, the economies boomed.

Structural adjustment had a profoundly negative impact on public health. Governments were forced to cut social welfare budgets, including those for public health and health care. Recipient countries were often required to cap the public-sector wage bill, resulting in the emigration of large numbers of doctors and nurses to high-income countries. In the 1980s, the number of doctors in Ghana fell by half, and only one-sixth of Senegal's nurses remained, compared to the start of the decade.[46] Structural adjustment programs frequently introduced user fees for health care that mimicked the U.S. model. As a result, the poor were unable to access even the most basic care. For example, when the World Bank forced Kenya to impose a charge of thirty-three cents to see a doctor, patient visits fell by half.[47] (The number of patients almost doubled when the fee was suspended.) And it has been shown that structural adjustment caused an increase in some infectious diseases, including TB.[48] From 1980 to 2000, life expectancy in sub-Saharan Africa barely increased at all, remaining stuck at around fifty years.

As we saw in the previous chapter, the process of democratization and state-directed sanitary reform led to a marked decline in infectious diseases and to improvements in public health in the UK and other high-income countries in the late nineteenth and early twentieth centuries. A similar process occurred in China during the last half-century. But at the same time, low-income countries, predominately in sub-Saharan Africa, have been denied the opportunity to follow a similar strategy; in effect, high-income countries "kicked away the ladder" that they had used to climb out of the poverty trap. Instead, sub-Saharan African countries were encouraged to use an untested approach to public health that stressed medicine and technology.[49] But states in low-income countries weren't able to take full advantage of the exciting new possibilities offered by advances in medical science. How could they, after being hollowed out first by colonialism and then by structural adjustment?

Shit Life Syndrome

On my cycle to work from west to east London, I pass through the Borough of Kensington and Chelsea, which is home to Kensington

Palace, where Princess Diana once lived; the Victoria and Albert, one of the world's foremost museums of art and design; and Harrods and Harvey Nichols, where the capital's elite do their shopping. This is one of the wealthiest and healthiest parts of the UK: men here can expect to live to ninety-five.[50] Even within Kensington and Chelsea there are big disparities in health, however. In the most salubrious parts of the borough, life expectancy is twenty-two years higher than in the immediate vicinity of Grenfell Tower, a social housing block in North Kensington where seventy-two people—mainly poor immigrants—died in a fire in 2017.[51] Health inequalities are even starker when we compare Kensington and Chelsea to other parts of the country. If I jump on a train at Euston station that is heading north, I can be in the seaside resort of Blackpool in less than three hours. Male life expectancy in the town is a full twenty-seven years lower than in Kensington and Chelsea—the same as the difference between the UK or the U.S. and the unhealthiest countries in sub-Saharan Africa.

Prior to the Covid-19 pandemic, the disparities in life expectancy within the UK were not explained by the differential impact of infectious diseases, as they killed far too few people to make a mark. Rather, inequalities in health outcomes were the result of disparities in premature deaths from non-communicable diseases, most notably cardiovascular disease, cancers and diabetes. While such illnesses obviously aren't transmitted from one person to another by pathogens, their distribution is not random. Just as the urban working classes in Victorian slums were more likely to be affected by cholera or TB, these modern "plagues" disproportionately impact the poor—hence the inequalities in health outcomes between places like Kensington and Chelsea on the one hand and Blackpool on the other. According to the Office for National Statistics, men and women in the most deprived areas of England were, respectively, 4.5 times and 3.9 times more likely to die young from preventable causes than those in the wealthiest areas.[52] Health is so closely linked to wealth and social status that Michael Marmot, the influential British epidemiologist, has likened contemporary Britain to Aldous Huxley's *Brave New World*, in which the lower castes were given chemicals—with the most lowly group receiving the highest dosage—to inhibit their intellectual and physical development.[53]

In order to emphasize the way in which poor people are dispropor-tionately affected by non-communicable diseases, some epidemiolo-gists argue that these afflictions are "socially transmitted": people who live in poverty are subjected to similar pressures and tend to respond to them in similar ways, as if a certain behavior were contagious.[54] One link between deprivation and non-communicable diseases is unhealthy eating. A recent study found that the poorest 10 percent of households in the UK would have to spend over 70 percent of their income in order to follow healthy eating guidelines.[55] As a result, we see higher levels of obesity in low-income areas. For example, 20 percent of five-year-olds in the most deprived areas of the UK are obese, almost three times the figure in the least deprived areas.[56] In addition, the dopamine rush from eating sugary, fatty food is the most affordable way of buying mo-mentary relief from the misery and helplessness of poverty. At the ex-treme end of the spectrum, deprivation-induced stress and anxiety cause severe mental health problems and deaths of despair from sui-cides, alcohol abuse and drug overdoses.

The connection between poverty and non-communicable disease is clear when we look at towns such as Blackpool. In the second half of the nineteenth century and the first half of the twentieth, workers from industrial centers like Manchester and Liverpool would decamp here during their summer holidays. The resort still has sandy beaches, donkey rides and a 158-meter-high replica of the Eiffel Tower, but its best days are behind it. Since the 1960s, vacationers have preferred to take advantage of cheap package holidays and flights to travel abroad where the sun is more reliable. Many of the small hotels where visitors once stayed have been converted into tiny rental apartments—the modern equivalent of slum housing. Today, people with little money and few prospects are drawn to Blackpool by the cheapest rent in the UK. Along with the lowest male life expectancy, it has some of the highest levels of unemployment, disability benefit claimants and anti-depressant prescriptions in the country. The local doctors have coined the phrase "Shit Life Syndrome" to refer to the common denominator for most of the maladies they see: destitution and hopelessness.[57]

The suffering we see in Blackpool is a consequence of deindus-trialization—or what some economists have called the "deindustrial revolution."[58] Work in factories, as well as mines and docks, was often hard and dirty, but it gave people a sense of security, identity and com-munity. Over the past fifty years, most of these jobs disappeared, lost to machines and the flight of manufacturing to countries like China, where production costs are cheaper. In the 1970s, almost 8 million people were employed in the manufacturing sector in the UK; now the figure is 2.5 million, even though the population has grown by a fifth.[59]

Deindustrialization has had a very limited impact on London and its surrounding areas, where people have benefited from the boom in the financial sector. But in the former industrial heartlands of northern England, manufacturing jobs have been replaced by precarious and poorly paid employment in the service sector—or they haven't been replaced at all. The disruption of the deindustrial revolution has had a devastating impact on health. While life expectancy has steadily in-creased over the last decade in Kensington and Chelsea, as well as in other wealthy, predominately southern parts of the UK, it has fallen in Blackpool and poor urban areas that were once the center of the Industrial Revolution such as Manchester and Liverpool, causing national-level figures to stall over the last decade.[60]

Health inequalities in the UK stem from policy choices made by the government. When Margaret Thatcher became prime minister in 1979 she reintroduced many ideas that had been popular in the mid-nineteenth century: not just the emphasis on free-market economics and an aversion to state intervention, but also the belief that people who are left behind by these brutal macroeconomic transformations are un-deserving scroungers who must be shamed into working harder. This was self-imposed, structural adjustment. Since 2010, the Conservative-led government has continued to push for limited state intervention in society. Welfare payments for families were cut, it became more diffi-cult for disabled people to qualify for benefits, and money for public health services fell. Funding for the National Health Service failed to rise at a rate that would have allowed it to keep up with the demands of an increasingly elderly and unhealthy population. A recent study esti-mates that since 2010, cuts in UK government spending have been re-sponsible for more than 10,000 extra deaths a year.[61] The British experience demonstrates that, even when a country has passed through the epidemiological transition, disruption and deprivation can still create new, non-communicable plagues that have a similar impact as infectious diseases.

Like the UK, the United States is characterized by marked inequalities in life expectancy driven by disparities in non-communicable diseases and deaths of despair. Historically, the most shocking inequalities have been between white and Black people. Although the life expectancy of the two groups has been converging in recent years, whites still live almost six years longer than Blacks.[62] This is, of course, a legacy of slavery. The stress of existing in a racist society has a devastating impact on both physical and mental health. But African Americans are not the only people in the U.S. affected by health inequalities.

Since 2015, life expectancy at the national level has been in decline. The Nobel Prize–winning economist Angus Deaton and his collaborator Anne Case point out that this is driven by an increase in suicides, alcohol abuse and drug overdoses, which kill about 190,000 people each year—three times more than in the 1990s.[63] The surge in deaths of despair is almost exclusively accounted for by white middle-aged males without a university degree; the death rate for this group has risen by a quarter in the last three decades. Although middle-aged African Americans are still more likely to die than their white counterparts, their death rate declined by a third in the same period. In the past, blue-collar workers could realistically aspire to the American Dream—a secure job, health insurance, a pension, a house in the suburbs, and so on. Today these things are little more than a fantasy for many people. There were 19.5 million well-paying manufacturing jobs in the United States in 1979 compared to around 12 million today, even though the population is now one and a half times as big. Wages for workers who don't have a university education have fallen by 15 percent in this period but have increased by a tenth for those with a bachelor's and by a quarter for those with a higher degree. Today, the most that someone with a high-school education can realistically hope for is a precarious, poorly paid job without health insurance or a pension.[64] Just as the bottle was the quickest way to get out of Manchester in the early nineteenth century, the fastest way to escape the North American version of Shit Life Syndrome in the early twenty-first century is alcohol, crystal meth or fentanyl.

There is, of course, one major difference between the UK and the

U.S.: their health care systems. Despite a decade of Thatcherism in the 1980s and another decade of austerity in the 2010s, Britain's National Health Service more or less survived as a system funded by national taxation that provides free health care to anyone who needs it. This contrasts starkly with the brutally inefficient privatized system in the U.S. The United States spends more on health care than any other country—almost $11,000 per person every year, compared to $4,300 in the UK, for example.[65] And yet health coverage is patchy. Those Americans who can afford to pay benefit from the best health care anywhere in the world. Yet tens of thousands of people die prematurely every year because they are unable to access health care.[66] More than 30 million are uninsured, and even people with insurance face such high costs that a quarter of the population have reported delaying seeking medical treatment and half a million people are declared bankrupt each year because they can't pay the costs of their health care.[67] Life expectancy is four years lower than in the UK. The system is so inefficient that if the U.S. had a national health service like the UK's, its health outcomes would improve *and* it would save almost 2.5 trillion dollars every year. Deaton and Case point out that the dysfunction in the U.S. health care system is, in monetary terms, more of a handicap than the reparations that Germany had to pay following the First World War.

When the Covid-19 pandemic became widespread in 2020, it shone an unforgiving light on a broader sickness in society: not just the deprivation of poor and marginalized groups in Britain and America but also the Chinese Communist Party's lack of respect for human rights, as well as indifference to the suffering of millions of people in sub-Saharan Africa.

The Coronavirus Syndemic

The December 2021 cover of *Time* magazine proclaimed that the scientists who developed Covid-19 vaccines were not just "heroes of the year" but "miracle workers." Within a month of the first patients being identified in Wuhan, researchers had decoded the virus's genome and posted it online. Less than a year later, multiple groups of scientists had successfully developed vaccines that provided a great deal of protection against Covid-19. That medical science can reduce the virus from an existential threat to a vaccine-preventable disease in a matter of months is a remarkable—even miraculous—achievement. Governments in high-income countries cut deals with pharmaceutical companies to buy vaccines and began jabbing their populations as soon as possible. By the time that edition of *Time* magazine was published, more or less everyone in Western Europe and North America who wanted to be jabbed had been fully vaccinated. In fact, many had already received a third booster shot to top up their immune system. Not everyone in the world has benefited from the miracles of modern medicine, however.

In sub-Saharan Africa, fewer than 5 percent of the population had been vaccinated by the end of 2021.[68] There were enough vaccines to go round, but the self-interested actions of high-income countries created artificial scarcity in low-income countries. Rich nations bought far more vaccines than they actually needed; one study estimates that by the end of 2021 they had stockpiled 1.2 billion doses, despite having vaccinated their populations already.[69] That is more than enough to vaccinate all adults in sub-Saharan Africa twice. In addition, several high-income countries, including the UK and Germany, repeatedly blocked proposals to waive the intellectual property rights for Covid-19 vaccines. This would have suspended patents related to the vaccines and allowed anyone to produce them—not just big pharmaceutical companies whose supplies were almost exclusively going to people in rich nations. It is as if no one has learned from the deaths of more than 10 million people in low-income countries from HIV-AIDS in the late 1990s and early 2000s, when pharmaceutical companies supported by wealthy nations blocked production of generic ARVs.

The stark disparity in supplies of vaccine between rich and poor nations has been condemned as "vaccine apartheid" and "vaccine colonialism." It clearly demonstrates that high-income countries regard their citizens' lives as more valuable than those of sub-Saharan Africans. Sadly, this is nothing new. As we have seen, millions of people in the region continue to die from preventable and treatable diseases such as cholera, TB, malaria and HIV-AIDS because treatment and prevention are not a priority for international politicians and policymakers. Just as Conrad's *Heart of Darkness* is so chilling because it ignores the experiences of the local people that Marlow encounters on his journey up the Congo, it has long been clear that, in public health, Black lives matter less than white ones—or at least that the lives of almost exclusively Black people in low-income countries matter less than those of people in high-income, predominantly white countries. Because Covid-19 is such an infectious pathogen, the hoarding of vaccines is not just callous selfishness on the part of high-income countries: it is potentially a massive own goal that could very well prolong the pandemic and increase the likelihood of new, more dangerous variants emerging.[70]

The Covid-19 pandemic has not only highlighted stark inequalities between countries. It has also drawn attention to deprivation within high-income countries. Richard Horton, editor of *The Lancet*, argues that the devastation wrought by coronavirus in the UK and the U.S. should be understood as a "syndemic" or "synergistic epidemic." In other words, the impact of the coronavirus pandemic can only be understood if we take into account the pre-existing pandemics of poverty and obesity that were already ravaging wealthy societies. In rich nations, poor people tend to have jobs which they cannot do from home; they travel by public transport and live in crowded housing, often with multiple generations. As a result, they are more likely to be exposed to the pathogens than wealthier people. To make matters worse, poor people are also more likely to have risk factors that could make them very ill if they contract Covid-19. These include obesity and noncommunicable diseases such as diabetes, asthma or chronic lung disease. In the UK, adults in the poorest parts of the country were almost four times more likely to die from coronavirus than those in the wealthiest areas.[71] In the U.S., death rates were four and a half times higher among the poorest people than those with the highest incomes at the height of the pandemic.[72]

Governments' policy responses haven't tried to tackle the twin pandemics of poverty and obesity that make the impact of Covid so much worse. In fact, before effective vaccines were developed, the main strategy was very similar to those of Italian Renaissance city-states in response to the plague, which went on to be applied halfheartedly in the nineteenth century when cholera hit. The state restricted movement, both between and within countries, and isolated people suspected of having the disease in order to reduce transmission of the virus. The extent to which these policies were implemented varied markedly between countries. At one extreme is the laissez-faire approach taken by the U.S. government. Citing concerns about the economic impact and curtailing individual freedom, President Trump let the virus rip through the country. As a result, over a million people in the U.S. died—0.31 percent of the total population.[73] In the UK, the government imposed several lockdowns with the intention of slowing rather than halting the spread of the virus. Covid-19 killed 200,000—0.27 percent of the population.

The outbreak developed into a pandemic only because of the Chinese authorities' reluctance to share information about the disease. Indeed, Doctor Li Wenliang was admonished by police for trying to raise the alarm about a new, deadly disease in late 2019.* But eventually China responded with strictly enforced lockdown measures that aimed to fully stop virus transmission. In affected cities, millions of people were effectively consigned to their houses for weeks, even months on end. Purely in terms of disease control, this was a remarkable success. Although China was the original source of Covid-19, the pandemic has killed fewer than 15,000 people there, according to official statistics: 0.001 percent of the population.[†] This achievement has come at an enormous cost, however, as it involved a massive curtailment of individual freedom and brought economic activity to a standstill—an approach that is unthinkable in most other parts of the world, where states have neither the will nor the capacity to enforce such stringent restrictions.

The Chinese example illustrates just how radical the societal response must be to stop a virus like Covid-19 from having a devastating impact: it entails not seeing our family and friends, going to school or work, eating in restaurants or playing sports. Essentially, we must stop living, which makes sense because viruses and bacteria are such an

---

* Tragically, Dr. Li died from Covid-19 in early 2020 at the age of thirty-three.

† The fact that China maintains such strict control on information inhibits comparisons. Some academics have cast doubt on the country's official statistics, but it seems clear that even if China is understating the number of deaths, mortality rates are still markedly lower than in the U.S. or UK.

inextricable part of human life—and death. China's "zero Covid" strategy can be seen as the modern-day equivalent of Mao's efforts to "conquer nature" during the Great Leap Forward. And just as efforts to "exterminate the four pests" disrupted the balance of nature with disastrous consequences in the 1950s and 1960s, the policy of extreme lockdowns has the potential to disturb the social world—causing mental health problems, political protest and economic hardship.

A century after Klimt's *Medicine* shocked the faculty at the University of Vienna, medical knowledge remains just a small part of dealing with infectious diseases. Pathogens thrive on inequality and injustice. And even in societies that have seemingly passed through the epidemic revolution, new communicable and non-communicable diseases continue to emerge which disproportionately strike down the poor. Although global life expectancy has increased over the last seventy-five years, there remains an enormous amount of pain and suffering that science and rationality haven't been able—or willing—to resolve. Public intellectuals who ignore this reality risk looking like the twenty-first-century avatar of Klimt's Hygeia, standing proudly and prominently in the foreground of our field of vision shouting loudly that everything is getting better while seemingly oblivious to the miserable scenes unfolding behind their backs. The Enlightenment has put some lucky people on what seems like a "perpetual path of progress," but much of the world's population lives in what must feel more like a dystopia.

Conclusion

> *This whole thing is not about heroism. It's about*
> *decency. It may seem a ridiculous idea, but the only*
> *way to fight the plague is with decency.*
> —ALBERT CAMUS

The Next Alexander the Great

Over the last couple of years, Covid-19 has affected all our lives to such an extent that it has become a cliché to say that the pandemic is unprecedented and extraordinary. But when we place coronavirus in its historical and scientific context, it becomes very clear that there is little about it that is new or remarkable. Recurring outbreaks of infectious disease have been a feature of human existence for millennia. Epidemics have played a critical role in, among other things, the transformation from a planet inhabited by multiple species of human to one in which *Homo sapiens* reigned supreme; the replacement of nomadic foraging with sedentary agriculture; the decline of the great empires of antiquity; the rise of new world religions; the transition from feudalism to capitalism; European colonialism; and the Agricultural and Industrial Revolutions. In other words, bacteria and viruses have been instrumental in the emergence of the modern world.

Emphasizing the role that infectious diseases play doesn't exclude the possibility that humans can have an impact on the world. It's just that very often we don't make history in circumstances of our own choosing, but in circumstances created by microbes—as well as other impersonal forces like the climate.[1] Many of Thomas Carlyle's "Great Men" appear in this book, including Alexander the Great, Muhammad, Charlemagne, Martin Luther and George Washington. But these "heroes" didn't bend the arc of history with their genius and force of personality; rather, these qualities allowed them to take advantage of the opportunities that had been created by devastating epidemics.

Similarly, class struggles played an important role in transforming the world. The decline of feudalism and emergence of capitalism was the outcome of centuries of conflict between peasants and lords in England, for example. And in Haiti it took a decade of war before the oppressed and exploited Black population brought slavery and colonialism crashing down. Leadership, organization and mass participation all played a crucial role in the successful outcome of these conflicts. But so did infectious diseases. The Black Death killed 60 percent of the European population, and it was the impact of this demographic crash that triggered the struggle between feudal lords and serfs in the first place. And while the Haitians were up against the French army, one of the best-trained, best-equipped forces the world had ever seen, they managed to devise a strategy that used yellow fever as a deadly weapon.

Covid-19 will be another crucial inflection point in the story of our species. Even before the pandemic hit, the world seemed to be in the midst of what might, with the benefit of hindsight, be seen as an epochal shift. The pandemic will accelerate the pace and alter the trajectory of history.

The pandemic appears to be changing *how humans see their place in the world*. The looming climate disaster was already forcing people not just to consider alternative ways of feeding a growing population and powering the economy, but to rethink how we fit into the ecosystem. The pandemic has sped this process along. It has reminded us of Darwin's most profound insight—what has been referred to as "the darkest of his truths, well known and persistently forgotten"—that humans are just another species of animal and, like everything else in the animal kingdom, we are vulnerable to the threat posed by pathogens.[2] If we *Homo sapiens* don't strive to live in balance with the other living things on our planet, we face a very bleak future.

Covid-19 is also transforming *how humans live in the world*. For the last couple of decades it has been increasingly possible to occupy not just the real world but also a parallel, virtual world. In the past, when diseases hit, humans frequently responded by running away—like Galen did as the Antonine Plague closed in on Rome, or parish priests in the east of England during the Black Death. But when Covid-19 struck, many of us began to live our work and social lives in the online realm.[3] We worked from home rather than commuting to the office, ordered our groceries online instead of going to the supermarket, got food delivered instead of eating in restaurants, and caught up with friends on Zoom rather than over a coffee in town. Schools, churches and even courts moved online. Since the pandemic died down, many people have continued to spend much more time in the virtual world than before coronavirus. This shift seems to be permanent.

And coronavirus also seems to be changing *how humans think the world should be organized*. The pandemic will aid China's re-emergence as a global superpower and at the same time undermine the U.S.'s— and to a lesser extent the UK's—status as a beacon of progress that other countries aspire to emulate. The liberal democracies' laissez-faire approach to dealing with Covid-19 was disastrous in health terms. Despite the fact that the virus originated in Wuhan, the official death rate in the U.S. is more than 300 times higher than in China; in the UK it is more than 250 times higher than in China.[4] The U.S., one of the richest countries in the world, was overwhelmed with disruption, deprivation, disease and death. China—one of the poorest societies on the planet fifty years ago—airlifted medical equipment to North America to help ease the crisis. A quarter of a century ago, American scholars could claim with straight faces that liberal democracy had demonstrated once and for all that it was superior to all other ways of organizing society.[5] Not anymore.

Taken as a whole, the Chinese system still doesn't look particularly appealing to most people in the West. And we still don't know how the country will fare over the longer term—especially if restrictions are eventually lifted and Covid-19 gains a foothold. But North America and Europe can no longer delude themselves that their political and economic system is an enticing model for the rest of the world. The American economist Lawrence Summers is a firm defender of free markets, but even he argues that "Covid-19 may mark a transition from western democratic leadership of the global system."[6] The crucial question is: what follows? The emergence of China as a world power, coupled with the waning power of the West, may well lead to geopolitical turmoil. As the American historian Graham Allison demonstrates, the vast majority of cases in world history when a rising power displaced another that was in decline resulted in war.[7] He refers to this phenomenon as "Thucydides' Trap," after the historian's suggestion that "it was the rise of Athens and the fear that this instilled in Sparta that made war inevitable." But the Peloponnesian War was so devastating that it wasn't Athens or even Sparta that took over as the hegemon of Hellenic civilization. Rather, it was Macedon, a state in the far north of the Greek world that no one paid much attention to in the middle of the fifth century BCE. Who might be the twenty-first-century iterations of Philip and Alexander the Great?

Being Human in the Age of Microbes

William McNeill's *Plagues and Peoples* is an epic tale in which humans inadvertently created plagues, struggled against them for thousands of years and then finally, with the help of modern medicine, won. This confidence seemed to have been vindicated in 1980, when smallpox—a disease that had killed 300 million in the twentieth century alone—was eradicated. But since then old diseases have refused to disappear and new ones have emerged. One of the deadliest viral diseases capable of infecting humans was discovered in a village near the Ebola River in what is now the Democratic Republic of Congo in 1976—the very same year that *Plagues and Peoples* was published. And the last fifty years have turned out to be a golden age for infectious diseases. HIV-AIDS appeared in the 1980s and for a while there were fears that it posed an existential threat to humanity. SARS, Zika and Covid-19 are more recent examples of emerging threats.

A number of factors are driving the emergence of new pathogens. Population growth means that humans are encroaching on animal environments that harbor viruses and bacteria that can jump the species barrier and infect humans. Climate change—including rising temperatures, increasing rainfall and flooding—will aid the spread of diseases, especially those transmitted by mosquitoes such as malaria and yellow fever, and waterborne infections like diarrheal disease and cholera. The increased ease of travel between distant places makes the spread of pathogens much more likely than ever before, particularly airborne ones. When we bear all this in mind, it seems likely that the Covid-19 pandemic isn't an aberration but merely the latest in a long line of infectious diseases to emerge over the last fifty years or so. This trend will almost certainly continue, and another pandemic will hit again before too long.

But the next pandemic might not look much like the last. Antimicrobial resistance (AMR) could well be the source of the next great pandemic. When antibiotics were discovered in the 1940s they had an almost miraculous impact: diseases that had killed people in the most gruesome manner—including plague and cholera—and all sorts of other infections that would have lingered in our bodies for years became treatable for the first time. But now it's clear that antibiotics only granted a temporary reprieve. More than 1.2 million people die each year as a direct result of common, previously treatable infections because the bacteria that cause them have evolved to be resistant to antibiotics.[8] Young children are at particularly high risk—one in five of these deaths are under the age of five. The figures will get worse as bacteria—which, remember, can horizontally transfer genes between species—take advantage of over-prescribing and misuse of antibiotics. An AMR pandemic would likely consist of many chronic and untreatable infections that slowly but surely wear down the population. Sally Davies, the former Chief Medical Officer in the UK, neatly captures the difference between the coronavirus pandemic and one caused by AMR. "Covid's a lobster dropped into boiling water, making a lot of noise as it expires, whereas AMR is a lobster put into cold water, heating up slowly, not making any noise."[9] The water already seems to be uncomfortably hot.

Humans are in a very precarious position. We live on a planet that is by almost any measure dominated by microbes. We are surrounded by innumerable viruses and bacteria that are mutating all the time. Some are evolving in ways to help us. Others are developing new ways to harm us. The age-old struggle between *plagues and peoples* does not necessarily have to end as a tragedy or even a farce. But if we are to avoid a bad outcome, it is crucial that we learn from history. So how should we respond to the existential threat posed by infectious diseases?

There is one universally incorrect choice: to do nothing. This didn't work when humans thought that plagues were a punishment sent by angry gods. Nor does a laissez-faire approach help stop disease when it is a deliberate policy choice. Lack of state intervention in the mid-nineteenth century ensured that Europe's urban poor lived in crowded, unsanitary conditions and suffered the lowest life expectancy since the Black Death. In the late twentieth century, structural adjustment resulted in cutbacks to health care in the world's poorest countries. Between 1980 and 2000, life expectancy in Africa barely increased at all, despite massive improvements in medical technology. Tens of millions of people—many of them children—died from preventable and treatable diseases because they didn't have access to health care. And then, in the last couple of years, Covid-19 has underlined the damage caused by the retrenchment of the state in countries like the UK and the U.S.: the poorest parts of the population have been hit hardest by the pandemic.

So what should we do instead? As a species, our best chance of surviving the threat posed by pathogens will come from working collaboratively. The great improvement in health that high-income countries experienced in the nineteenth and twentieth centuries was not a result of better medicine—as William McNeill claimed—or even economic growth per se. It was, rather, the consequence of political decisions to make massive investments in drinking water, sanitation, housing and poverty reduction. Just as cholera and other waterborne diseases forced cities to undertake vast infrastructure projects, Covid-19 should encourage us to tackle the causes of ill health. This might include ventilation in buildings and in public transport. But in order to prepare society to be resistant to future pandemics, it is crucial to address the more fundamental problems that make some people more vulnerable to infectious diseases than others. Reducing stark inequalities both within and between countries would be a very good start, as would improving lack of access to basic health care across the world.

Although such profound changes might seem unachievable in the current political climate, we should take inspiration from the fact that, throughout history, pandemics have driven momentous political and economic transformations. They shine a light on corrupt and incompetent leaders, reveal and exacerbate pre-existing social divisions, and encourage people to question the status quo. The Covid-19 pandemic has highlighted many of the problems that blight modern society. It is now up to us to seize the opportunity to address these iniquities and to build a happier and healthier world.

Acknowledgments

This book brings together an enormous amount of primary research carried out by archeologists, geneticists, historians, anthropologists, sociologists and economists, among others. In a review of William McNeill's *Plagues and Peoples*, the British historian Keith Thomas described the people who undertake such studies as "small peasants, intensively cultivating tiny tracts of the past."* Such an analogy doesn't do them justice. To my eyes these researchers are alchemists who are capable of generating priceless insights from a fragment of old bone, vial of spit, arctic ice core, centuries-old text or numbers in a spreadsheet. It would not have been possible to write this book without their inspired and painstaking work.

I have spent most of adult life studying and then working in universities, and these experiences have contributed to the book in various ways. I count myself very lucky to have had the opportunity take part in Frank Welz's Global Studies Program, which allowed me to study for two years in Germany, South Africa and India. In particular, living in Durban and Delhi changed the way I see the world. At Cambridge, my PhD supervisor Lawrence King had a profound impact on my intellectual development. Among other things, it was Larry who first encouraged me to look at the link between politics and economics and health. He also introduced me to the work of people like Robert Brenner and Simon Szreter, which features prominently in this book.

---

* The quote goes on: "their labor is arduous and indispensable, but if they pause to raise their heads their vision is usually bounded by their neighbor's fence." Thomas, Keith, "Epidemic Man," *New York Review of Books*, 30 September 1976: 3–4.

And I am grateful to Rhys Hopkins, Paul Kelley, Seth Schindler and Rosamund Conroy for making my years as a student a lot of fun.

In 2016, I began working at what was then the Barts and the London School of Medicine at Queen Mary University of London. I have been there ever since. My office is located in east London, not far from where the capital's last cholera outbreak occurred in 1866—after the municipal authorities decided to connect the poorest part of the capital to the sewage system last. The area surrounding our campus remains among the most deprived part of the country, despite being a few minutes' walk from the City—the UK's financial center. Many of the students I have taught over the last six years grew up locally and they have taught me a great deal that is relevant to this book. I am also fortunate to have incredibly kind, encouraging and inspiring colleagues, including Meg Clinch, Jonathan Filippon, Andrew Harmer, Jen Randall and the person who brought us all together, Dave McCoy.

This is my first book and I couldn't have asked for a better guide to the world of trade publishing than Jessica Woollard, my agent at David Higham Associates. At different times her enthusiasm and calmness have helped me to keep everything on track. I am also very grateful to Jessica for setting me up with my UK editor, Alex Cristofi at Transworld; and, along with Simon Lipskar of Writers House, my U.S. editor, Amanda Cook at Crown—and her colleague Katie Berry. Alex, Amanda and Katie's advice made this book much more concise, focused and clear than it would have otherwise been.

I must thank my parents, Alison and David, for all their encouragement over the last four decades. But more than anyone, I need to acknowledge the role of my partner, Farrah Jarral. Over the last couple of years I have spent many evenings, weekends and holidays working on this book. Farrah has been slow to complain and quick to offer words of support. But her role has been much more important than just tolerating my absence and cheering me on from the sidelines. If I was to dream up the perfect person to act as a sounding board for this book, they wouldn't be too far off her. In 2020, Farrah gave birth to our first child. Since then, I haven't had time to do much except write and play with Zaha, but it has been the most enjoyable time of my life.

Notes

Introduction

1. Freud, Sigmund, *A General Introduction to Psychoanalysis*. Boni and Liveright, 1920.
2. British journalist Scott Oliver notes: "If this all sounds like the ramblings of a man who's just snorted an industrial-sized line of cocaine, then that's probably because psychoanalysis owes its emergence to Freud's protracted dabbling with the stuff, which back then was a freely available over-the-counter medicine." Oliver, Scott, "A Brief History of Freud's Love Affair with Cocaine," *Vice*, 23 June 2017.
3. Stephen Jay Gould suggests that another example of a scientific revolution that undermined the anthropocentric worldview is the discovery of what he calls "deep time." The Book of Genesis claims that the earth is only a few thousand years old, and humans were the dominant life-form on the planet from the sixth day. As Gould points out, if one believes this to be the case, "Why not, then, interpret the physical universe as existing for and because of us?" But, of course, in the last couple of centuries paleontologists have come to realize that the world is in fact several billion years old and humans have only existed for a tiny fraction of that time. Gould, Stephen Jay, *Full House: The Spread of Excellence from Plato to Darwin*. Harvard University Press, 2011.
4. Falkowski, Paul, *Life's Engines: How Microbes Made Earth Habitable*. Princeton University Press, 2015.
5. Ball, Philip, *Curiosity: How Science Became Interested in Everything*. University of Chicago Press, 2013.
6. Mora, Camilo, et al., "How many species are there on Earth and in the ocean?," *PLoS Biology* 9:8 (2011): e1001127.
7. Locey, Kenneth, and Jay Lennon, "Scaling laws predict global microbial diversity," *Proceedings of the National Academy of Sciences* 113:21 (2016): 5970–75.
8. Gould, *Full House*.

9. Langergraber, Kevin, et al., "Generation times in wild chimpanzees and gorillas suggest earlier divergence times in great ape and human evolution," *Proceedings of the National Academy of Sciences* 109:39 (2012): 15716–21.

10. Richter, Daniel, et al., "The age of the hominin fossils from Jebel Irhoud, Morocco, and the origins of the Middle Stone Age," *Nature* 546:7657 (2017): 293–96.

11. Yong, Ed, *I Contain Multitudes: The Microbes Within Us and a Grander View of Life.* Random House, 2016.

12. Joung, Young Soo, Zhifei Ge, and Cullen R. Buie, "Bioaerosol generation by raindrops on soil," *Nature Communications* 8:1 (2017): 1–10.

13. Bar-On, Yinon M., Rob Phillips, and Ron Milo, "The biomass distribution on Earth," *Proceedings of the National Academy of Sciences* 115:25 (2018): 6506–11.

14. Dartnell, Lewis, *Origins: How the Earth Shaped Human History.* Random House, 2019.

15. Warke, Matthew R., et al., "The great oxidation event preceded a paleoproterozoic 'snowball Earth,'" *Proceedings of the National Academy of Sciences* 117:24 (2020): 13314–20.

16. The rising oxygen levels and plummeting temperatures resulted in the planet's first mass extinction. Oxygen is toxic to anaerobic bacteria, so what had been the most abundant forms of life for over a billion years were vanquished to the margins of the earth. Today, anaerobic bacteria survive in what humans see as inhospitable environments and are referred to as extremophiles.

17. Field, Christopher, et al., "Primary production of the biosphere: Integrating terrestrial and oceanic components," *Science* 281:5374 (1998): 237–40.

18. "Viruses have big impacts on ecology and evolution as well as human health," *Economist,* 20 August 2020.

19. Mushegian, A. R., "Are there 10^{31} virus particles on earth, or more, or fewer?," *Journal of Bacteriology* 202:9 (2020): e00052-20.

20. Woolhouse, Mark, et al., "Human viruses: Discovery and emergence," *Philosophical Transactions of the Royal Society B: Biological Sciences* 367:1604 (2012): 2864–71.

21. Suttle, Curtis A., "Marine viruses—major players in the global ecosystem," *Nature Reviews Microbiology* 5:10 (2007): 801–12.

22. Horie, Masayuki, et al., "Endogenous non-retroviral RNA virus elements in mammalian genomes," *Nature* 463:7277 (2010): 84–87.

23. Pastuzyn, Elissa D., et al., "The neuronal gene arc encodes a repurposed retrotransposon gag protein that mediates intercellular RNA transfer," *Cell* 172:1–2 (2018): 275–88.

24. Mi, Sha, et al., "Syncytin is a captive retroviral envelope protein involved in human placental morphogenesis," *Nature* 403:6771 (2000): 785–89.

Chuong, Edward B., "The placenta goes viral: Retroviruses control gene expression in pregnancy," *PLoS Biology* 16:10 (2018): e3000028.

25. Enard, David, et al., "Viruses are a dominant driver of protein adaptation in mammals," *Elife* 5 (2016): e12469.

26. Benedictow, Ole Jørgen, *The Black Death, 1346–1353: The Complete History.* Boydell & Brewer, 2004.

27. Kwiatkowski, Dominic, "How malaria has affected the human genome and what human genetics can teach us about malaria," *The American Journal of Human Genetics* 77:2 (2005): 171–92.

28. Gilbert, Jack A., et al., "Current understanding of the human microbiome," *Nature Medicine* 24:4 (2018): 392–400.

29. Liang, Shan, Xiaoli Wu, and Feng Jin, "Gut-brain psychology: Rethinking psychology from the microbiota–gut–brain axis," *Frontiers in Integrative Neuroscience* 12 (2018): 33.

30. Yong, *I Contain Multitudes.*

31. Valles-Colomer, Mireia, et al., "The neuroactive potential of the human gut microbiota in quality of life and depression," *Nature Microbiology* 4:4 (2019): 623–32.

32. "Germ-free" rodents are born by aseptic cesarean section and then kept in a sterile environment for the rest of their lives. Studies demonstrate that they are unable to recognize other mice that they interact with, and display behavior that is similar to human anxiety and depression. It is possible to restore more normal behavior by introducing certain strains of bacteria into their intestines. In another study, germ-free mice that are colonized by bacteria taken from the intestines of another mouse strain are shown to take on aspects of the donor's personality. Naturally timid mice become more gregarious, and vice versa. The microbiome even seems to impact on the structure of the brain. The amygdala, an almond-shaped part of the brain that plays a crucial role in the response to fear and anxiety, looks different in germ-free animals. Luczynski, Pauline, et al., "Growing up in a bubble: Using germ-free animals to assess the influence of the gut microbiota on brain and behavior," *International Journal of Neuropsychopharmacology* 19:8 (2016): 1–17.

33. Carlyle, Thomas, *On Heroes, Hero-worship, and the Heroic in History.* University of California Press, 1993.

34. Powerful men and women—not all of them great—continue to dominate national and international politics. Angela Merkel, Donald Trump, Boris Johnson, Vladimir Putin, Narendra Modi and Xi Jinping have left their mark in the last few years, for example. The idea that individual leaders can change the world still plays an important role in our hopes and fears for the future, as evidenced by the fact that many of us vote, pray or protest for new heroes to come and save us from our problems.

35. Febvre, Lucien, "Albert Mathiez: Un tempérament, une éducation," *Annales d'histoire économique et sociales* 4:18 (1932): 573–76.

Chapter 1 **Paleolithic Plagues**

1. McIlwaine, Catherine, *Tolkien: Maker of Middle-earth: A Storyteller's History*. Bodleian Library, 2018.
2. Patterson, Nick, et al., "Genetic evidence for complex speciation of humans and chimpanzees," *Nature* 441:7097 (2006): 1103–8. Langergraber, Kevin, et al., "Generation times in wild chimpanzees and gorillas suggest earlier divergence times in great ape and human evolution," *Proceedings of the National Academy of Sciences* 109:39 (2012): 15716–21.
3. Richter, Daniel, et al., "The age of the hominin fossils from Jebel Irhoud, Morocco, and the origins of the Middle Stone Age," *Nature* 546:7657 (2017): 293–96.
4. In terms of archeological evidence, *Homo naledi*—a human species of around 40 kilograms—lived in southern Africa until about 50,000 years ago. DNA degrades quickly in the tropics, so geneticists have not yet been able to extract genetic material from ancient skeletons found in Africa. Researchers have, however, managed to glean some fascinating insights by analyzing the DNA of present-day Africans and comparing their genomes with those of other modern humans, as well as Neanderthals and Denisovans. A study published in 2020 revealed that the genomes of some West African populations contain gene variants belonging to a "ghost population"—an extinct species of humans that have left no physical remains on earth but interbred with *Homo sapiens* or their ancestors and can be identified by the traces of their DNA in the genome of humans alive today. Remarkably, the researchers found that contemporary Yoruba and Mende people in West Africa derive between 2 and 19 percent of their genomes from a ghost species that split from *Homo sapiens* between 360,000 and 975,000 years ago and interbred about 50,000 years ago. The introgressed gene variants that have been retained in the genome of modern Yoruba and Mende appear to give their carriers some advantages, for example in suppressing tumors and regulating hormones. Durvasula, Arun, and Sriram Sankararaman, "Recovering signals of ghost archaic introgression in African populations," *Science Advances* 6:7 (2020): eaax5097.
5. Huerta-Sánchez, Emilia, et al., "Altitude adaptation in Tibetans caused by introgression of Denisovan-like DNA," *Nature* 512:7513 (2014): 194–97.
6. Sutikna, Thomas, et al., "Revised stratigraphy and chronology for *Homo floresiensis* at Liang Bua in Indonesia," *Nature* 532:7599 (2016): 366–69.
7. Détroit, Florent, et al., "A new species of Homo from the Late Pleistocene

of the Philippines," *Nature* 568:7751 (2019): 181–86. This is an abridged list of species of humans that were alive at the same time as *Homo sapiens*. Other examples include *Homo longi* or Dragon Man, who lived in northwest China 150,000 years ago and had an anatomy similar to Neanderthals and Denisovans.

8. *Homo sapiens* did not reach the Americas until about 17,000 years ago because ice sheets in what are now Alaska and Canada made it impossible. They were the first species of humans to inhabit this part of the world.

9. Sutikna et al., "Revised stratigraphy and chronology." Détroit et al., "A new species of Homo."

10. Douka, Katerina, et al., "Age estimates for hominin fossils and the onset of the Upper Paleolithic at Denisova Cave," *Nature* 565:7741 (2019): 640–44. Jacobs, Guy, et al., "Multiple deeply divergent Denisovan ancestries in Papuans," *Cell* 177:4 (2019): 1010–21.

11. Higham, Tom, et al., "The timing and spatiotemporal patterning of Neanderthal disappearance," *Nature* 512:7514 (2014): 306–9. There is evidence that archaic species of humans may have held on longer in Africa. For example, a skull found in Iho Eleru in Nigeria is about 13,000 years old but doesn't appear to belong to *Homo sapiens*. Bergström, Anders, et al., "Origins of modern human ancestry," *Nature* 590:7845 (2021): 229–37.

12. Thurman, Judith, "First impressions: What does the world's oldest art say about us?," *New Yorker*, 23 June 2008.

13. Quiles, Anita, et al., "A high-precision chronological model for the decorated Upper Paleolithic cave of Chauvet-Pont d'Arc, Ardèche, France," *Proceedings of the National Academy of Sciences* 113:17 (2016): 4670–75.

14. Pike, Alistair, et al., "U-series dating of Paleolithic art in 11 caves in Spain," *Science* 336:6087 (2012): 1409–13.

15. Conard, Nicholas, "A female figurine from the basal Aurignacian of Hohle Fels Cave in southwestern Germany," *Nature* 459:7244 (2009): 248–52.

16. Conard, Nicholas, "Paleolithic ivory sculptures from southwestern Germany and the origins of figurative art," *Nature* 426:6968 (2003): 830–32.

17. Higham, Thomas, et al., "Testing models for the beginnings of the Aurignacian and the advent of figurative art and music: The radiocarbon chronology of Geißenklösterle," *Journal of Human Evolution* 62:6 (2012): 664–76.

18. Archeologists recently found paintings of two wild pigs on the wall of a cave in Sulawesi, Indonesia. At over 45,000 years old these are the oldest known examples of figurative art. But they are nowhere near the scale of Chauvet. Brumm, Adam, et al., "Oldest cave art found in Sulawesi," *Science Advances* 7:3 (2021): eabd4648.

19. Leroi-Gourhan, Arlette, "The archeology of Lascaux cave," *Scientific American* 246:6 (1982): 104–13.

20. Thurman, "First impressions."

21. Harari, Yuval Noah, *Sapiens: A Brief History of Humankind*. Random House, 2014.

22. Deacon, Terrence William, *The Symbolic Species: The Co-evolution of Language and the Brain*. W. W. Norton, 1998. Henshilwood, Christopher S., and Francesco d'Errico (eds), *Homo Symbolicus: The Dawn of Language, Imagination and Spirituality*. John Benjamins, 2011.

23. Henshilwood, Christopher S., et al., "The origin of modern human behavior: Critique of the models and their test implications," *Current Anthropology* 44:5 (2003): 627–51. Klein, Richard G., "Whither the Neanderthals?," *Science* 299:5612 (2003): 1525–27.

24. A recent study suggests that *Homo sapiens* carry a gene mutation that allowed them to develop more neurons in the frontal lobe of the brain than Neanderthals. This is not definitive proof of modern humans' superior cognitive ability, however, and as we'll see in the next few pages, there is overwhelming evidence that Neanderthals engaged in all sorts of sophisticated behavior. Pinson, Anneline, et al., "Human TKTL1 implies greater neurogenesis in frontal neocortex of modern humans than Neanderthals," *Science* 377:6611 (2022): eabl6422.

25. Zilhão, João, et al., "Last Interglacial Iberian Neandertals as fisher-hunter-gatherers," *Science* 367:6485 (2020).

26. Brooks, Alison S., et al., "Long-distance stone transport and pigment use in the earliest Middle Stone Age," *Science* 360:6384 (2018): 90–94.

27. Sommer, Marianne, "Mirror, mirror on the wall: Neanderthal as image and 'Distortion' in early 20th-century French science and press," *Social Studies of Science* 36:2 (2006): 207–40. Hammond, Michael, "The expulsion of the Neanderthals from human ancestry: Marcellin Boule and the social context of scientific research," *Social Studies of Science* 12:1 (1982): 1–36.

28. Mooallem, Jon, "Neanderthals were people, too," *New York Times Magazine*, 15 January 2017.

29. Flannery, Tim, *Europe: A Natural History*. Text Publishing, 2018.

30. Walker, James, David Clinnick, and Mark White, "We are not alone: William King and the naming of the Neanderthals," *American Anthropologist* 123:4 (2021): 805–8.

31. Villa, Paola, and Wil Roebroeks, "Neandertal demise: An archeological analysis of the modern human superiority complex," *PLoS One* 9:4 (2014): e96424.

32. Aranguren, Biancamaria, et al., "Wooden tools and fire technology in the early Neanderthal site of Poggetti Vecchi (Italy)," *Proceedings of the National Academy of Sciences* 115:9 (2018): 2054–59.

33. Ferentinos, George, et al., "Early seafaring activity in the southern Ionian Islands, Mediterranean Sea," *Journal of Archeological Science* 39:7 (2012):

2167–76. Strasser, Thomas F., et al., "Dating Paleolithic sites in southwestern Crete, Greece," *Journal of Quaternary Science* 26:5 (2011): 553–60.

34. Kozowyk, P. R. B., et al., "Experimental methods for the Paleolithic dry distillation of birch bark: Implications for the origin and development of Neandertal adhesive technology," *Scientific Reports* 7:1 (2017): 1–9.

35. Spikins, Penny, et al., "Living to fight another day: The ecological and evolutionary significance of Neanderthal healthcare," *Quaternary Science Reviews* 217 (2019): 98–118. Weyrich, Laura S., et al., "Neanderthal behavior, diet, and disease inferred from ancient DNA in dental calculus," *Nature* 544:7650 (2017): 357–61.

36. D'Anastasio, Ruggero, et al., "Micro-biomechanics of the Kebara 2 hyoid and its implications for speech in Neanderthals," *PLoS One* 8:12 (2013): e82261. If you're curious what Neanderthals sounded like, I suggest you watch a YouTube clip from a BBC documentary titled "High-pitched voice theory."

37. Dediu, Dan, and Stephen C. Levinson, "Neanderthal language revisited: Not only us," *Current Opinion in Behavioral Sciences* 21 (2018): 49–55.

38. Solecki, Ralph S., *Shanidar: The First Flower People*. Knopf, 1971. Trinkaus, Erik, *The Shanidar Neandertals*. Academic Press, 2014.

39. Sommer, Jeffrey D., "The Shanidar IV 'flower burial': A re-evaluation of Neanderthal burial ritual," *Cambridge Archeological Journal* 9:1 (1999): 127–29.

40. Trinkaus, Erik, and Sébastien Villotte, "External auditory exostoses and hearing loss in the Shanidar 1 Neandertal," *PLoS One* 12:10 (2017): e0186684.

41. But this argument is based on the assumption that nature is red in tooth and claw, and humans have a unique ability to opt out of the brutal struggle for existence. As we saw in the previous chapter, there is plenty of evidence that the natural world is far more collaborative that the Malthusian-Darwinian worldview allows for.

42. Hoffmann, Dirk, et al., "Symbolic use of marine shells and mineral pigments by Iberian Neandertals 115,000 years ago," *Science Advances* 4:2 (2018): eaar5255.

43. Roebroeks, Wil, et al., "Use of red ochre by early Neandertals," *Proceedings of the National Academy of Sciences* 109:6 (2012): 1889–94.

44. Jaubert, Jacques, et al., "Early Neanderthal constructions deep in Bruniquel Cave in southwestern France," *Nature* 534:7605 (2016): 111–14.

45. Hoffmann, Dirk, et al., "U-Th dating of carbonate crusts reveals Neandertal origin of Iberian cave art," *Science* 359:6378 (2018): 912–15.

46. Higham, Tom, et al., "The timing and spatiotemporal patterning of Neanderthal disappearance," *Nature* 512:7514 (2014): 306–9. Slimak, Ludovic, et al., "Modern human incursion into Neanderthal territories 54,000 years ago at Mandrin, France," *Science Advances* 8:6 (2022): eabj9496.

244 NOTES TO PAGES 26 TO 29

47. Galway-Witham, Julia, James Cole, and Chris Stringer, "Aspects of human physical and behavioral evolution during the last 1 million years," *Journal of Quaternary Science* 34:6 (2019): 355–78.

48. Villa and Roebroeks, "Neandertal demise." Mooallem, "Neanderthals were people, too."

49. Greenbaum, Gili, et al., "Was inter-population connectivity of Neanderthals and modern humans the driver of the Upper Paleolithic transition rather than its product?," *Quaternary Science Reviews* 217 (2019): 316–29.

50. Reich, David, *Who We Are and How We Got Here: Ancient DNA and the New Science of the Human Past.* Oxford University Press, 2018.

51. Green, Richard, et al., "A draft sequence of the Neandertal genome," *Science* 328:5979 (2010): 710–22. Prüfer, Kay, et al., "The complete genome sequence of a Neanderthal from the Altai Mountains," *Nature* 505:7481 (2014): 43–49.

52. Recent research shows that modern-day Africans have more Neanderthal ancestry than previously thought, although not as much as Europeans and Asians. This is a consequence of *Homo sapiens* mating with Neanderthals between 80,000 and 60,000 years ago in the Eastern Mediterranean and then returning to Africa. The retained Neanderthal gene variants spread throughout the continent because they provided ancient Africans with a survival advantage. Chen, Lu, et al., "Identifying and interpreting apparent Neanderthal ancestry in African individuals," *Cell* 180:4 (2020): 677–87.

53. Sankararaman, Sriram, et al., "The genomic landscape of Neanderthal ancestry in present-day humans," *Nature* 507:7492 (2014): 354–57.

54. Posth, Cosimo, et al., "Deeply divergent archaic mitochondrial genome provides lower time boundary for African gene flow into Neanderthals," *Nature Communications* 8:1 (2017): 1–9. Petr, Martin, et al., "The evolutionary history of Neanderthal and Denisovan Y chromosomes," *Science* 369:6511 (2020): 1653–56.

55. Sankararaman, Sriram, et al., "The date of interbreeding between Neandertals and modern humans," *PLOS Genetics* 8:10 (2012): e1002947. Kuhlwilm, Martin, et al., "Ancient gene flow from early modern humans into Eastern Neanderthals," *Nature* 530:7591 (2016): 429–33.

56. Weyrich et al., "Neanderthal behavior, diet, and disease."

57. Harvati, Katerina, et al., "Apidima Cave fossils provide earliest evidence of *Homo sapiens* in Eurasia," *Nature* 571:7766 (2019): 500–504.

58. Grün, Rainer, et al., "U-series and ESR analyzes of bones and teeth relating to the human burials from Skhul," *Journal of Human Evolution* 49:3 (2005): 316–34. Valladas, Heléne, et al., "Thermoluminescence dates for the Neanderthal burial site at Kebara in Israel," *Nature* 330:6144 (1987): 159–60.

59. Gittelman, Rachel, et al., "Archaic hominin admixture facilitated adaptation to out-of-Africa environments," *Current Biology* 26:24 (2016): 3375–82.

60. Greenbaum, Gili, et al., "Disease transmission and introgression can explain the long-lasting contact zone of modern humans and Neanderthals," *Nature Communications* 10:1 (2019): 1–12.

61. Enard, David, and Dmitri Petrov, "Evidence that RNA viruses drove adaptive introgression between Neanderthals and modern humans," *Cell* 175:2 (2018): 360–71.

62. This includes: the major histocompatibility complex (MHC), a group of genes that code for proteins found on the surfaces of cells that help the immune system to recognize pathogens and other foreign substances; the OAS gene cluster that produces proteins involved in the immune response to viral infections, including the tick-borne encephalitis virus still found in northern Europe; STAT2, a gene that codes for a protein that plays an important role in the signalling pathways that help cells to resist viral infections; PNMA1, which codes for a protein that binds with the flu virus; and genes that code for Toll-like receptors (TLR), a class of proteins that play a key role in recognizing pathogens and triggering an immune response. Gouy, Alexandre, and Laurent Excoffier, "Polygenic patterns of adaptive introgression in modern humans are mainly shaped by response to pathogens," *Molecular Biology and Evolution* 37:5 (2020): 1420–33.

63. Enard and Petrov, "RNA viruses drove adaptive introgression."

64. Duffy, Siobain, "Why are RNA virus mutation rates so damn high?," *PLoS Biology* 16:8 (2018): e3000003. Wolff, Horst, and Alex D. Greenwood, "Did viral disease of humans wipe out the Neandertals?," *Medical Hypotheses* 75:1 (2010): 99–105.

65. Sankararaman, Sriram, et al., "The combined landscape of Denisovan and Neanderthal ancestry in present-day humans," *Current Biology* 26:9 (2016): 1241–47. Prüfer, "The complete genome sequence."

66. Vespasiani, Davide Maria, et al., "Denisovan introgression has shaped the immune system of present-day Papuans," *bioRxiv* (2020).

67. Huerta-Sánchez, Emilia, et al., "Altitude adaptation in Tibetans caused by introgression of Denisovan-like DNA," *Nature* 512:7513 (2014): 194–97.

68. Ilardo, Melissa A., et al., "Physiological and genetic adaptations to diving in sea nomads," *Cell* 173:3 (2018): 569–80.

69. Racimo, Fernando, et al., "Archaic adaptive introgression in TBX15/WARS2," *Molecular Biology and Evolution* 34:3 (2017): 509–24.

70. Enard and Petrov, "RNA viruses drove adaptive introgression."

71. Bocquet-Appel, Jean-Pierre, and Anna Degioanni, "Neanderthal demographic estimates," *Current Anthropology* 54.S8 (2013): 202–13.

72. Prüfer, "The complete genome sequence."

73. Sjödin, Per, et al., "Resequencing data provide no evidence for a human bottleneck in Africa during the penultimate glacial period," *Molecular Biology and Evolution* 29:7 (2012): 1851–60.

74. Reich, *Who We Are and How We Got Here*.

75. Laurance, William, "Reflections on the tropical deforestation crisis," *Biological Conservation* 91:2–3 (1999): 109–17.

76. Greenbaum, Gili, "Disease transmission and introgression."

Chapter 2 Neolithic Plagues

1. Pearson, Mike Parker, et al., "The original Stonehenge? A dismantled stone circle in the Preseli Hills of west Wales," *Antiquity* 95:379 (2021): 85–103.

2. Nash, David J., et al., "Origins of the sarsen megaliths at Stonehenge," *Science Advances* 6:31 (2020): eabc0133.

3. Renfrew, Colin (ed.), *The Explanation of Culture Change: Models in Prehistory: Proceedings*. University of Pittsburgh Press, 1973.

4. Madgwick, Richard, et al., "Multi-isotope analysis reveals that feasts in the Stonehenge environs and across Wessex drew people and animals from throughout Britain," *Science Advances* 5:3 (2019): eaau6078. "Madge" is actually my old classmate from secondary school but he's here on merit—even Graeber and Wengrow cite him!

5. Brace, Selina, et al., "Ancient genomes indicate population replacement in Early Neolithic Britain," *Nature Ecology & Evolution* 3:5 (2019): 765–71.

6. Diamond, Jared, *The World Until Yesterday: What Can We Learn from Traditional Societies?* Penguin, 2013.

7. Graeber, David, and David Wengrow, *The Dawn of Everything: A New History of Humanity*. Penguin, 2021.

8. Scott, James C., *Against the Grain: A Deep History of the Earliest States*. Yale University Press, 2017.

9. Graeber and Wengrow, *The Dawn of Everything*.

10. Gurven, Michael, and Hillard Kaplan, "Longevity among hunter-gatherers: A cross-cultural examination," *Population and Development Review* 33:2 (2007): 321–65.

11. Graeber and Wengrow, *The Dawn of Everything*.

12. Ibid.

13. This process was aided by the fact that the land mass runs along an east–west axis—and therefore has much less variation in climate than the Americas or Africa, which runs on a North to South axis. Diamond, Jared, *Guns, Germs and Steel: A Short History of Everybody for the Last 13,000 Years*. Random House, 2013.

14. Scott, *Against the Grain*.

15. Ibid.

16. Diamond, Jared, "The Worst Mistake in the History of the Human Race," *Discover Magazine*, 1 May 1999.

17. Ibid.

18. Burger, Joseph, and Trevor Fristoe, "Hunter-gatherer populations inform modern ecology," *Proceedings of the National Academy of Sciences* 115:6 (2018): 1137–9.

19. Graeber and Wengrow, *The Dawn of Everything*.

20. Gignoux, Christopher R., Brenna M. Henn, and Joanna L. Mountain, "Rapid, global demographic expansions after the origins of agriculture," *Proceedings of the National Academy of Sciences* 108:15 (2011): 6044–49.

21. Bocquet-Appel, Jean-Pierre, "When the world's population took off: The springboard of the Neolithic Demographic Transition," *Science* 333:6042 (2011): 560–61. Bocquet-Appel, Jean-Pierre, "Paleoanthropological traces of a Neolithic demographic transition," *Current Anthropology* 43:4 (2002): 637–50.

22. Diamond, "The worst mistake."

23. Page, Abigail E., et al., "Reproductive trade-offs in extant hunter-gatherers suggest adaptive mechanism for the Neolithic expansion," *Proceedings of the National Academy of Sciences* 113:17 (2016): 4694–99.

24. Bocquet-Appel, "Paleoanthropological traces of a Neolithic demographic transition."

25. Lee, Richard Borshay, *The !Kung San: Men, Women and Work in a Foraging Society*. Cambridge University Press, 1979.

26. Armelagos, George J., and Mark Nathan Cohen (eds), *Paleopathology at the Origins of Agriculture*. Academic Press, 1984. Mummert, Amanda, et al., "Stature and robusticity during the agricultural transition: evidence from the bioarchaeological record," *Economics and Human Biology* 9.3 (2011): 284–301.

27. Scott, *Against the Grain*.

28. Page et al., "Reproductive trade-offs in extant hunter-gatherers suggest adaptive mechanism for the Neolithic expansion."

29. Armelagos, George J., and Kristin N. Harper, "Genomics at the origins of agriculture, part one," *Evolutionary Anthropology: Issues, News, and Reviews* 14:2 (2005): 68–77. Barrett, Ronald, Christopher W. Kuzawa, Thomas McDade, and G. J. Armelagos, "Emerging and re-emerging infectious diseases: The third epidemiologic transition," *Annual Review of Anthropology* 27 (1998): 247–71.

30. Krause-Kyora, Ben, et al., "Neolithic and medieval virus genomes reveal complex evolution of hepatitis B," *Elife* 7 (2018): e36666.

31. Rascovan, Nicolás, et al., "Emergence and spread of basal lineages of *Yersinia pestis* during the Neolithic decline," *Cell* 176:1–2 (2019): 295–305.

32. Sabin, Susanna, et al., "A seventeenth-century Mycobacterium tuberculosis genome supports a Neolithic emergence of the Mycobacterium tuberculosis complex," *Genome Biology* 21:1 (2020): 1–24. Other studies suggest that tuberculous emerged earlier but then spread widely through the population

after the adoption of settled agriculture. Kerner, Gaspard, et al., "Human ancient DNA analyses reveal the high burden of tuberculosis in Europeans over the last 2,000 years," *The American Journal of Human Genetics* 108:3 (2021): 517–24.

33. Düx, Ariane, et al., "Measles virus and rinderpest virus divergence dated to the sixth century BCE," *Science* 368:6497 (2020): 1367–70.

34. Thèves, Catherine, Eric Crubézy, and Philippe Biagini, "History of smallpox and its spread in human populations," *Microbiology Spectrum* 4:4 (2016): 1–10.

35. Paul, John Rodman, *A History of Poliomyelitis.* Yale University Press, 1971.

36. Livingstone, Frank, "Anthropological implications of sickle cell gene distribution in West Africa 1," *American Anthropologist* 60:3 (1958): 533–62.

37. Joy, Deirdre, et al., "Early origin and recent expansion of Plasmodium falciparum," *Science* 300:5617 (2003): 318–21.

38. Not to be confused with his father, William. McNeill, John, *Mosquito Empires: Ecology and War in the Greater Caribbean, 1620–1914.* Cambridge University Press, 2010.

39. Deschamps, Matthieu, et al., "Genomic signatures of selective pressures and introgression from archaic hominins at human innate immunity genes," *The American Journal of Human Genetics* 98:1 (2016): 5–21.

40. Bocquet-Appel, "When the world's population took off."

41. During these summer forays, early humans left their mark on the archeological record. We see tantalizing early evidence of humans in the muddy footsteps left by a small group of adults and children on the beach at Happisburgh in the east of England between 850,000 and 950,000 years ago. Modern humans continued these forays: a 40,000-year-old *Homo sapiens* jawbone fragment from Kent's Cavern in the southwest of England is the oldest anatomically modern human found anywhere in northwest Europe.

42. Brace et al., "Ancient genomes indicate population replacement."

43. Western Hunter-gatherers lacked versions of genes that are responsible for lighter skin in modern-day Europeans and instead had genetic markers of skin pigmentation that are associated with contemporary sub-Saharan Africans. Versions of genes that were responsible for lighter skin did exist at this time among groups in parts of Scandinavia and Western Asia.

44. Even so, vitamin D deficiency is still a health issue for people living in the UK today. The NHS recommends that children under five are given vitamin D supplements, and everyone should take them in the autumn and winter. Alex Ferguson, the former Manchester United manager, was so concerned about the ill-effects of vitamin D deficiency on his players that he installed tanning booths at their training ground and allowed players to go on holiday during the football season.

45. Bocquet-Appel, Jean-Pierre, et al., "Understanding the rates of expansion of the farming system in Europe," *Journal of Archeological Science* 39:2 (2012): 531–46.

46. Pinkowski, Jennifer, "Ötzi the Iceman: What we know 30 years after his discovery," *National Geographic*, 15 September 2021.

47. Keller, Andreas, et al., "New insights into the Tyrolean Iceman's origin and phenotype as inferred by whole-genome sequencing," *Nature Communications* 3:1 (2012): 1–9. Lazaridis, Iosif, et al., "Ancient human genomes suggest three ancestral populations for present-day Europeans," *Nature* 513:7518 (2014): 409–13.

48. Brace et al., "Ancient genomes indicate population replacement." In the most remote regions of northern Europe, such as Scotland and Scandinavia, such a marked population turnover did not occur. Instead, some indigenous hunter-gatherers survived and adopted farming. Skoglund, Pontus, et al., "Genomic diversity and admixture differs for Stone-Age Scandinavian foragers and farmers," *Science* 344:6185 (2014): 747–50.

49. Reich, *Who We Are and How We Got Here*.

50. Goldberg, Amy, et al., "Ancient X chromosomes reveal contrasting sex bias in Neolithic and Bronze Age Eurasian migrations," *Proceedings of the National Academy of Sciences* 114:10 (2017): 2657–62.

51. Crosby, Alfred W., *Ecological Imperialism: The Biological Expansion of Europe, 900–1900*. Cambridge University Press, 2004.

52. McNeill, William Hardy, *Plagues and Peoples*. Anchor, 1998.

53. Castillo, Beatriz Huertas, *Indigenous Peoples in Isolation in the Peruvian Amazon: Their Struggle for Survival and Freedom*. IWGIA, 2004.

54. Colledge, Sue, et al., "Neolithic population crash in northwest Europe associated with agricultural crisis," *Quaternary Research* 92:3 (2019): 686–707.

55. Brace et al., "Ancient genomes indicate population replacement."

56. A couple of centuries after the Western Steppe Herders swept into northern and central Europe, artifacts from the Bell Beaker culture—named after distinctive bell-shaped drinking vessels that they were buried with—started appearing across western and central Europe. This phenomenon began in the Iberian Peninsula but spread throughout northern Europe and as far east as the Danube. Ancient DNA analysis of 200 skeletons that were buried with Bell Beaker artifacts from across Europe shows that the north- and eastward expansion of this new culture about 4,700 years ago wasn't accompanied by significant migration. In Iberia, Bell Beaker people were mostly of Neolithic Farmer ancestry, whereas in northern Europe they had predominantly Steppe Herder ancestry. While the expansion of Corded Ware pottery accompanied the spread of Steppe Herders across Europe, Bell Beaker culture was transmitted horizontally, as one community learned

from and imitated their neighbors. Olalde, Iñigo, et al., "The Beaker phenomenon and the genomic transformation of northwest Europe," *Nature* 555:7695 (2018): 190–96.

57. Ibid.

58. Anthony, David, *The Horse, the Wheel, and Language: How Bronze-Age Riders from the Eurasian Steppes Shaped the Modern World*. Princeton University Press, 2015. Reich, *Who We Are and How We Got Here*.

59. Allentoft, Morten E., et al., "Population genomics of Bronze Age Eurasia," *Nature* 522:7555 (2015): 167–72. Haak, Wolfgang, et al., "Massive migration from the steppe was a source for Indo-European languages in Europe," *Nature* 522:7555 (2015): 207–11.

60. Evershed, Richard P., et al., "Dairying, diseases and the evolution of lactase persistence in Europe," *Nature* 608 (2022): 336–45.

61. Haak et al., "Massive migration from the steppe."

62. Bellwood, Peter, *First Migrants: Ancient Migration in Global Perspective*. John Wiley & Sons, 2014.

63. Goldberg et al., "Ancient X chromosomes."

64. Reich, *Who We Are and How We Got Here*.

65. Shennan, Stephen, et al., "Regional population collapse followed initial agriculture booms in mid-Holocene Europe," *Nature Communications* 4:1 (2013): 1–8.

66. Stevens, Chris, and Dorian Fuller, "Did Neolithic farming fail? The case for a Bronze Age agricultural revolution in the British Isles," *Antiquity* 86:333 (2012): 707–22.

67. Skoglund et al., "Genomic diversity and admixture."

68. Rascovan et al., "*Yersinia pestis* during the Neolithic decline."

69. Valtueña, Aida Andrades, et al., "The Stone Age plague and its persistence in Eurasia," *Current Biology* 27:23 (2017): 3683–91. Rasmussen, Simon, et al., "Early divergent strains of *Yersinia pestis* in Eurasia 5,000 years ago," *Cell* 163:3 (2015): 571–82.

70. Rasmussen et al., "Early divergent strains of *Yersinia pestis*."

71. Rascovan et al., "*Yersinia pestis* during the Neolithic decline."

72. Chapman, John, Bisserka Gaydarska, and Marco Nebbia, "The origins of Trypillia megasites," *Frontiers in Digital Humanities* 6 (2019): 10.

73. Müller, Johannes, Knut Rassmann, and Mykhailo Videiko (eds), *Trypillia Mega-sites and European Prehistory: 4100–3400 BCE*. Routledge, 2016.

74. Rassmann, Knut, et al., "High precision Tripolye settlement plans, demographic estimations and settlement organization," *Journal of Neolithic Archaeology* (2014): 96–134.

75. Graeber and Wengrow, *The Dawn of Everything*.

76. Payne, Joan Crowfoot, "Lapis lazuli in early Egypt," *Iraq* 30:1 (1968): 58–61.

77. Vandkilde, H., "Bronzization: The Bronze Age as pre-modern globalization,"

Prähistorische Zeitschrift 91:1 (2016): 103–23. Ratnagar, Shereen, et al., "The Bronze Age: Unique instance of a preindustrial world system?," *Current Anthropology* 42:3 (2001): 351–79.

78. One particularly curious piece of evidence for long-distance interactions between Neolithic populations is a species of vole that is found in the Orkney Islands but not mainland Britain. Genetic analysis has shown that the Orkney vole was most likely introduced to the Scottish archipelago over 5,000 years ago from what is now Belgium. Martínková, Natália, et al., "Divergent evolutionary processes associated with colonization of offshore islands," *Molecular Ecology* 22:20 (2013): 5205–20.

79. Lazaridis et al., "Ancient human genomes."

80. Although hunter-gatherers were routed by Neolithic Farmers, they were not completely wiped out. In fact, after their initial decimation, the proportion of hunter-gatherer DNA in the European genome started to increase. This could be because the hunter-gatherers developed immunity to the Neolithic pathogens by adaptive introgression. Haak et al., "Massive migration from the steppe."

81. At a time when the concept of indigenous Britishness is wheeled out by cynical politicians to incite anger against more recent migrants, it is heartening to be reminded how wrong this assertion is. In 2013, the British comedian Stewart Lee skewered right-wing politicians' concerns about Bulgarians and Romanians being allowed to work in the UK. He notes the repeated xenophobic sentiments expressed ten years earlier about "bloody Poles . . . coming over here fixing all the stuff we have broken and are too illiterate to read the instructions for and doing it better than us in a second language." Lee then goes back through multiple waves of immigration: "Pakistanis and Indians coming over here and inventing us a national cuisine"; the Huguenots doubting transubstantiation—"we don't want your lace here, we've got corduroy"; the Anglo-Saxons with their inlaid jewelry, shit burial tradition, miserable epic poetry; all the way back to the "bloody Beaker folk coming over here with their drinking vessels." The Amesbury Archer was one of the first Beaker folk to arrive in the British Isles, bringing Steppe Herder ancestry with him.

82. Marcus, Joseph H., et al., "Genetic history from the Middle Neolithic to present on the Mediterranean island of Sardinia," *Nature Communications* 11:1 (2020): 1–14.

83. Günther, Torsten, et al., "Ancient genomes link Neolithic Farmers from Atapuerca in Spain to modern-day Basques," *Proceedings of the National Academy of Sciences* 112:38 (2015): 11917–22.

84. Haak et al., "Massive migration from the steppe."

85. Anthony, *The Horse, the Wheel, and Language.*

86. Steppe Herder DNA is the common link between European and South

Asian people, who both speak Indo-European languages. It began to appear in South Asia between 4,000 and 3,000 years ago. The migrants mixed with the people already there to form the population that inhabits North India today. Crucially, those contemporary Indians who carry the largest proportion of Steppe Herder DNA tend to speak Indo-European languages such as Hindi. Often, but not always, people with more fair-skinned Steppe ancestry belong to upper castes. Haak et al., "Massive migration from the steppe."

Chapter 3 Ancient Plagues

1. Sontag, Susan, *Illness as Metaphor and AIDS and Its Metaphors*. Penguin, 2013. The way of understanding disease is also apparent in the Bible. For example, the Book of Exodus in the Old Testament explains the ten plagues of Egypt as God's response to the pharaoh's taunts.

2. Littman, Robert J., "The plague of Athens: Epidemiology and paleopathology," *Mount Sinai Journal of Medicine* 76:5 (2009): 456–67.

3. In 2006, scientists claimed to have identified typhoid bacteria in teeth that were found in a mass grave in Athens dating to around 430 BCE; but the methods used in this study have come in for heavy criticism, so we are still none the wiser. Papagrigorakis, Manolis J., et al., "DNA examination of ancient dental pulp incriminates typhoid fever as a probable cause of the Plague of Athens," *International Journal of Infectious Diseases* 10:3 (2006): 206–14. Shapiro, Beth, Andrew Rambaut, and M. Thomas P. Gilbert, "No proof that typhoid caused the Plague of Athens (a reply to Papagrigorakis et al.)," *International Journal of Infectious Diseases* 10:4 (2006): 334–35.

4. Littman, "The plague of Athens."

5. Ibid.

6. Mitchell-Boyask, Robin, "Plague and theatre in ancient Athens," *The Lancet* 373:9661 (2009): 374–75.

7. Cartledge, Paul, *The Spartans: An Epic History*. Pan Macmillan, 2003.

8. Littman, "The plague of Athens."

9. Toynbee, Arnold J., *A Study of History*. Oxford Paperbacks, 1987.

10. By the beginning of the first millennium CE, the population of Rome consisted mostly of people who were similar to modern-day Greeks, Maltese, Cypriots and Syrians. Antonio, Margaret, et al., "Ancient Rome: A genetic crossroads of Europe and the Mediterranean," *Science* 366:6466 (2019): 708–14.

11. Harper, Kyle, *The Fate of Rome: Climate, Disease and the End of an Empire*. Princeton University Press, 2017.

12. Ibid.

13. Moss, Henry St. Lawrence Beaufort, *The Birth of the Middle Ages, 395–814*. Clarendon Press, 1935.

14. Scheidel, Walter, *Escape from Rome: The Failure of Empire and the Road to Prosperity*. Princeton University Press, 2019. Harper, *The Fate of Rome*.

15. Harper, *The Fate of Rome*.

16. McConnell, Joseph R., et al., "Lead pollution recorded in Greenland ice indicates European emissions tracked plagues, wars, and imperial expansion during antiquity," *Proceedings of the National Academy of Sciences* 115:22 (2018): 5726–31.

17. Harper, *The Fate of Rome*.

18. Bruun, Christer, "Water supply, drainage and watermills," in Paul Erdkamp (ed.), *The Cambridge Companion to Ancient Rome*, Cambridge University Press, 2013, pp. 297–313.

19. Galen described three different types of intestinal worms, but following Hippocrates' theory he believed they were created by humoral imbalances within the body rather than transmitted by insanitary practices. Mitchell, Piers, "Human parasites in the Roman World: Health consequences of conquering an empire," *Parasitology* 144:1 (2017): 48–58.

20. Koloski-Ostrow, Ann Olga, "Talking heads: What toilets and sewers tell us about ancient Roman sanitation," *The Conversation* (2015).

21. Jansen, Gemma C. M., Ann Olga Koloski-Ostrow, and Eric M. Moormann (eds), *Roman Toilets: Their Archaeology and Cultural History*. Peeters, 2011.

22. Ingemark, Camilla Asplund, "The octopus in the sewers: An ancient legend analogue," *Journal of Folklore Research* (2008): 145–70.

23. Koloski-Ostrow, Ann Olga, *The Archaeology of Sanitation in Roman Italy: Toilets, Sewers, and Water Systems*. University of North Carolina Press, 2015.

24. Mitchell, "Human parasites in the Roman World."

25. Harper, *The Fate of Rome*.

26. Sallares, Robert, *Malaria and Rome: A History of Malaria in Ancient Italy*. Oxford University Press, 2002.

27. Winegard, Timothy C., *The Mosquito: A Human History of Our Deadliest Predator*. Text Publishing, 2019.

28. Brown, Peter, *Late Antiquity*. Harvard University Press, 1998.

29. Harper, *The Fate of Rome*.

30. Ibid.

31. Jones, Christopher P., "An amulet from London and events surrounding the Antonine Plague," *Journal of Roman Archaeology* 29 (2016): 469–72.

32. Harper, *The Fate of Rome*.

33. McConnell, "Lead pollution recorded in Greenland ice."

34. Harper, *The Fate of Rome*.

35. Marcus Aurelius wrote *Meditations* during the Antonine Plague and the trials of being Roman emperor during such a devastating epidemic are likely to have influenced his Stoic philosophy. Robertson, Donald, *How to Think*

Like a Roman Emperor: The Stoic Philosophy of Marcus Aurelius. St. Martin's Press, 2019.

36. Harper, *The Fate of Rome.*

37. This is an apocryphal tale but one that demonstrates that stereotypes about the brutality of oriental despots were already present in Ancient Rome.

38. McConnell, "Lead pollution recorded in Greenland ice."

39. Harper, *The Fate of Rome.*

40. Ibid.

41. Hackett, Conrad, Marcin Stonawski, Michaela Potančoková, Vegard Skirbekk, Phillip Connor, David McClendon, and Stephanie Kramer, *The Changing Global Religious Landscape.* Pew Research Center, 2017.

42. Harper, *The Fate of Rome.*

43. The U.S. figure comes from Harvard University's Pluralism Project, while the UK number is based on the latest Census data.

44. Harper, *The Fate of Rome.*

45. Ibid.

46. Ibid.

47. Stark, Rodney, *The Triumph of Christianity: How the Jesus Movement Became the World's Largest Religion.* HarperOne, 2011.

48. McNeill, *Plagues and Peoples.*

49. Harper, *The Fate of Rome.*

50. The Goths were a Germanic people, but the identity of the Huns is more complicated, as they appear to have been shifting alliances of diverse nomadic groups that lived on the Steppe, including Scythians and Xiongnu. Damgaard, Peter de Barros, et al., "137 ancient human genomes from across the Eurasian steppes," *Nature* 557:7705 (2018): 369–74.

51. Galassi, Francesco, et al., "The sudden death of Alaric I (c.370–410 AD), the vanquisher of Rome: A tale of malaria and lacking immunity," *European Journal of Internal Medicine* 31 (2016): 84–87.

52. Harper, *The Fate of Rome.*

53. Ibid.

54. Gibbons, Ann, "Eruption made 536 'the worst year to be alive,'" *Science* (2018): 733–34.

55. Sarris, Peter, "New approaches to the 'Plague of Justinian,'" *Past & Present* 254:1 (2022): 315–46.

56. Rasmussen et al., "Early divergent strains of *Yersinia pestis.*"

57. The black rat is much more gregarious than the brown rat that now dominates Eurasia. McCormick, Michael, "Rats, communications, and plague: Toward an ecological history," *Journal of Interdisciplinary History* 34:1 (2003): 1–25.

58. Harper, *The Fate of Rome.*

59. Damgaard et al., "137 ancient human genomes."

60. Schmid, Boris V., et al., "Climate-driven introduction of the Black Death and successive plague reintroductions into Europe," *Proceedings of the National Academy of Sciences* 112:10 (2015): 3020–25.

61. Harper, *The Fate of Rome*.

62. Russell, Josiah, "That earlier plague," *Demography* 5:1 (1968): 174–84.

63. Bowersock, Glen Warren, *Empires in Collision in Late Antiquity*. UPNE, 2012.

64. Dols, Michael Walters, *The Black Death in the Middle East*. Princeton University Press, 2019.

65. Bowersock, Glen Warren, *The Crucible of Islam*. Harvard University Press, 2017.

66. Aslan, Reza, *No God but God: The Origins, Evolution, and Future of Islam*. Random House, 2011.

67. Harper, *The Fate of Rome*.

68. Mackintosh-Smith, Tim, *Arabs: A 3,000-Year History of Peoples, Tribes and Empires*. Yale University Press, 2019.

69. Bowersock, *The Crucible of Islam*. Bulliet, Richard, *Conversion to Islam in the Medieval Period*. Harvard University Press, 2013.

70. Mackintosh-Smith, *Arabs*.

71. Dols, *The Black Death in the Middle East*.

72. Ibid. Russell, "That earlier plague."

73. Brown, Peter, "'Mohammed and Charlemagne' by Henri Pirenne," *Daedalus* (1974): 25–33.

74. Scheidel, *Escape from Rome*.

Chapter 4 Medieval Plagues

1. Tuchman, Barbara W., *A Distant Mirror: The Calamitous 14th Century*. Random House, 2011.

2. Herlihy, David, and Samuel H. Cohn, *The Black Death and the Transformation of the West*. Harvard University Press, 1997.

3. Ibid.

4. Lavigne, Franck, et al., "Source of the great AD 1257 mystery eruption unveiled, Samalas volcano, Rinjani Volcanic Complex, Indonesia," *Proceedings of the National Academy of Sciences* 110:42 (2013): 16742–47.

5. Phillips, Rod, *French Wine: A History*. University of California Press, 2016.

6. Ziegler, Philip, *The Black Death*. Faber & Faber, 2013.

7. Jones, Michael (ed.), *The New Cambridge Medieval History*. Cambridge University Press, 1995.

8. Ziegler, *The Black Death*.

9. McNeill, *Plagues and Peoples*. In 1986, William Dalrymple set off from the Church of the Holy Sepulchre in Jerusalem to retrace Marco Polo's journey

to the Far East. His first book, *In Xanadu* (1989), describes the trip. Dalrymple is acutely aware that the *pax Mongolica* was a historical exception. In fact, with the Soviet Army withdrawing from Afghanistan and China opening up, he suggests that it was the first time in several centuries that it was possible to travel overland on the Silk Road as Polo had done.

10. Spyrou, Maria, et al., "The source of the Black Death in fourteenth-century central Eurasia," *Nature* 606:7915 (2022): 718–24.

11. Sussman, George D., "Was the black death in India and China?," *Bulletin of the History of Medicine* (2011): 319–55.

12. McNeill, *Plagues and Peoples*.

13. Benedictow, *The Black Death*. A recent study that found evidence of *Yersinia pestis* in the dental pulp of thirty-four people suspected to have died during the Black Death and in subsequent waves of plague from ten sites across Europe seems to confirm this. Spyrou, Maria A., et al., "Phylogeography of the second plague pandemic revealed through analysis of historical *Yersinia pestis* genomes," *Nature Communications* 10:1 (2019): 1–13.

14. Wheelis, Mark, "Biological warfare at the 1346 siege of Caffa," *Emerging Infectious Diseases* 8:9 (2002): 971–75.

15. Ziegler, *The Black Death*.

16. Ibid.

17. Benedictow, *The Black Death*.

18. Ibid.

19. More, Alexander, et al., "Next-generation ice core technology reveals true minimum natural levels of lead (Pb) in the atmosphere: Insights from the Black Death," *GeoHealth* 1:4 (2017): 211–19.

20. Ziegler, *The Black Death*.

21. Benedictow, *The Black Death*.

22. Cantor, Norman, *In the Wake of the Plague: The Black Death and the World It Made*. Simon and Schuster, 2001.

23. Cohn Jr., Samuel K., "The Black Death and the burning of Jews," *Past & Present* 196:1 (2007): 3–36.

24. Astonishingly, a recent study demonstrated that the "same places that witnessed violent attacks on Jews during the plague in 1349 also showed more anti-Semitic attitudes more than half a millennium later: their inhabitants engaged in more anti-Semitic violence in the 1920s, were more likely to vote for the Nazi Party before 1930, wrote more letters to the country's most anti-Semitic newspaper, organized more deportations of Jews, and engaged in more attacks on synagogues during the *Reichskristallnacht* in 1938." Voigtländer, Nico, and Hans-Joachim Voth, "Persecution perpetuated: The medieval origins of anti-Semitic violence in Nazi Germany," *The Quarterly Journal of Economics* 127:3 (2012): 1339–92.

25. Ziegler, *The Black Death*. Also see Cohn Jr., Samuel, "Plague violence and

abandonment from the Black Death to the early modern period," *Annales de démographie historique* 2017/2 (134): 39–61.

26. Cantor, *In the Wake of the Plague.*

27. Ziegler, *The Black Death.*

28. Gottfried, Robert S., *The Black Death: Natural and Human Disaster in Medieval Europe.* Simon and Schuster, 2010.

29. Ibid.

30. A recent study demonstrates that new outbreaks in Europe tended to occur a few years after climate fluctuations in the gerbils' and marmots' mountainous habitats in Asia. Schmid, Boris V., et al., "Climate-driven introduction of the Black Death and successive plague reintroductions into Europe," *Proceedings of the National Academy of Sciences* 112:10 (2015): 3020–25.

31. Gottfried, *The Black Death.*

32. Alfani, Guido, "Plague in seventeenth-century Europe and the decline of Italy: An epidemiological hypothesis," *European Review of Economic History* 17:4 (2013): 408–30.

33. Pamuk, Şevket, "The Black Death and the origins of the 'Great Divergence' across Europe, 1300–1600," *European Review of Economic History* 11:3 (2007): 289–317.

34. Snowden, Frank M., *Epidemics and Society: From the Black Death to the Present.* Yale University Press, 2019.

35. Foucault, Michel, *Security, Territory, Population: Lectures at the Collège de France, 1977–78.* Springer, 2007.

36. Cohn, Samuel K., "Epidemiology of the Black Death and successive waves of plague," *Medical History* 52.S27 (2008): 74–100.

37. Dols, Michael W., "The second plague pandemic and its recurrences in the Middle East: 1347–1894," *Journal of the Economic and Social History of the Orient* (1979): 162–89.

38. Benedictow, *The Black Death.*

39. Speros Vryonis refers to this process as the "nomadization" and "Islamization" of Asia Minor. Recent studies have demonstrated that the population that currently lives in Turkey has close genetic links with the Middle East, Europe and the Caucuses. Vryonis, Speros, *The Decline of Medieval Hellenism in Asia Minor and the Process of Islamization from the Eleventh through the Fifteenth Century.* University of California Press, 1971. Kars, M. Ece, et al., "The genetic structure of the Turkish population reveals high levels of variation and admixture," *Proceedings of the National Academy of Sciences* 118:36 (2021): e2026076118.

40. Finkel, Caroline, *Osman's Dream: The History of the Ottoman Empire.* Hachette UK, 2007.

41. Dunn, Ross E., *The Adventures of Ibn Battuta.* University of California Press, 2012.

42. Ayalon, Yaron, "The Black Death and the rise of the Ottomans," in *Natural Disasters in the Ottoman Empire: Plague, Famine and Other Misfortunes*. Cambridge University Press, 2015, pp. 21–60. Kasaba, Resat, *A Moveable Empire: Ottoman Nomads, Migrants, and Refugees*. University of Washington Press, 2011.

43. Mikhail, Alan, *God's Shadow: Sultan Selim, His Ottoman Empire, and the Making of the Modern World*. Liveright Publishing, 2020.

44. Dols, "The second plague pandemic and its recurrences in the Middle East."

45. Neustadt, David, "The plague and its effects upon the Mamlûk Army," *Journal of the Royal Asiatic Society* 78:1–2 (1946): 67–73. Dols, *The Black Death in the Middle East*.

46. Kasaba, *A Moveable Empire*.

47. McNeill, *Plagues and Peoples*.

48. Mikhail, *God's Shadow*.

49. Ziegler, *The Black Death*.

50. Ekelund, Robert B., et al., *Sacred Trust: The Medieval Church as an Economic Firm*. Oxford University Press, 1996.

51. Gottfried, *The Black Death*.

52. Herlihy and Cohn, *The Black Death*.

53. Cantor, *In the Wake of the Plague*.

54. Gottfried, *The Black Death*.

55. "Lollard" is thought to come from a Dutch word meaning to mutter or mumble. The name was meant to be derogatory but was adopted by these proto-Protestants.

56. German, Lindsey, and John Rees, *A People's History of London*. Verso, 2012.

57. Herlihy and Cohn, *The Black Death*.

58. A contemporary equivalent is the manner in which Twitter transformed politics by allowing outsiders like Donald Trump to communicate directly with massive numbers of supporters. To continue the social media analogy, woodcuts were the TikTok of the Late Middle Ages.

59. Eisenstein, Elizabeth L., *The Printing Press as an Agent of Change*. Cambridge University Press, 1980.

60. Edwards Jr., Mark U., *Printing, Propaganda, and Martin Luther*. Fortress Press, 2004.

61. Poe, Marshall T., *A History of Communications: Media and Society from the Evolution of Speech to the Internet*. Cambridge University Press, 2010.

62. Herlihy and Cohn, *The Black Death*.

63. Tuchman, *A Distant Mirror*.

64. Peterhouse (1284) is the oldest Cambridge college, followed by Clare (1326) and Pembroke (1347). It should be noted that sometimes the donations

were not motivated by a desire to further learning, however. Corpus Christi was founded in 1352 by two guilds which stipulated that the scholars must pray for their deceased members because it was cheaper than employing clergy, who had become both scarce and expensive after the Black Death. Gottfried, *The Black Death*.

65. Herlihy and Cohn, *The Black Death*.

66. See for example Ryrie, Alec, *Protestants: The Radicals Who Made the Modern World*. William Collins, 2017.

67. Outram, Quentin, "The socio-economic relations of warfare and the military mortality crises of the Thirty Years' War," *Medical History* 45:2 (2001): 151–84.

68. The figures are based on estimates from the Pew Research Center.

69. Bloch, Marc, *Feudal Society*. Folio Society, 2012.

70. Brenner, Robert, "The agrarian roots of European capitalism," *Past & Present* 97 (1982): 16–113.

71. Brenner, Robert, "Property and progress: Where Adam Smith went wrong," in Chris Wickham (ed.), *Marxist History-Writing for the Twenty-First Century*. British Academy, 2007, pp. 49–111.

72. Across Europe, feudal lords made war with one another, attempting to compensate for their lost income by plundering and conquering their neighbors. This is why the Hundred Years' War lasted so long. Economic necessity pushed impoverished hidalgos to wage continuous war against Muslim Spain and then, when the Emirate of Granada was defeated in 1491, the indigenous people of the New World. Brenner, "The agrarian roots of European capitalism." Brenner, "Property and progress."

73. Ibid.

74. Cohn, Samuel, "After the Black Death: Labor legislation and attitudes toward labor in late-medieval western Europe," *The Economic History Review* 60:3 (2007): 457–85.

75. MacArthur, Brian (ed.), *The Penguin Book of Historic Speeches*. Penguin, 1996.

76. Brenner, "The agrarian roots of European capitalism." Brenner, "Property and progress."

77. Allen, Robert, "Economic structure and agricultural productivity in Europe, 1300–1800," *European Review of Economic History* 4:1 (2000): 1–25.

78. Appleby, Andrew, "Grain prices and subsistence crises in England and France, 1590–1740," *The Journal of Economic History* 39:4 (1979): 865–87.

79. Ibid.

80. Brenner, "The agrarian roots of European capitalism." Brenner, "Property and progress."

81. In France, the urbanization rate increased from 9 percent to 13 percent in the same period, and in Germany from 8 percent to 9 percent. Ibid.

Chapter 5 Colonial Plagues

1. Bell, Julian, "Werner Herzog and the World's Oldest Paintings," *New York Review of Books*, 4 May 2011.

2. "Aztec" is a nineteenth-century invention, so contemporary historians tend to avoid it. The Mexica Empire was controlled by an alliance of three militarized city-states located in what is now the middle of Mexico: Texcoco, Tlacopan and Tenochtitlan—with Tenochtitlan being by far the most powerful partner.

3. The film's events and characters are inspired by history. The real-life Aguirre set off from Quito in search of the City of Gold in 1560 CE, mutinied somewhere in the Amazon, and actually made it all the way to the Caribbean before being killed.

4. Thomas, Hugh, *The Conquest of Mexico*. Random House, 1993.

5. Hemming, John, *The Conquest of the Incas*. Pan Macmillan, 2004. At the time of writing, a kilo of gold is worth about $55,000 or £48,000.

6. Cortés, Hernán, *Letters from Mexico,* ed. Anthony Pagden. Yale University Press, 2001.

7. Maddison, Angus, *Contours of the World Economy 1–2030 AD: Essays in Macro-economic History*. Oxford University Press, 2007. According to World Bank data, the USA's GDP per capita was $69,000, compared to $50,000 in the UK in 2021 (PPP, current international $).

8. Horses had lived in North America but became extinct between 10,000 and 15,000 years ago, possibly as a result of hunting after humans arrived on the continent.

9. This is when using the measure of GDP that is most generous to the Afghans. World Bank figures. GDP per capita (PPP, current international $).

10. Koch, Alexander, Chris Brierley, Mark M. Maslin, and Simon L. Lewis, "Earth system impacts of the European arrival and Great Dying in the Americas after 1492," *Quaternary Science Reviews* 207 (2019): 13–36.

11. Reséndez, Andrés, *The Other Slavery: The Uncovered Story of Indian Enslavement in America*. HarperCollins, 2016.

12. Mann, Charles C., *1493: How Europe's Discovery of the Americas Revolutionized Trade, Ecology and Life on Earth*. Granta Books, 2011. A recent study showed that the modern-day Caribbean population still retain some Taíno gene variations as a result of interbreeding with Europeans and Africans in the immediate aftermath of colonization. In addition, some present-day Caribbean inhabitants identify as "neo-Taíno" and claim to practice Taíno culture. Schroeder, Hannes, et al., "Origins and genetic legacies of the Caribbean Taino," *Proceedings of the National Academy of Sciences* 115:10 (2018): 2341–46.

13. Cook, Noble David, "Disease and the Depopulation of Hispaniola, 1492–1518," *Colonial Latin American Review* 2:1–2 (1993): 213–45.

14. Clendinnen, Inga, *Ambivalent Conquests: Maya and Spaniard in Yucatan, 1517–1570*. Cambridge University Press, 2003.

15. Restall, Matthew, *When Montezuma Met Cortés: The True Story of the Meeting That Changed History*. HarperCollins, 2018.

16. Koch et al., "Earth system impacts of the European arrival."

17. Crosby, *Ecological Imperialism*. Also see McNeill, *Plagues and Peoples*.

18. Crosby, Alfred W., *The Columbian Exchange: Biological and Cultural Consequences of 1492*. Greenwood Publishing Group, 1972.

19. McNeill, *Plagues and Peoples*.

20. Restall, *When Montezuma Met Cortés*.

21. Koch et al., "Earth system impacts of the European arrival."

22. Cook, Sherburne Friend, and Lesley Byrd Simpson, *The Population of Central Mexico in the Sixteenth Century*. University of California Press, 1948.

23. Vågene, Åshild J., et al., "Salmonella enterica genomes from victims of a major sixteenth-century epidemic in Mexico," *Nature Ecology & Evolution* 2:3 (2018): 520–28.

24. McNeill, *Plagues and Peoples*.

25. Koch et al., "Earth system impacts of the European arrival."

26. Ibid.

27. The mortality rates were similar to those of Central America. The population of the Inka heartland had fallen from about 9 million to about 670,000 by 1620, largely as a result of these epidemics. Ibid.

28. Ibid.

29. Diamond, Jared, and Peter Bellwood, "Farmers and their languages: The first expansions," *Science* 300:5619 (2003): 597–603.

30. Sontag, *Illness as Metaphor and AIDS and Its Metaphors*.

31. Diamond, *Guns, Germs and Steel*.

32. The lack of domesticated animals in the New World reflects the lack of domesticable wild animals. According to Diamond, 80 percent of large mammals in the Americas became extinct around 11,000 years ago, a point in prehistory that coincides with the arrival of the first humans on the continent. Ibid.

33. Crosby, *Ecological Imperialism*. Also see McNeill, *Plagues and Peoples*.

34. According to statistics from the Pew Research Center.

35. Similarly, many indigenous communities adopted their conquerors' language. Spanish remains the second-most spoken language in the world after Mandarin. But only 10 percent of Spanish-speakers live in Spain—almost all the rest are in Latin America.

36. Simpson, Lesley Byrd, *The Encomienda in New Spain: The Beginning of Spanish Mexico*. University of California Press, 1982.

37. Mann, *1493*.

38. Lane, Kris, *Potosí: The Silver City That Changed the World*. University of California Press, 2019.

39. Dell, Melissa, "The persistent effects of Peru's mining *mita*," *Econometrica* 78:6 (2010): 1863–1903.

40. Lane, *Potosí*. Mann, *1493*.

41. Flynn, Dennis, and Arturo Giráldez, "Born with a 'silver spoon': The origin of world trade in 1571," *Journal of World History* 6:2 (1995): 201–21.

42. Mann, *1493*.

43. Flynn and Giráldez, "Born with a 'silver spoon.'"

44. Mann, *1493*.

45. Keller, Christian, "Furs, fish, and ivory: Medieval Norsemen at the Arctic fringe," *Journal of the North Atlantic* 3:1 (2010): 1–23.

46. Kuitems, Margot, et al., "Evidence for European presence in the Americas in AD 1021," *Nature* 601:7893 (2022): 388–91.

47. Barraclough, Eleanor Rosamund, *Beyond the Northlands: Viking Voyages and the Old Norse Sagas*. Oxford University Press, 2016.

48. Crosby, *Ecological Imperialism*.

49. Fenner, Frank, et al., *Smallpox and Its Eradication*. World Health Organization, 1988.

50. Crosby, *Ecological Imperialism*.

51. Hopkins, Donald, *The Greatest Killer: Smallpox in History*. University of Chicago Press, 2002.

52. Crosby, *Ecological Imperialism*.

53. Mann, Charles C., *1491: New Revelations of the Americas Before Columbus*. Alfred Knopf, 2005.

54. Crosby, *Ecological Imperialism*.

55. Ibid.

56. Mann, *1493*.

57. Mann, *1491*.

58. Fischer, David Hackett, *Albion's Seed: Four British Folkways in America*. Oxford University Press, 1989.

59. Crosby, *Ecological Imperialism*.

60. Ibid. The British weren't always willing to leave something as important as the spread of infectious disease up to God. In 1763 General Jeffery Amherst justified distributing blankets from a nearby smallpox hospital to Native American communities by saying that "We must, on this occasion, Use Every Stratagem in our power to Reduce them"—by which he means kill the indigenous population. Fenn, Elizabeth A., *Pox Americana: The Great Smallpox Epidemic of 1775–82*. Macmillan, 2001.

61. Fischer, *Albion's Seed*.

62. In fact, when the Pilgrims were trying to decide where to settle, they weighed the pros and cons of several possible locations. William Bradford,

who led the foundation of Plymouth Colony, notes how back in Leiden the Pilgrims considered the Dutch colony of Essequibo in the Guiana region, which "was both fruitful and pleasant, and might yield riches and maintenance to the possessors more easily than the other; yet, other things considered, it would not be so fit for them . . . Such hot countries are subject to grievous diseases and many noisome impediments which other more temperate places are freer from, and would not so well agree with our English bodies." Instead, the Pilgrims sailed to New England, the epitome of a "more temperate place" and free from devastating infectious diseases—at least those that kill Europeans. Crosby, *Ecological Imperialism*. In North America, about 1.5 percent of European settlers would die every year on average—a mortality rate that was only marginally higher than in England. Acemoglu, Daron, Simon Johnson, and James A. Robinson, "The colonial origins of comparative development: An empirical investigation: Reply," *American Economic Review* 102:6 (2012): 3077–110.

63. Acemoglu, Johnson and Robinson, "The colonial origins of comparative development."

64. "Do They Know It's Christmas?" lyrics © Chappell Music Ltd. Songwriters: Midge Ure and Bob Geldof.

65. It is often said that Mansa Musa was the richest person who ever lived—that is, not just wealthier than Bill Gates, Jeff Bezos and Elon Musk, but also the Rockefellers, Rothschilds and Fuggers. Such comparisons are impossible from a methodological perspective, but Arab historians leave us in little doubt that his wealth was extraordinary.

66. Fauvelle, François-Xavier, *The Golden Rhinoceros: Histories of the African Middle Ages*. Princeton University Press, 2021.

67. Bennett, Herman, *African Kings and Black Slaves: Sovereignty and Dispossession in the Early Modern Atlantic*. University of Pennsylvania Press, 2018. Green, Toby, *A Fistful of Shells: West Africa from the Rise of the Slave Trade to the Age of Revolution*. Penguin, 2019.

68. Herbst, Jeffrey, *States and Power in Africa: Comparative Lessons in Authority and Control*. Princeton University Press, 2014.

69. Curtin, Philip D., "Epidemiology and the slave trade," *Political Science Quarterly* 83:2 (1968): 190–216.

70. Curtin, Philip D., "'The White Man's Grave': Image and reality, 1780–1850," *The Journal of British Studies* 1:1 (1961): 94–110.

71. Ibid.

72. Some West Africans have even evolved genetic immunity to malaria. For example, sickle-cell anemia discourages the multiplication of parasites in the blood but has other negative effects for carriers. Kwiatkowski, "How malaria has affected the human genome." However, the limitations of genetic immunity were revealed when Britain shipped manumitted enslaved

Africans to the Province of Freedom—now Sierra Leone—in the later eighteenth century. In 1787, the first year of the project, 46 percent of European settlers died but so did 39 percent of the Black settlers. There were similarly high levels of mortality among African Americans who settled in Liberia in the first half of the nineteenth century. Crosby, *Ecological Imperialism*.

73. Kallas, Esper G., et al., "Predictors of mortality in patients with yellow fever: An observational cohort study," *The Lancet Infectious Diseases* 19:7 (2019): 750–58.

74. Crosby, *Ecological Imperialism*.

75. Curtin, "The White Man's Grave."

76. Curtin, Philip D., *Death by Migration: Europe's Encounter with the Tropical World in the Nineteenth Century*. Cambridge University Press, 1989, p. 30.

77. Curtin, Philip D., "The end of the 'white man's grave'? Nineteenth-century mortality in West Africa," *The Journal of Interdisciplinary History* 21:1 (1990): 63–88.

78. Gelfand, Michael, "Rivers of death in Africa," *Central African Journal of Medicine* 11:8 (1965): 1–46.

79. Crosby, *Ecological Imperialism*.

80. Shepperson, George, "Mungo Park and the Scottish contribution to Africa," *African Affairs* 70:280 (1971): 277–81.

81. Headrick, Daniel R., "The tools of imperialism: Technology and the expansion of European colonial empires in the nineteenth century," *The Journal of Modern History* 51:2 (1979): 231–63.

82. Green, *A Fistful of Shells*.

83. Chinua Achebe, the Nigerian novelist, famously denounced Conrad as a "bloody racist" in the 1970s. Clearly, Marlow's lack of interest in the Africans that he meets on his journey is disturbing, but this myopia is what makes *Heart of Darkness* such a chilling account of colonialism.

84. Headrick, Daniel R., *Power Over Peoples: Technology, Environments, and Western Imperialism, 1400 to the Present*. Princeton University Press, 2012.

85. Winegard, *The Mosquito*.

86. Curtin, "The White Man's Grave."

87. Ibid.

88. Barrett, Michael P., and Federica Giordani, "Inside Doctor Livingstone: A Scottish icon's encounter with tropical disease," *Parasitology* 144:12 (2017): 1652–62.

89. Gelfand, Michael, *Livingstone the Doctor: His Life and Travels. A Study in Medical History*. Blackwell, 1957. Headrick, "The tools of imperialism."

90. Curtin, "The White Man's Grave."

91. The Andean foothills couldn't satisfy the growing demand for cinchona bark, so in the 1850s and 1860s seeds smuggled out of Bolivia were used to start cinchona plantations in British India and Dutch East India. By the

early twentieth century European colonies in Asia supplied almost all of the world's quinine. Ibid.

92. Acemoglu, Johnson and Robinson, "The colonial origins of comparative development."

93. Hochschild, Adam, *King Leopold's Ghost: A Story of Greed, Terror, and Heroism in Colonial Africa*. Houghton Mifflin Harcourt, 1999.

94. Ibid.

95. Ibid.

96. Ibid.

97. Ibid.

98. Ibid.

Chapter 6 Revolutionary Plagues

1. Buchanan, Larry, Quoctrung Bui, and Jugal K. Patel, "Black Lives Matter may be the largest movement in US history," *The New York Times,* 3 July 2020.

2. Federal Reserve, "Recent Trends in Wealth-Holding by Race and Ethnicity: Evidence from the Survey of Consumer Finances." Accessible Data, 2017.

3. Carson, E. Ann, "Prisoners in 2018." Bureau of Justice Statistics, 2020.

4. Data is from the Slave Voyages website.

5. Edward Colston was deputy governor of the Royal African Company, which was formed in 1672 and would go on to transport more African children, women and men across the Atlantic than any other institution: 150,000 in roughly fifty years. Pettigrew, William, *Freedom's Debt: The Royal African Company and the Politics of the Atlantic Slave Trade, 1672–1752*. University of North Carolina Press, 2013.

6. Davis, David Brion, *Inhuman Bondage: The Rise and Fall of Slavery in the New World*. Oxford University Press, 2006. Slavery did, in fact, exist in some hunter-gatherer societies—for example, in the northwest coast of America. Graeber and Wengrow point out that in such situations, enslaved people were treated more like pets than beasts of burden—"they had to be nurtured, cooked for." But then they were killed at collective feasts and sometimes even eaten.

7. Wood, Ellen Meiksins, *Peasant-Citizen and Slave: The Foundations of Athenian Democracy*. Verso Books, 2015.

8. Hunt, Peter, *Ancient Greek and Roman Slavery*. John Wiley & Sons, 2017.

9. Barker, Hannah, *That Most Precious Merchandise: The Mediterranean Trade in Black Sea Slaves, 1260–1500*. University of Pennsylvania Press, 2019.

10. Davis, David Brion, *The Problem of Slavery in Western Culture*. Oxford University Press, 1988.

11. Greenfield, Sidney M., "Plantations, sugar cane and slavery," *Historical Reflections/Réflexions Historiques* 6:1 (1979): 85–119.

12. Galloway, Jock H., *The Sugar Cane Industry: An Historical Geography from Its Origins to 1914.* Cambridge University Press, 2005.

13. Greenfield, "Plantations, sugar cane and slavery."

14. Madeira was discovered in 1419 by a group including a Lisbon-based Genoese navigator called Bartolomeu Perestrello, who would later become a sugar plantation owner on the archipelago and the father-in-law of Christopher Columbus.

15. Greenfield, "Plantations, sugar cane and slavery."

16. Pike, Ruth, "Sevillian society in the sixteenth century: Slaves and freedmen," *Hispanic American Historical Review* 47:3 (1967): 344–59.

17. The Taíno's lack of resistance to the infectious diseases was apparent when, in 1495, Columbus trafficked 550 indigenous people to Seville to be sold as slaves. Two hundred didn't even survive the journey, and the majority of those who made it to Spain died soon after their arrival. Crosby, *Ecological Imperialism.*

18. Rouse, Irving, *The Tainos: Rise and Decline of the People Who Greeted Columbus.* Yale University Press, 1992.

19. Mann, *1493.*

20. Curtin, "Epidemiology and the slave trade."

21. Ibid.

22. McNeill, John Robert, *Mosquito Empires: Ecology and War in the Greater Caribbean, 1620–1914.* Cambridge University Press, 2010.

23. Ibid.

24. Curtin, "Epidemiology and the slave trade."

25. You'll recall from the previous chapter that the situation was even worse in the White Man's Grave of West Africa, with a European soldier having about a fifty-fifty chance of surviving a year.

26. Based on the assumption that malaria, as an endemic disease, will account for a similar number of deaths every year, while there will be major fluctuations in yellow fever mortality because it is epidemic, Curtin calculates that malaria caused about 60 percent of the "fever" deaths and yellow fever was responsible for the rest. In contrast, just over a tenth of African troops in the Lesser Antilles died from fever. Their biggest killer was "diseases of the lungs," most likely pneumonia and tuberculosis. Ibid.

27. Ibid.

28. McNeill, *Mosquito Empires.* Mann, *1493.*

29. Mann, *1493.*

30. McNeill, *Mosquito Empires.* Mann, *1493.* The French encountered similar problems in the 1880s, when they tried to build a canal that linked the Atlantic and Pacific Oceans. But no money was allocated to infectious dis-

eases and 20,000 workers died, most of them from yellow fever. After eight years the project was abandoned and investors in Compagnie Universelle du Canal Interocéanique de Panama lost all their money. When the U.S. took over in 1904 they employed 4,000 people to destroy the mosquitoes' breeding sites. Death rates plummeted and the project finally became viable. It was completed in 1914. Birn, Anne-Emanuelle, Yogan Pillay, and Timothy H. Holtz, *Textbook of International Health: Global Health in a Dynamic World*. Oxford University Press, 2009.

31. Galloway, *The Sugar Cane Industry*.
32. Davis, *The Problem of Slavery in Western Culture*.
33. Beckles, Hilary McDonald., "The economic origins of Black slavery in the British West Indies, 1640–1680: A tentative analysis of the Barbados model," *The Journal of Caribbean History* 16 (1982): 36–56.
34. Kempadoo, Kamala, " 'Bound Coolies' and other indentured workers in the Caribbean: Implications for debates about human trafficking and modern slavery," *Anti-Trafficking Review* 9 (2017).
35. Block, Kristen, and Jenny Shaw, "Subjects without an empire: The Irish in the early modern Caribbean," *Past & Present* 210:1 (2011): 33–60.
36. Blackburn, Robin, *The Making of New World Slavery: From the Baroque to the Modern 1492–1800*. Verso, 1997.
37. Lewis, Linden, "Barbadian society and the camouflage of conservatism," in Brian Meeks and Folke Lindahl (eds), *New Caribbean Thought: A Reader*. University of the West Indies Press, 2001, pp. 144–95.
38. McNeill, *Mosquito Empires*.
39. Mann, *1493*.
40. Beckles, "The economic origins of Black slavery in the British West Indies, 1640–1680." Some of the buckra survived, however. For example, the Barbadian singer Rhianna's surname is Fenty, which is common among the descendants of Irish indentured laborers.
41. Mintz, Sidney W., *Sweetness and Power: The Place of Sugar in Modern History*. Penguin, 1986.
42. Mancke, Elizabeth, and Carole Shammas (eds), *The Creation of the British Atlantic World*. Johns Hopkins University Press, 2005.
43. Burnard, Trevor, *Mastery, Tyranny, and Desire: Thomas Thistlewood and His Slaves in the Anglo-Jamaican World*. University of North Carolina Press, 2004.
44. Micheletti, Steven J., et al., "Genetic consequences of the transatlantic slave trade in the Americas," *The American Journal of Human Genetics* 107:2 (2020): 265–77.
45. Davis, *Inhuman Bondage*.
46. Curtin, "Epidemiology and the slave trade."
47. The figure fell to about 40 percent in the eighteenth century. Tomlins,

Christopher, "Reconsidering indentured servitude: European migration and the early American labor force, 1600–1775," *Labor History* 42:1 (2001): 5–43.

48. Census Bureau, *Bicentennial Edition: Historical Statistics of the United States, Colonial Times to 1970*. United States Government, 1975.

49. Berlin, Ira, *Many Thousands Gone: The First Two Centuries of Slavery in North America*. Harvard University Press, 2009.

50. Degler, Carl, "Slavery and the genesis of American race prejudice," *Comparative Studies in Society and History* 2:1 (1959): 49–66.

51. Census Bureau, *Bicentennial Edition*.

52. Tomlins, "Reconsidering indentured servitude." Wiecek, William M., "The statutory law of slavery and race in the thirteen mainland colonies of British America," *The William and Mary Quarterly: A Magazine of Early American History* 34:2 (1977): 258–80.

53. Blackburn, Robin, *The Overthrow of Colonial Slavery, 1776–1848*. Verso, 1988. Gosse, Van, *The First Reconstruction: Black Politics in America from the Revolution to the Civil War*. University of North Carolina Press, 2021.

54. Tomlins, "Reconsidering indentured servitude."

55. Or at least not until much later. In 1930, the *Anopheles gambiae* was found in Brazil. Over the next decade, the number of people dying from malaria increased by about 25 percent but, after a concerted effort, the mosquito was eradicated in the region by 1940. Parmakelis, Aristeidis, et al., "Historical analysis of a near disaster: Anopheles gambiae in Brazil," *The American Journal of Tropical Medicine and Hygiene* 78:1 (2008): 176–78.

56. McNeill, *Mosquito Empires*.

57. Esposito, Elena, "The side effects of immunity: Malaria and African slavery in the United States," *American Economic Journal: Applied Economics* 14:3 (2022): 290–328.

58. Ibid.

59. Mann, *1493*.

60. Menard, Russell R., *Migrants, Servants and Slaves: Unfree Labor in Colonial British America*. Routledge, 2001.

61. Esposito, Elena. "The side effects of immunity."

62. Ibid.

63. Census Bureau, *Bicentennial Edition*.

64. McNeill, *Mosquito Empires*.

65. Fick, Carolyn E., *The Making of Haiti: The Saint Domingue Revolution from Below*. University of Tennessee Press, 1990.

66. Makandal's fame has endured and he is a character in Alejo Carpentier's magical realist novella *The Kingdom of This World* (1949) and the video game *Assassin's Creed*.

67. Allewaert, Monique, "Super fly: François Makandal's colonial semiotics," *American Literature* 91:3 (2019): 459–90.

68. Geggus, David Patrick, *Haitian Revolutionary Studies*. Indiana University Press, 2002.

69. Snowden, *Epidemics and Society*.

70. Census Bureau, *Bicentennial Edition*.

71. James, C.L.R., *The Black Jacobins: Toussaint L'Ouverture and the San Domingo Revolution*. Penguin, 2001.

72. Dubois, Laurent, *Haiti: The Aftershocks of History*. Metropolitan Books, 2012.

73. Snowden, *Epidemics and Society*.

74. Blackburn, Robin, "Haiti, slavery, and the age of the democratic revolution," *The William and Mary Quarterly* 63:4 (2006): 643–74.

75. Geggus, *Haitian Revolutionary Studies*.

76. Marr, John S., and John T. Cathey, "The 1802 Saint-Domingue yellow fever epidemic and the Louisiana Purchase," *Journal of Public Health Management and Practice* 19:1 (2013): 77–82.

77. Snowden, *Epidemics and Society*.

78. McNeill, *Mosquito Empires*.

79. Ibid.

80. Snowden, *Epidemics and Society*.

81. Blackburn, *The Overthrow of Colonial Slavery*.

82. Drescher, Seymour, *Econocide: British Slavery in the Era of Abolition*. University of North Carolina Press, 2010.

83. Blackburn, "Haiti, slavery, and the age of the democratic revolution."

84. Rugemer, Edward Bartlett, *The Problem of Emancipation: The Caribbean Roots of the American Civil War*. Louisiana State University Press, 2009.

85. McPherson, James M., *The War That Forged a Nation: Why the Civil War Still Matters*. Oxford University Press, 2015.

86. McPherson, James M., *Battle Cry of Freedom: The Civil War Era*. Oxford University Press, 2003.

87. Mann, *1493*.

88. McNeill, *Mosquito Empires*.

89. Jones, Howard, *Abraham Lincoln and a New Birth of Freedom: The Union and Slavery in the Diplomacy of the Civil War*. University of Nebraska Press, 2002.

Chapter 7 Industrial Plagues

1. Hobsbawm, Eric, *The Age of Revolution: Europe 1789–1848*. Hachette, 2010.

2. Allen, Robert, "Why the industrial revolution was British: Commerce, induced invention, and the scientific revolution," *The Economic History Review* 64:2 (2011): 357–84.

3. Galloway, *The Sugar Cane Industry*. Mintz, Sidney W., *Sweetness and Power:*

The Place of Sugar in Modern History. Penguin, 1986. Potatoes, which were brought to Europe from the Americas in the sixteenth century and are a richer source of calories and nutrients than Old World foods, had an even bigger impact. The American economist Nathan Nunn calculates that this root vegetable was responsible for at least one-quarter of the continent's increase in population and urbanization in the eighteenth and nineteenth centuries. Nunn, Nathan, and Nancy Qian, "The potato's contribution to population and urbanization: Evidence from a historical experiment," *The Quarterly Journal of Economics* 126:2 (2011): 593–650.

4. Solow, Barbara L., *The Economic Consequences of the Atlantic Slave Trade*. Lexington Books, 2014.

5. Ray, Indrajit, "Identifying the woes of the cotton textile industry in Bengal: Tales of the nineteenth century," *The Economic History Review* 62:4 (2009): 857–92. There is a clear link, therefore, between Britain's economic boom and the impoverishment of the regions the British colonized. In the early eighteenth century, India accounted for about a quarter of the world's economic output, but by the time the British left in 1947 the figure was 4 percent. Maddison, *Contours of the World Economy 1–2030 AD*.

6. Hobsbawm, *The Age of Revolution*.

7. Keynes, John Maynard, "Economic possibilities for our grandchildren," in *Essays in Persuasion*. Palgrave Macmillan, 2010, pp. 321–32.

8. Szreter, Simon, "Economic growth, disruption, deprivation, disease, and death: On the importance of the politics of public health for development," *Population and Development Review* 23:4 (1997): 693–728.

9. Marx, Karl, and Friedrich Engels, *The Communist Manifesto*. Penguin, 1967.

10. McKeown, Thomas, *The Role of Medicine: Dream, Mirage, or Nemesis?* Princeton University Press, 1980. Szreter, "Economic growth, disruption, deprivation, disease, and death."

11. Szreter, "Economic growth, disruption, deprivation, disease, and death."

12. In fact, there were just forty-eight towns with more than 10,000 inhabitants. Ibid.

13. Law, Christopher M., "The growth of urban population in England and Wales, 1801–1911," *Transactions of the Institute of British Geographers* 41 (1967): 125–43.

14. Szreter, Simon, and Graham Mooney, "Urbanization, mortality, and the standard of living debate: New estimates of the expectation of life at birth in nineteenth-century British cities," *The Economic History Review* 51:1 (1998): 84–112.

15. Omran, Abdel R., "The epidemiological transition: A theory of the epidemiology of population change," *Millbank Memorial Fund Quarterly* 49 (1971): 509–38.

16. Szreter, Simon, "Industrialization and health," *British Medical Bulletin* 69:1 (2004): 75–86.

17. Szreter, Simon, "The importance of social intervention in Britain's mortality decline *c.* 1850–1914: A re-interpretation of the role of public health," *Social History of Medicine* 1:1 (1988): 1–38.

18. Szreter and Mooney, "Urbanization, mortality, and the standard of living debate."

19. Ibid.

20. Szreter, Simon, and Michael Woolcock, "Health by association? Social capital, social theory, and the political economy of public health," *International Journal of Epidemiology* 33:4 (2004): 650–67.

21. Green, Mark A., Danny Dorling, and Richard Mitchell, "Updating Edwin Chadwick's seminal work on geographical inequalities by occupation," *Social Science & Medicine* 197 (2018): 59–62.

22. The sketch was written and first performed by Tim Brooke-Taylor, Marty Feldman, John Cleese and Graham Chapman on their TV show *At Last the 1948 Show*. Cleese and Chapman were members of *Monty Python* and went on to perform it at their live shows.

23. Chang, Ha-Joon, *Kicking Away the Ladder: Development Strategy in Historical Perspective*. Anthem Press, 2002.

24. Despite the economic importance of children to their parents, infanticide was a common feature of Britain's towns and cities in the nineteenth century. One contemporary observer noted that the police "think no more of finding the dead body of a child in the streets than of picking up a dead cat or dog." Mathieson, Paige, "Bad or Mad? Infanticide: Insanity and morality in nineteenth-century Britain," *Midlands Historical Review* 4 (2020): 1–44.

25. Mooney, Graham, "Infectious diseases and epidemiologic transition in Victorian Britain? Definitely," *Social History of Medicine* 20:3 (2007): 595–606.

26. Evans, Richard, "Epidemics and revolutions: Cholera in nineteenth-century Europe," *Past & Present 120* (1988): 123–46.

27. Snowden, *Epidemics and Society*.

28. Ibid.

29. Evans, "Epidemics and revolutions."

30. Ibid.

31. Ibid.

32. Ibid.

33. Ibid. Burrell, Sean, and Geoffrey Gill, "The Liverpool cholera epidemic of 1832 and anatomical dissection—medical mistrust and civil unrest," *Journal of the History of Medicine and Allied Sciences* 60:4 (2005): 478–98.

34. Evans, "Epidemics and revolutions."

35. Szreter, "Industrialization and health."

36. Hobsbawm, *The Age of Revolution*.

37. Szreter and Woolcock, "Health by association?"

38. Szreter, "Economic growth, disruption, deprivation, disease, and death."

39. Szreter and Woolcock, "Health by association?"

40. Szreter, Simon, "Rapid economic growth and 'the four Ds' of disruption, deprivation, disease and death: Public health lessons from nineteenth-century Britain for twenty-first-century China?," *Tropical Medicine & International Health* 4:2 (1999): 146–52.

41. Thompson, E. P., *The Making of the English Working Class*. Penguin, 1968.

42. Szreter, Simon, "The right of registration: Development, identity registration, and social security—a historical perspective," *World Development* 35:1 (2007): 67–86.

43. Snowden, *Epidemics and Society*.

44. Ibid.

45. Johnson, Steven, *The Ghost Map: The Story of London's Most Terrifying Epidemic—and How It Changed Science, Cities, and the Modern World*. Penguin, 2006.

46. Briggs, Asa, "Cholera and society in the nineteenth century," *Past & Present* 19:1 (1961): 76–96.

47. Szreter, "Economic growth, disruption, deprivation, disease, and death."

48. Szreter, "Rapid economic growth and 'the four Ds.'" Szreter, "Economic growth, disruption, deprivation, disease, and death."

49. Szreter and Woolcock, "Health by association?"

50. Szreter, "Economic growth, disruption, deprivation, disease, and death." Szreter, "The importance of social intervention in Britain's mortality decline." Szreter, "Industrialization and health." Szreter and Woolcock, "Health by association?"

51. Johnson, *The Ghost Map*.

52. Halliday, Stephen, "Death and miasma in Victorian London: An obstinate belief," *British Medical Journal* 323:7327 (2001): 1469–71.

53. Snow's 1858 obituary read as follows: "This well-known physician died at noon, on the 16th instant, at his house in Sackville Street, from an attack of apoplexy. His researches on chloroform and other anaesthetics were appreciated by the profession." In 2013—almost 150 years after his death—the journal published a lengthier obituary. Hempel, Sandra, "John Snow," *The Lancet* 381:9874 (2013): 1269–70.

54. Black, Mary E., "Our relationship with poo," *British Medical Journal* (2012): 344:e2354.

55. Luckin, William, "The final catastrophe—cholera in London, 1866," *Medical History* 21:1 (1977): 32–42. Johnson, *The Ghost Map*.

56. Szreter, "Industrialization and health."

57. Szreter, "Economic growth, disruption, deprivation, disease, and death." Szreter and Woolcock, "Health by association?"

58. Szreter, "Economic growth, disruption, deprivation, disease, and death."
59. Szreter and Woolcock, "Health by association?"
60. Szreter, "Economic growth, disruption, deprivation, disease, and death."
61. Szreter, "The importance of social intervention in Britain's mortality decline."
62. Ibid. This contrasts with what we see in the contemporary world: a "race to the bottom" between countries with regard to taxes, as well as other related costs such as labor laws and environmental regulation, in order to attract investment. Szreter calls this "a macabre inversion" of late-nineteenth-century municipal politics.
63. Szreter, "Industrialization and health."
64. Mooney, "Infectious diseases and epidemiologic transition in Victorian Britain?" Szreter, "Economic growth, disruption, deprivation, disease, and death." Szreter, "The importance of social intervention in Britain's mortality decline."
65. Evans, Richard J. *Death in Hamburg: Society and Politics in the Cholera Year.* Clarendon, 1987.
66. Ibid.
67. Ibid.
68. Szreter, Simon, "The population health approach in historical perspective," *American Journal of Public Health* 93:3 (2003): 421–31.
69. Szreter, "Industrialization and health."
70. Szreter and Woolcock, "Health by association?"
71. Szreter, "Industrialization and health."

Chapter 8 Plagues of Poverty

1. Schorske, Carl, *Fin-De-Siècle Vienna: Politics and Culture.* Vintage Books, 1981.
2. The Spanish flu also had a massive influence on the world, but I don't explore it in detail in this book as it is covered elsewhere, most notably in Spinney, Laura, *Pale Rider: The Spanish Flu of 1918 and How It Changed the World.* PublicAffairs, 2017.
3. Kenny, Anthony, *The Enlightenment: A Very Brief History.* Society for Promoting Christian Knowledge, 2017.
4. Adam, David, "15 million people have died in the pandemic, WHO says," *Nature* 605:7909 (2022): 206.
5. All data on life expectancy and poverty in this chapter are from the World Bank unless otherwise stated. You might recall from Chapter 2 that, based on observations of foraging communities over the last fifty years or so, researchers estimate hunter-gathers' average life expectancy to be around the mid-seventies. So although these recent improvements in global life expec-

tancy may seem impressive at first sight, they actually only illustrate that human society is finally managing to overcome the damage that the Neo-lithic and then the Industrial Revolution did to our health.

6. According to a statement by the United Nations on World Toilet Day 2021.

7. Unless otherwise stated, all figures for the numbers of deaths caused by infectious disease come from the latest Global Burden of Disease study, which is carried out by the Institute for Health Metrics and Evaluation, University of Washington.

8. According to World Bank data.

9. See Dylan Mohan Gray's 2013 film *Fire in the Blood*.

10. According to data from UNAIDS for 2021.

11. Niyibitegeka, Fulgence, et al., "Economic burden of childhood diarrhea in Burundi," *Global Health Research and Policy* 6:1 (2021): 1–12.

12. Muttamba, Winters, et al., "Households experiencing catastrophic costs due to tuberculosis in Uganda: Magnitude and cost drivers," *BMC Public Health* 20:1 (2020): 1–10.

13. The figures were calculated by KPMG and the World Health Organization's Global TB Programme and published in Global TB Caucus's 2017 "The Price of a Pandemic" report.

14. Sachs, Jeffrey, and Pia Malaney, "The economic and social burden of malaria," *Nature* 415:6872 (2002): 680–85.

15. Dixon, Simon, Scott McDonald, and Jennifer Roberts, "The impact of HIV and AIDS on Africa's economic development," *British Medical Journal* 324:7331 (2002): 232–4.

16. Bonds, Matthew H., et al., "Poverty trap formed by the ecology of infectious diseases," *Proceedings of the Royal Society B: Biological Sciences* 277:1685 (2010): 1185–92.

17. Milanovic, Branko, *Global Inequality: A New Approach for the Age of Globalization*. Harvard University Press, 2016. Pinker cites the global decline in the number of people living in extreme poverty—currently classified as $1.90 a day by the World Bank—as a cause for optimism. The number of people living below this threshold has fallen, from over a third of the world's population in 1990 to less than a tenth today. The decline in extreme poverty in sub-Saharan Africa has been much less steep: from 55.1 percent to 40.4 percent in the same period. But as the continent's population has more than doubled in this time, the absolute number of destitute Africans has actually doubled, from 280.7 to 548.9 million. Liswati anthropologist Jason Hickel points out that $1.90 a day is too low to be a meaningful measure of poverty, however. If we instead use a higher threshold of $5.50 a day, which is just about enough to provide for one's basic survival needs, then the proportion of the sub-Saharan African population living under the pov-

erty line has hardly shifted between 1990 (89.1 percent) and today (86.1 percent), while the absolute numbers have boomed from 454 million to 978.1 million.

18. Quoted in Lampton, David M., "Public health and politics in China's past two decades," *Health Services Reports* 87:10 (1972): 895–904.

19. Needham, Joseph, *Science and Civilisation in China. Volume VI: 6.* Cambridge University Press, 2000.

20. Hipgrave, David, "Communicable disease control in China: From Mao to now," *Journal of Global Health* 1:2 (2011): 224–38.

21. Ibid.

22. Lampton, "Public health and politics in China's past two decades."

23. Hipgrave, "Communicable disease control in China."

24. Roberts, John Anthony George, *A History of China.* Macmillan, 1999.

25. Dikötter, Frank, *Mao's Great Famine: The History of China's Most Devastating Catastrophe, 1958–62.* Bloomsbury, 2018.

26. Dikötter, Frank, *The Cultural Revolution: A People's History, 1962–1976.* Bloomsbury, 2016.

27. Hipgrave, "Communicable disease control in China."

28. Ibid. Lampton, "Public health and politics in China's past two decades."

29. Lampton, "Public health and politics in China's past two decades."

30. Rosenthal, Marilynn, and Jay Greiner, "The barefoot doctors of China: From political creation to professionalization," *Human Organization* 41:4 (1982): 330–41.

31. Hipgrave, "Communicable disease control in China." Gong, You-Long, and L. M. Chao, "The role of barefoot doctors," *American Journal of Public Health* 72:9 (1982): 59–61.

32. Beach, Marilyn, "Beijing China's rural health care gradually worsens," *The Lancet* 358:9281 (2001): 567.

33. Ibid.

34. Cook, Ian G., and Trevor J. B. Dummer, "Changing health in China: Re-evaluating the epidemiological transition model," *Health Policy* 67:3 (2004): 329–43.

35. Yu, Hao, "Universal health insurance coverage for 1.3 billion people: What accounts for China's success?," *Health Policy* 119:9 (2015): 1145–52.

36. Dong, Yanhui, et al., "Infectious diseases in children and adolescents in China: Analysis of national surveillance data from 2008 to 2017," *British Medical Journal* 369 (2020).

37. These figures comes from the Xinhua News Agency, the official state press agency of the People's Republic of China.

38. Almost a quarter of the population still make do with less than $5.50, although this is down from just less than 90 percent at the turn of the millennium.

39. Acemoglu, Johnson, and Robinson, "The colonial origins of comparative development."

40. Hochschild, *King Leopold's Ghost*. Compare the situation in New England with the Congo. The leaders of the Massachusetts Bay Colony founded Harvard University in 1636, Protestant clergyman John Harvard being the college's first donor.

41. Clift, Charles, "The role of the World Health Organization in the international system," Chatham House Center on Global Health Security Working Group Papers (2013).

42. Brown, Theodore M., Marcos Cueto, and Elizabeth Fee, "The World Health Organization and the transition from 'international' to 'global' public health," *American Journal of Public Health* 96.1 (2006): 62–72. Fee, Elizabeth, and Theodore M. Brown, "A return to the social justice spirit of Alma-Ata," *American Journal of Public Health* 105:6 (2015): 1096-97.

43. Ibid.

44. Chang, *Kicking Away the Ladder*. Chang, Ha-Joon, *Bad Samaritans: The Guilty Secrets of Rich Nations and the Threat to Global Prosperity*. Random House, 2008.

45. According to World Bank Data.

46. Forster, Timon, et al., "How structural adjustment programs affect inequality: A disaggregated analysis of IMF conditionality, 1980–2014," *Social Science Research* 80 (2019): 83–113.

47. Skosireva, Anna K., and Bonnie Holaday, "Revisiting structural adjustment programs in Sub-Saharan Africa: A long-lasting impact on child health," *World Medical & Health Policy* 2:3 (2010): 73–89.

48. Nosrati, Elias, et al., "Structural adjustment programs and infectious disease mortality," *PloS One* 17:7 (2022): e0270344.

49. This is a deliberate allusion to Ha Joon Chang's magisterial *Kicking Away the Ladder*, in which he demonstrates that most high-income countries—including the U.S. and UK—became wealthy by protecting domestic industries with tariffs and subsidies. But, once wealthy, they adopted free-trade policies and forced them upon the rest of the world, through violence if necessary. In doing this, Chang argues that the world's richest countries denied poorer countries the opportunity to industrialize and grow rich. In other words, they were "kicking away the ladder."

50. Rashid, Theo, et al., "Life expectancy and risk of death in 6791 communities in England from 2002 to 2019: High-resolution spatiotemporal analysis of civil registration data," *The Lancet Public Health* 6:11 (2021): e805–e816.

51. Marmot, Michael, "Society and the slow burn of inequality," *The Lancet* 395:10234 (2020): 1413-14.

52. Office for National Statistics, "Socioeconomic inequalities in avoidable

mortality, England and Wales: 2001 to 2017." Government of the United Kingdom, 2019.

53. Marmot, Michael, "The health gap: The challenge of an unequal world," *The Lancet* 386:10011 (2015): 2442–44.

54. Allen, Luke N., and Andrea B. Feigl, "Reframing non-communicable diseases as socially transmitted conditions," *The Lancet Global Health* 5:7 (2017): e644–e646.

55. Scott, Courtney, Jennifer Sutherland, and Anna Taylor, "Affordability of the UK's Eatwell Guide." The Food Foundation, 2018.

56. These figures are from the NHS's "National Child Measurement Program, England 2020/21 School Year" report.

57. Hutton, Will, "The bad news is we're dying early in Britain—and it's all down to 'shit-life syndrome,'" *Guardian,* 19 August 2018.

58. Kitson, Michael, and Jonathan Michie, "The Deindustrial Revolution: The Rise and Fall of UK Manufacturing, 1870–2010." Working Paper 459, Centre for Business Research, University of Cambridge, 2014.

59. Berry, Craig, "UK manufacturing decline since the crisis in historical perspective," SPERI British Political Economy Brief No. 25 (2016).

60. Marmot, Michael, et al., *Build Back Fairer: The COVID-19 Marmot Review.* The Health Foundation, 2020.

61. Martin, Stephen, et al., "Causal impact of social care, public health and healthcare expenditure on mortality in England: Cross-sectional evidence for 2013/2014," *BMJ Open* 11:10 (2021): e046417.

62. Arias, Elizabeth, et al., "Provisional life expectancy estimates for January through June, 2020." National Center for Health Statistics (U.S.), NVSS vital statistics rapid release report No. 010, 2021.

63. Case, Anne, and Angus Deaton, *Deaths of Despair and the Future of Capitalism.* Princeton University Press, 2020.

64. Ibid.

65. According to World Bank data.

66. Wilper, Andrew P., et al., "Health insurance and mortality in US adults," *American Journal of Public Health* 99:12 (2009): 2289–95.

67. Figures for people without health insurance are from the Centers for Disease Control and Prevention. Himmelstein, David U., et al., "Medical bankruptcy: Still common despite the Affordable Care Act," *American Journal of Public Health* 109:3 (2019): 431–33.

68. Hakobyan, Shushanik, "In the race to vaccinate sub-Saharan Africa continues to fall behind," https://blogs.imf.org/2021/11/22/in-the-race-to-vaccinate-sub-saharan-africa-continues-to-fall-behind/ (2020).

69. Paton, James, "Wealthy nations will have 1.2 billion doses they don't need," https://www.bloomberg.com/news/articles/2021-09-04/wealthy-nations-will-have-1-2-billion-doses-they-don-t-need (5 September 2021).

70. Ye, Yang, et al., "Equitable access to COVID-19 vaccines makes a life-saving difference to all countries," *Nature Human Behavior* 6 (2022): 207–16.

71. Suleman, Mehrunisha, et al., *Unequal Pandemic, Fairer Recovery: The COVID-19 Impact Inquiry Report.* The Health Foundation, 2021.

72. This statistic is from the Poor People's Campaign's "A poor people's pandemic report: Mapping the intersections of poverty, race and COVID-19."

73. Covid figures are from Johns Hopkins' Coronavirus Resource Center. They are correct as of July 2022.

Conclusion

1. This is, of course, a conscious allusion to Marx's famous remark that "Men make their own history, but they do not make it just as they please; they do not make it under circumstances chosen by themselves, but under circumstances directly encountered, given and transmitted from the past. The tradition of all the dead generations weighs like a nightmare on the brain of the living."

2. Quammen, David, *Spillover: Animal Infections and the Next Human Pandemic.* W. W. Norton, 2012.

3. As Yuval Noah Harari points out, this mass migration into the digital realm has made society more able to survive a pandemic in the real world but increasingly vulnerable to malware and cyber warfare. Harari, Yuval Noah, "Lessons from a year of Covid," *Financial Times*, 26 February 2021.

4. Covid figures are from Johns Hopkins' Coronavirus Resource Center. They are correct as of July 2022.

5. Fukuyama, Francis, *The End of History and the Last Man.* Simon and Schuster, 2006.

6. Summers, Lawrence, "Covid-19 looks like a hinge in history," *Financial Times*, 14 May 2020.

7. Allison, Graham, *Destined for War: Can America and China Escape Thucydides's Trap?* Houghton Mifflin Harcourt, 2017.

8. Murray, Christopher J. L., et al., "Global burden of bacterial antimicrobial resistance in 2019: A systematic analysis," *The Lancet* 399:10325 (2022): 629–55.

9. Spinney, Laura, "The next pandemic? It may already be upon us," *Guardian*, 15 February 2021.

Art Credits

Index

JONATHAN KENNEDY teaches global public health at Queen Mary University of London. He has a PhD in sociology from the University of Cambridge.

Twitter: @J_J_Kennedy

About the Type

This book was set in Fairfield, the first typeface from the hand of the distinguished American artist and engraver Rudolph Ruzicka (1883–1978). Ruzicka was born in Bohemia (in the present-day Czech Republic) and came to America in 1894. He set up his own shop, devoted to wood engraving and printing, in New York in 1913 after a varied career working as a wood engraver, in photoengraving and banknote printing plants, and as an art director and freelance artist. He designed and illustrated many books, and was the creator of a considerable list of individual prints—wood engravings, line engravings on copper, and aquatints.